Also by Les Brown
Live Your Dreams!

It's Not Over Until You Win!

How to Become the Person You Always Wanted to Be— No Matter What the Obstacle

Les Brown

SIMON & SCHUSTER

SIMON & SCHUSTER
Rockefeller Center
1230 Avenue of the Americas
New York, NY 10020

SIMON & SCHUSTER and colophon are registered trademarks
of Simon & Schuster Inc.
Designed by Irving Perkins Associates
Manufactured in the United States of America
10 9 8 7 6 5 4 3 2
Library of Congress Cataloging-in-Publication Data
Brown, Les.
It's not over until you win!: how to become the person you always
wanted to be, no matter what the obstacle / Les Brown.
p.   cm.
1. Life-change events—Psychological aspects.   2. Adjustment
(Psychology)   3. Adaptability (Psychology)   I. Title.
BF637.L53B76   1997
158'.1—dc20   96-35856
                                                        CIP

ISBN 0-684-81560-5

To the memory of my mother, Mamie Brown, and to all the people who have dreams and pursue them relentlessly.

Acknowledgments

I would not have been able to write this book about some very emotionally charged periods in my life without the love and support of my wife, Gladys Knight, whose strength and integrity have bolstered me in hard times and sent me soaring in good ones. My children, too, helped me through the challenging times that are documented in this book. They are my greatest motivators.

To my brothers and sisters, and to Alexander Bou Whyms, thank you for strengthening me during my moments of weakness.

I would also like to thank those people who watched and supported *The Les Brown Show,* and stayed with me in spite of its flaws.

For the second time, and certainly not the last, writer Wes Smith has helped me put my thoughts and feelings and experiences on the page, and I am grateful for his insight and for his frequent reminders of the importance of the task at hand.

My longtime friend and adviser Mike Williams also served as my personal reality checker in this book and in life, and I thank him for his loyalty and friendship.

I am indebted also to my caring agent, Jan Miller, and to Simon & Schuster editor Dominick Anfuso, who shared my vision and saw it through.

To my supporters around the country, most notably the Reverend Johnnie Colemon, Dexter and Birdie Yager, Michael and Sharon Kelly, Willie and Dee Jolley, Dr. Myles and Ruth Munroe, Bishop Chandler Owens, Pastors Clinton and Sarah Utterbach, Juanita Sanders Cribb, Traci Lynn, Hattie Hill, and Otis Williams, thank you for being there when I most needed you.

My appreciation goes to my wonderful staff, Sue Burkhart, Celeste Johnson, and Marcia Snow, for all their hard work.

And for her prayers, love, and support, my thanks to my mother-in-law, Elizabeth Gram Knight.

Contents

- Overcoming defeat and hard times in your personal and professional lives
- Fostering self-awareness
- Developing an optimistic and dynamic approach to life

CHAPTER 1

Taking Life On

In January of 1993, I was eighteen feet tall, emotionally, spiritually, and in cardboard too. As I descended an escalator to the convention floor of the National Association of Television Program Executives in San Francisco's Moscone Convention Center, I looked directly into the eyes of an eighteen-foot-tall cardboard version of myself on display to promote the new *Les Brown Show*.

I had just signed the agreement to do the nationally syndicated talk show after many months of negotiations and so there I was, suddenly sharing the limelight with Vanna White, Phil Donahue, Regis and Kathie Lee too. I was on top of the world. My first book, *Live Your Dreams!*, had just been released and I was fresh off a twenty-city book tour. Toastmasters International had just named me one of the top five public speakers in the world. And now, I was going to have my own television talk show produced by the same people who brought Oprah to the masses.

As someone well acquainted with life's ups and downs, I savored the moment as a gift. I basked in all the attention and congratulations that night, because I think it is important to enjoy those times when life smiles upon you. As I will relate in this book, I believe also that it is unrealistic to expect good times to last forever. For most of us, life offers abundant opportunities for both laughter and tears. The good times you put in your pocket to savor. The hard times go to your heart and into your soul.

Our ability to handle life's challenges is a measure of our strength of character. And yet, where do we learn *how* to deal with those challenges, hard times, and difficulties? In school, we are taught how to read and write, and how to add and subtract. Those are vital keys to learning and getting along in the world. But what about the keys to *living?* Where do we enroll in Life 101? Where are the classes for dealing with the loss of a job, the death of a loved one, the failure of a relationship? Unfortunately, those lessons are mostly learned through trial by fire, and the school of hard knocks. No wonder so many people feel lost and alone when they are going through hard times. No wonder so many turn to alcohol, drugs, and even suicide. How many times have you heard someone in distress say, *I can't see a way out. I feel so alone. It's over for me?*

But the message of this book is that no matter how difficult your life may become, no matter how hard it gets, *there is always reason to keep on going and fighting because you can survive and thrive.* This book is intended to serve as a guide on how to do that after encountering difficult times, setbacks, failures, losses, and defeats in your life. My goal is to inspire and to empower you so that no experience in your life is too difficult to overcome, no defeat is permanent, no failure overwhelms you. My intent is to motivate you to look beyond temporary setbacks and to fight your way through them by understanding that it is not only within your power, it is your absolute *right* to experience and enjoy the best that life has to offer.

As in my first book, *Live Your Dreams!,* I will serve as an example, both good and bad, of how to deal with difficulties in your life. In that book, I urged readers to be *unstoppable* in pursuing their goals and dreams. And in this one, I will offer ways to get through some of life's greatest challenges. We all hit hard times. We all must deal with defeats and tragedies. This book, then, is for everyone who needs encouragement and assistance along the way, for those on top and those who want to get there.

In these pages, I will offer advice, tips, and examples that will help you in both your job or career and in your personal life too. I also will encourage and, hopefully, inspire you to live a *dynamic* life by helping you understand that even experiencing pain is a sign of life. After someone has seriously injured an arm or a leg, doctors say that one of the first signs of recovery is to feel pain. But you must focus on the life, not the pain. You cannot let it overwhelm you or your pursuit of your dreams. As you will read later, my suggestion is that after you have been knocked down or pushed back by life, you should acknowledge the setback, understand why it happened, and then *make a leap* ahead of where you were when you were hit.

As I was writing this book, the actor and singer Dean Martin died. His many close friends, including Frank Sinatra and Shirley MacLaine, commented upon his death that Dean Martin had given up on life years earlier—after his son died in a plane crash. In fact, after his son was killed, Martin told his friends that he no longer wanted to live himself. He was simply waiting to die. They tried to help him. Sinatra even arranged for a concert tour to lift his friend's spirits. But Dean Martin felt that life was over for him. He became a virtual recluse. He refused to see friends. He watched television by himself most of the day. When he did go out, it was usually to dine alone. He allowed his son's tragic death to overwhelm his own desire to live.

Two people died in that plane crash, Dean Martin's son, and Dean Martin himself. That is an even greater tragedy. Although he had a great deal of life to live still, Dean Martin quit on life. He quit on those who loved him. He refused to see beyond the hurt and pain and heartache.

He is not alone in responding this way. Often, people do not consciously focus on dying as Dean Martin did, but they still stop living. It is wrong to do that. It is a waste of your gifts and talents to give up on life. It is a betrayal of the love others have granted you. You have to live *dynamically.* We all have to keep focused, even through the hard times, on our dreams and goals. We have to monitor our thoughts and reject negative thinking and negative people who hold us back.

We have to live life with a sense of *urgency,* so that not a minute is wasted. Failure and defeat and loss afflict us all. Expect it, and, from these pages, learn to deal with it. And then learn to get back after life without waiting for an invitation. One way to do that is to trust in a power greater than yourself, and to believe that *good things* are going to follow, that *great things* will occur when you get up, dust yourself off, and go after life with determination and courage.

To a large degree, this book will chronicle a couple of very challenging years in my life: *character-building* years. The first of the two main events is the saga of *The Les Brown Show,* which was the highest-rated, fastest-canceled talk show in the history of the universe. The second was a personal tragedy that occurred shortly after I lost the television show; my beloved mother, Mrs. Mamie Brown, died of breast cancer at the age of eighty-eight.

These were solemn events in my life, but there is joy and humor in these pages too. From this book, I want you to learn to take life on, to live it passionately and courageously, and to never let a failure or a defeat stop you for more than the time it takes you to acknowledge it, recognize its impact on your life, accept it, learn from it, and then move on.

Looking for Answers

As you will read in the pages to follow, life certainly has tested me and I have not always responded with the courage and determination that I'd like to claim. I don't have all the answers all the time. No one does. The person who tells you that a rewarding life will come to you if you follow a few easy steps is no different from the guy in the sharkskin suit selling you real estate on the San Andreas Fault.

Don't believe anyone who claims to have all the answers. But do listen to those who say they are still looking for answers, because in their search they are taking life on. *And what really matters is that when you take life on, you are using your talents and energies and knowledge to the fullest extent possible.* When you live in that dynamic manner, you waste nothing. You do the universe proud.

I believe that life is an adventure and a celebration, and so while this book may tell you about the loss of my television talk show and the death of Mama, it also celebrates the fact that someone who was abandoned at birth and labeled "mentally retarded" in school could rise to the level of one day having his own television show. In these pages, I celebrate also the life of my mother, who is responsible for any and all successes that I may claim, and the joy of her love, as well as the love of another woman who came into the center of my life just as these hard times hit. She is still there, as my wife now, and Gladys Knight is the primary reason I got through it all. She is also the primary reason I look forward to the rest of my life with such relish.

I survived the cancellation of my talk show and I survived the death of Mama. I am stronger for the experiences, wiser and more determined than ever to celebrate all that life throws at me, the good and the bad. I hope when you have finished reading, you will feel the same way.

Escape from the Dodo Ward

As I descended onto the floor of my first NAPTE convention in January of 1993 as King World's newly anointed, nationally syndicated talk show host, I had this feeling of invincibility. In spite of deep reservations about abandoning my highly successful and lucrative public speaking career, I had put all my fears aside and decided to dive into an entirely new adventure. In retrospect, I'm not at all sorry about having that attitude. I think you have to enjoy these times in your life. You have to breathe them in deeply and savor them. You can't be afraid to dance with life; I learned that early on.

My very first public speaking appearance—and my first public humiliation—occurred in my junior year of high school when my speech teacher and mentor, Mr. Washington, asked me to introduce a play that some other students were presenting. I was thrilled. And I was scared to death! You see, I was officially designated a member of the Dodo Ward. When I was in fifth grade, my teacher and principal decided that my hyperactivity and slow learning processes were indications of a mental disability. They forced me to go back into the fourth-grade special education class.

Mama fought to keep me in the mainstream classes. My mother

only had a third-grade education and the teachers took advantage of that by telling her that the best thing for me was to go into special education. They convinced my mother they were trying to help me, that this was good for me. Against her best instincts, she accepted their judgment, assuming that they knew what they were talking about.

I was devastated. Unless it has happened to you, you can't imagine how painful it is to be called "dumb" or "slow" by your classmates. How many people never live up to their potential because at some time in their lives someone told them they were stupid or dumb or somehow inferior, and then they took it to heart and lived down to that expectation?

I didn't want to be a member of the Dodo Ward. I wanted to be accepted by everybody. And so I had attached myself to Mr. Leroy Washington and his award-winning speech and drama program. Talking was the one thing I did *exceptionally* well, and even though speech class was considered off limits to special education students back then, I felt if I could win Mr. Washington over I might just *talk* my way into the mainstream curriculum and into acceptance by the other students.

Mr. Washington was taking a big chance when he put me up on that stage to introduce a play. He had a reputation as a star-maker among high school speech and drama students in Miami and across the state. I was definitely a loose cannon in those days, but he let me get up there, and I was determined to prove to him that I could do it.

My voice, however, had its own agenda. When I opened my mouth, *Alfalfa spoke!* My voice was caught in the door between adolescence and adulthood. It screeched like new chalk on a blackboard. The students in the audience cracked up. The play was not a comedy, but I was certainly shoving it in that direction. I was scared to death. I clapped my hands over my mouth—something I'm sure countless teachers had wanted to do many times—and then I ran off the stage.

"Get back up there," Mr. Washington commanded as I sprinted past him.

"I can't," I told him. "I can't remember what I'm supposed to say. I'll do it better next time, I promise."

He looked me over. As dignified and disciplined as a four-star general, Mr. Washington had molded scores of poor high school children into scholarship college students. He had no tolerance for quitters. Even squeaky-voiced ones.

"Get back up there and finish it, Leslie Brown!"

I drew a deep breath from somewhere down in my shoes, and returned to the stage, to the delight of the student body. I gave my five-minute introduction to the program, screeching and yelping all the way. The other students were doubled over in laughter. They were rolling in the aisles, calling me "Alfalfa," and "Squeaky," and "Girlie Boy."

Mr. Washington watched all of this intently, his eyes on me, his arms folded in front of him. "That was very good, Les," he said when I came down from my first, but certainly not my last, public humiliation.

From that day, I became Mr. Washington's special project. He worked and worked with me. He put me on the debate team and in the speech club. He built my voice up and helped me develop presentation and speaking skills, but more importantly he taught me that the only way I could fail was to accept failure as my destiny. He taught me to learn from my failures and not allow them to discourage me. In other words *failure is not final*. It is not real unless you make it real. The only reality is how you respond to it, whether it makes you better or bitter.

Psychiatric Shock Treatment

Thanks to the powerful lessons taught and lived by Mama and reinforced by Mr. Washington, I learned not to allow negative events in my life to affect my attitude. And I even learned to use the experiences of being labeled mentally retarded as a vehicle for carrying my motivational messages to audiences. Sometimes, even the wrong audiences.

I once appeared on *The MacNeil/Lehrer News Hour* on public television talking about my childhood and about the need for building self-esteem in children. A psychiatrist I'd met at a seminar saw the interview and, unbeknownst to me, he assumed I was nationally renowned educator Dr. Lester Brown, who is also from

Miami. A man called my office in Miami and had them schedule me to speak to a group of psychologists and psychiatrists meeting in Columbia, South Carolina, to discuss methods of building self-esteem and motivating children.

Weeks later, I arrived at the breakfast gathering and when I sat down at the head table I saw the name cards and every one of them had a Ph.D. after the name, including mine. I leaned over to the master of ceremonies before he stood to introduce me, and I said, "Listen, I am not Dr. Lester Brown."

Startled, he said, "You're not? Who are you?"

With a serious expression on my face, I said: "I'm Mrs. Mamie Brown's baby boy."

He did not appear to be at all relieved to hear that. I believe his response was something along the lines of "Oh my God!"

Calmly, I patted his shoulder and said, "Don't worry about it."

Again, he did not appear to be comforted.

"Don't worry about it?" he cried.

The audience awaited, so I stood up and announced, "I've got some good news and bad news, and I will tell you the bad news first. I am not Dr. Lester Brown. I have no college training what-soever. Not only that, but when I was in the fifth grade, they put me back in the fourth grade and labeled me 'EMR.' So not only am I the wrong man, I'm also 'educable mentally retarded.'"

There were a few gasps around the room. The master of cere-monies, who no doubt thought his professional reputation was about to be ruined, put his hand to his forehead and said aloud "Oh Lord!"

I think they were worried that they had invited a madman to speak at a psychiatric convention. But then I set out to prove to them that they had invited exactly the right person to talk to them.

"No, I am not the educator Dr. Lester Brown," I said. "However, when it comes to sharing techniques on how to motivate our chil-dren, I can talk to you about that through my own experiences and what I have used to transform my own life."

I was the only one in the room that day without a Ph.D. but I took those psychiatrists to school. I gave them an inside look at what it is like to be poor and powerless, not from a textbook but from the school of life. I gave them insight into what it means to be raised in poverty and what it takes to get people to see beyond their circumstances and mental conditioning.

Those psychiatrists learned something that day. I know because they gave a standing ovation to me, the wrong Mr. Brown. I filled their ears with information about motivating children that came straight from the mouth of someone who had been there, a child raised in poverty and stigmatized by the unfair label of mental retardation, but a child who'd been taught how to take life on. Think about that. Something that very well could have held me back in life, something that could have permanently damaged my self-esteem and my ability to develop my gifts, instead was transformed into a powerful tool for good that I could pull out and apply to what could have been a very awkward and embarrassing situation.

Tackling Hard Times Head-On

I have noticed that many people who do well in life carry that same ability with them. They find the hope in every desperate situation. They find the positive message in negative experiences. I am not alone in noticing that. The Little brothers lived with their mother on 22nd Street in Overtown. They went to school with me.

The youngest, Larry, was a good kid but he was quiet and didn't stand out in school. His older brother, George, was an outstanding student and was one of Mr. Washington's star speech and drama students. He was a high achiever in a school full of children who had no high expectations to live up to. When I was in high school, the *Miami Herald* did a story noting that students in our school tested lower than all others in south Florida. We were all born of poverty, and I guess they expected all of us to be impoverished in our dreams too. George Little, though, was obviously not buying into that mentality. He knew he was going to make it and we all agreed. But he didn't.

In his senior year in high school, he was shot and killed. We were all affected, but not in the way his quiet, younger brother was. Larry had idolized George, as we all had to some extent. But while we all grieved and then went on, Larry avenged his brother's death by transforming his own life. Never much of an achiever prior to George's death, Larry took on his brother's striving spirit. He made greatness his goal.

Not particularly big or fast, Larry had never been a natural athlete. But what he wasn't given, he worked to obtain. I can still remember seeing him running laps around Dixie Park while the rest of us played around, that look of fierce determination on his face. After high school, where he was a standout tackle on the football team, he went to Bethune-Cookman College in Florida, a small school where again he was a standout, but received little attention. He was not selected in either the NFL or AFL football drafts, but he signed as a free agent with the AFL's San Diego Chargers and was traded to the Miami Dolphins in 1969.

At six foot one, 265 pounds, he was small, but Larry became the point man in Miami's legendary running attack of that era. He was named to the All-AFC team four years in a row and, with him leading the charge as an offensive guard, Miami won all seventeen games in its 1972 season, including the Super Bowl. They came back the next year, and won it again, with undersized Larry Little on the offensive line. Larry's vengeance against his brother's killers was to become a Hall of Fame pro football player. When life slapped him in the face with the death of his brother, Larry Little took the hit, gathered his strength, and then took life on.

Sometimes the Hits Just Keep on Coming

We are living in very challenging times today. Pressured in the workplace, stressed out at home, people are trying to make sense of their lives. While there is tension on one hand there is introspection and exploration on the other. How do you keep on going when life knocks you down? It's one thing to be positive when things are going well. But it is something altogether different when life catches you on the blind side:

- When someone you love is taken away.
- When a debilitating illness strikes you or a family member.

- When your "lifetime" job is suddenly downsized.
- When the relationship that has kept you going falls apart.
- When you go through the emotional torment of a divorce.
- When your grown children refuse to grow up.
- When your teenagers decide they are adults.

There are times when you want to say to life: "Please give me a break, just give me a chance to catch my breath." But life doesn't listen. Sometimes, as soon as we raise our heads, it knocks us back down. Such is life.

I'm reminded of Anna Price, a friend of mine who was stunned one day to get a telephone call that her daughter had died in a car accident. She said she felt as though life had knocked her down, broken every bone in her body, and then told her to get back up. It has been said that pain, sickness, disappointment, tragedies, death, and other adversities are always chasing us, and that at least three or four times a year one or more will catch up to us or someone we care about.

Reflect over the past year on your own life and list three adverse things that have happened to you or someone you care about:

1. _____

2. _____

3. _____

Reflect on how each affected you and how you handled the effects. Does it continue to affect your mood and behavior adversely?

_____

_____

_____

How do you wish things had worked out instead?

_____

_____

_____

Now consider these questions, which I'll help you find answers to in the rest of the book:

- *How can you rebound from this setback and get your life on track?*
- *What is holding you back?*
- *Where can you find the strength to get unstuck?*
- *What small steps can you take to get going?*
- *What goals can you set to move your life ahead?*

In the pages that follow, I'm going to share a great deal of my life with you.

No Condition Is Permanent

A married couple I know visited South Africa recently, and when they returned they told me that the most inspiring thing they saw was what they found in a crumbling old school building. The roof was half torn off. The windows were nearly all boarded up. The classrooms had floors of dirt. The schoolchildren sat on boxes and crates. But my friends were struck by the spirits of those children. Their eyes were bright and their minds eager. They laughed and sang and seemed totally unaffected by the squalor in which they were gathered.

My friends were awed by the indomitable nature of these children and wondered what it was that empowered them. And then, as they walked through the school, they saw this sign posted in a prominent place: "No condition is permanent!" it said.

Those South African schoolchildren were not focused on the dirt floor beneath their feet, nor were their minds occupied with the sky showing through the roof and the general dilapidation all around them. In this nation now headed by a man who for nearly twenty-eight years was a political prisoner, these children have been trained to look forward to the potential in their lives rather than any temporary condition.

Ralph was a Ph.D. psychologist and behaviorist from Salt Lake City whom I had hired to do some training program work for me. He had just started when I telephoned him one day because I heard he was going through hard times. He was in the middle of a divorce and, at the same time, having serious tax problems. The IRS had frozen his bank account and he had creditors breathing down his neck. When I called him, a friend of his answered the phone and he told me my call was too late. Ralph had hanged himself.

Ralph had been a smart guy. And sometimes smart people feel that if they can't see the way out of a problem, there must be no way. There is always a way. Nobody has all the answers all the time. But you have to understand that the answers will come eventually. Suicide is a permanent solution to a temporary problem. It is the result of people convincing themselves they can't make it. In order for us to take life on, even in the worst times, we have to say to ourselves *I am going to make it no matter what*. Not making it is not an option.

Making It Against All Odds

We all go through hard times. There have been periods in my life when my car was repossessed, the power to my house was shut off, and nobody believed in my dream. If I had accepted those times as permanent I would not be here now. There are times in life when it seems the harder you work, the deeper the hole you dig for yourself. But you've got to *dig down deep* within yourself and make a gut check. Whatever is pushing you down right now, you have to say *I'm going to make it no matter what!*

That is what Nelson Mandela had to say to himself each day of the twenty-seven and a half years he was in prison. That's what poet Maya Angelou, who was a rape victim and physically abused and became a teenage mother at sixteen, had to say. That's what Olympic speed skater Dan Jansen had to say after his sister died and he fell time and time again in front of millions of people. They all made it, against the odds.

I'm going to make it no matter what! That is what you are going to have to say to yourself when you are unemployed and creditors are banging on your door or you've lost all your money on a business plan that didn't work.

That is what Walt Disney had to say after he had filed for bankruptcy seven times and suffered two nervous breakdowns. That is what merchant J.C. Penney said, even though, at age fifty-six, he was $7 million in debt and committed to a mental institution. Walt Disney made it back and built an empire. J.C. Penney lived to be ninety-two. He had a certificate saying he was of sound mind, and he had $2 billion in assets. *What were the odds of them making it?*

You have that same power. You have powers in you to overcome anything you are facing right now. You are greater than your circumstances and anything that could ever happen to you. That's what L. C. Robinson meant when he said "Things may happen around you and things may happen to you but the only things that really count are things that happen in you."

Failure is a *temporary* condition. My goal is to encourage you to develop the spirit of those schoolchildren, the same spirit imparted to me by my Mama and Mr. Washington.

Life in the Challenged Lane

I've always taken life on because I had no other choice. If you are familiar with my background, you know that life came at me from the first breath I took on the linoleum floor of an abandoned shack on 62nd Street and 17th Avenue in a Miami ghetto. My twin brother and I were born there, to a woman we never knew. We were given away at birth and adopted by a devoted single woman, Mrs. Mamie Brown, who worked as a cafeteria cook, maid, and field-worker to support us. This great woman, my mother, had divorced after a brief and childless marriage as a young woman. She took us in out of love, and she taught me a great deal about taking life on.

When my brother and I were still children, she adopted my sister, Margaret, and later she took on an entire second family of four more. And after those four were gone, she took in physically handicapped children and worked with them. Mama was determined to provide for us, and we saw that love and determination in her every day. Sometimes, we felt it on our backsides because she was determined that we would stay out of trouble too. I say "we" but the truth is, I was the one who benefited the most from Mama's switch. I was the problem child in the family. Mama put me on a pedestal, and she was determined that I stay there or she was going to whup me until I couldn't jump down. Like most mothers, she wanted the best for me, and she was determined that I want it too. She used to cry while she whupped me, "I don't want you to end up in jail, or get killed by running with the Fourteenth Street Gang."

Her goals were very simple in scope, but difficult to achieve. She wanted a family that she could love and one that would love her in return. And most of all, she wanted us to be respectful, have good manners, and make something of ourselves.

My mother was a real winner in that regard. She persevered against some substantial odds. Each of those children she adopted was a risk. Obviously, Mama was unafraid. She went all out for us, which is what you have to do when you take life on. Life is not easy, even for people who make it look easy. As you will read in the following pages, I've been up in my life, I've enjoyed some of the best things life can offer. I've lived in splendor, and I have also lived on the charity of friends. There have been times when, as the song says, I've been down so long it looked like up to me. At no point in my life, whether things were going wonderfully, or terribly, did I think it was easy. Challenging, yes. Stimulating, yes. Intimidating, yes. But not easy. If you are waiting for Easy, you'd better take a seat, because that bus won't be coming by. Easy didn't leave the depot this morning! Easy had a mechanical breakdown.

I suggest that instead of waiting for life to give you an easy path, that you enter the flow of life and take it on as it comes to you, understanding that there will be hard times, good times, and times that try your soul. If you are looking for keys to life, that is an important one: *Know that life is a constant cycle of change and that conflict is part of that cycle.* And during the down cycle, awareness is our best weapon.

Stuck with a Label

I went through all of grade school and high school as a special education student. I was a slow learner, and so I needed special attention in the classroom, but I didn't need the label that went with it. I was held back in grade school while my twin brother passed. The other kids called me "the dumb twin." I was desperate not to be considered an outcast by the other students, and I did everything I could to mainstream myself. The other kids in special education seemed to accept their outcast status for the most part. They stuck together, ate together, played together.

I was in their class, but I was not one of them in my mind. I ran with the other kids. I attached myself to Mr. Washington's class where I thought I had a chance to fit in. Instinctively, I sought to avoid being shoved aside. Recently, I heard of a father whose son was physically deformed. The father refused to put his son in classes with other physically deformed children. He didn't want him to accept his handicap as the norm. He didn't want him to "learn" to be handicapped. He feared that isolating his son's contacts to other deformed children would lead to the son feeling isolated from other people. You can argue with his theory, but you cannot argue that the man was not trying to do what he thought was best for his child.

Though I was classified as a slow learner, what they call "learning-disabled" today, I sought out the smartest kids in the school, kids who were already focused and disciplined, kids who were smart and leaders. I hoped some of it would rub off on me. At first, they didn't want to accept me; to them, I was a Dodo who'd flown the coop. But eventually, I won them over with humor and my reputation as one of Mr. Washington's special projects. If you don't see how you fit, you become a misfit. *You have to have faith that you are part of the plan, and that life will yield to you if you are persistent and courageous.*

Twice the Courage for Twice the Challenges

Sometimes you have to have *double courage* because you will be confronted by people urging you to do the wrong thing. You have to have the courage to not do the wrong thing and the courage also to resist the people urging you to do it. Teenagers especially need to understand this because their identity is still forming and it makes them vulnerable. It takes courage not to buy into negative influences, whether gangs, drugs, or crime. You have to be the primary influence on your own life. Peer pressure does not go away with adolescence. It also shows up in adult life with pressure to have one more drink, to be unfaithful, to steal on the job, or to take a little longer on the lunch hour.

I helped a young man get a job at a McDonald's. He was from a good family and was a good student but he got caught giving food to his friends for free. They also caught him pocketing money from the cash register. I was upset. I demanded to know why he did it and his answer was *Everybody else was doing it.* Negative peer pressure got to him. He was listening to voices that did not speak to the best in him. He did not have the courage to resist.

Recall a time in your life when you had to display double courage when someone tried to influence you to make a bad decision:

_____

_____

_____

_____

_____

_____

Think about how you found the strength to do that, and when hard times hit, tap into that same source of strength. Sometimes we forget what we have overcome, but those memories can help you take on life down the line. Life is loaded with difficulties and you have to tap into your past exhibitions of strength, what I call your "victory bank." Those victories are part of you, they make you the person you are today. Hold on to those victories as if they were gold.

A social worker I know, Sally, developed a program to help women who have been physically, mentally, and sexually abused. And because of their histories when these women are asked to think of good things they have done, they often draw a blank. Sally then advises them to think about how hard it was for them just to show up for her session. Sally knows that these women have a high level of hopelessness and so taking the simple step of coming to a class that will help them requires a major effort. When Sally asks how hard it is for them to come to class, they all say "It is very hard." And she then tells them to give themselves credit for doing something good on that day. Those women come to class because they believe that it is possible for their lives to get better. With that one small step, they had begun to believe in themselves.

You Gotta Believe in Yourself

Often, small steps lead to great strides. It's not the distance you go that is important so much as the *going* itself. When you take control of your own life, it responds. Getting into Mr. Washington's class was a small step with great and lasting impact on my life. No longer was I simply Leslie Calvin Brown, special education student. I had found a new focus and new energy. Now, I was Les Brown, speech student. I was someone with potential! Mr. Washington believed in me at a time when I was struggling to believe in myself. He saw that I had an interest and a spark for public speaking. He was willing to give me a chance, and when I sensed that he recognized something in me, I was willing to take a chance.

My Mama had always instilled in us that we were special, and now I had found someone else willing to see me as something other than a special education student. And this was a man who had sent Liberty City children into talent competitions around the country and brought them back home with trophies. When Mr. Washington helped me see the potential for my life, suddenly I was willing to take life on, to act on it, rather than passively allowing life to act upon me. He felt there was something there and I was hoping he was right.

Believing Is Powerful

Believing in yourself requires knowing that your life has value and that there is hope for your life. You don't have to be on top of the world already in order to look up. No matter what your circumstances are, there is a reason for you still being here. How can you begin to believe in yourself more?

1. Get positive encouragement from others. Make it a point to be around people who make you feel good about yourself, whether friends, family, co-workers, or mentors such as teachers and coaches.

2. Give yourself internal encouragement. Concentrate on saying things and doing volunteer work, working out, taking a class, listening to music or motivational tapes, reading inspirational books and the Bible, anything that makes you feel good about yourself. Get in the habit of saying positive things to yourself. Find a positive expression or several that work for you and put them on a card where you can look at them during the day. One of my favorites was given to me by a friend. It goes: "Good things are going to happen to me." Say it repeatedly but each time put the emphasis on a different word or phrase.

GOOD things are going to happen to me.
Good THINGS are going to happen to me.
Good things ARE going to happen to me.
Good things are GOING to happen to me.
Good things are going TO HAPPEN to me.
Good things are going to happen TO me.
Good things are going to happen to ME.

3. Make deposits in a positive memory bank of achievements or good things you have done with your life. Savor your victories and achievements and moments of joy. Store them away for the hard times so that they can provide light in the darkness and hope when it seems like there is none.

4. Give yourself a break. Too many people blame themselves for hard times, when often it is just simply a down cycle that has caused the sky to fall down upon you. We all go through those cycles in our lives. Don't assume responsibility for matters that are out of your control.

5. Grant yourself permission to make mistakes now and then, realizing we are God's, not gods. Even if hard times in your life are the result of your actions, you should not condemn yourself. Has there ever been a life free of mistakes? I'll answer that one for you. NO! So, take responsibility, take time to contemplate where you went wrong, and then accept that you are not perfect. Learn from your mistakes, make a commitment to change, then move on.

6. Put together a book or other positive reference source to bring you up when you slide into low moments. I call my version of this my *Spirit Book* because I go to it when I need my spirits lifted. It has pictures of my friends and family members enjoying life with me. It reminds me that hard times don't last forever, and that better times are ahead.

7. Get busy on smaller steps that take you toward your dream. Do not overlook the need to have small victories. I love small victories and accomplishments because you can build upon them so easily to achieve *great* things. So take victories wherever you can find them, whether from cookies that come out of the oven just right, or a fifteen-minute exercise program that leaves you feeling exhilarated. One step at a time, day by day. Stay in pursuit of your dreams and goals.

8. Resolve to replace worry with work, avoid the idle mind when you are vulnerable. Fretting should be banned as a waste of natural resources. What is ever accomplished by worrying about what *might* happen? People who fret and worry and chew their nails waste too much time. Focus on solutions, not problems, and the way will become clear.

9. Look your best so that your appearance reflects how you see yourself and attracts the sort of people you want to attract. I don't know how people can expect to feel good on the inside when they look like thirty miles of dirt road on the outside. When you are feeling down and out, dress as though you feel like a million dollars. If nothing else, people will wonder what you are up to.

10. Make a list of prized possessions, such as photographs of those you hold dear, and note why they have meaning for you. This is simply a way of reminding yourself of the people and things you value most in life. It is difficult to stay down and out for long when you stay in touch with those things that give your life meaning.

Someone's Belief in You Empowers You

When you believe in yourself you believe you are entitled to great things, and so you are willing to commit yourself to doing what is necessary to get those great things. When Mr. Washington saw potential in me, I began to believe in myself and in my dreams. My dreams in those days often placed me in the radio broadcast booth alongside the deejays who were my heroes. I was glued to the radio. I loved listening to them.

I eventually followed my dreams into a Miami radio station where I volunteered to work for free, just to get experience. I soaked up all I could and when the opportunity presented itself one day, I filled in for a hard-drinking deejay called "Rock" who drank himself right off the air. I was ready for that opportunity, and when it came I seized it. Soon, I was working full-time on that radio station. The job there led to another in Columbus, Ohio, where I became well known not only as a radio personality but also a social activist, encouraging my listeners to become involved in the community.

My social activism eventually led to my being fired, but with the encouragement of friends I decided to run for the Ohio House of Representatives. I was elected to that position three times, but during my third term my mother fell ill, and for me there was no hesitation. I quit to be with her. I nursed her back to health for nearly a year, and when she was able to take care of herself again, I set out on a new career as a public speaker.

It was rough going at first. I had to beg people to listen. I spoke to pigeons in the park. Grade-school-children. Lampposts. Any audience I could find. And I studied the style and mannerisms of the best speakers I could find. I joined the National Speakers Association and I traveled to Orlando on a Greyhound bus from Miami to attend their convention.

My family and friends weren't always supportive. I had given up a prestigious political career and a secure income for the insecurity of public speaking. Who would pay to hear me talk? Not many in those early days of struggle. There were many times when strangers came to my rescue. People I did not know would come up to me after hearing me speak and offer to help me out. At one point, my car was repossessed. At another, I was forced to live in my office because I couldn't afford an apartment too. All of us have times when we feel "I don't know *how* I am going to get out of this jam."

Jammed Up

We all have periods in our lives when our problems seem insurmountable. The challenge is to stay focused on your goals in life, keeping your energy positive and relentlessly looking for ways to pull it out. If you can do that, you will overcome the problem. I guarantee you.

I'll never forget when I got fired from radio broadcasting in Columbus in 1978. I was in financial trouble. I had borrowed as much money as I could borrow. My house was near foreclosure. I'd been unemployed for months and applied for job after job. But you know, I never felt that I was really going to lose my house. I did the best that I could and with the limited money I did have, I took a trip to Miami with my wife and children. And on the day that the bank was supposed to foreclose, one of my friends called me in Florida and said the IRS had sent a refund check that was enough to pay the house note with money left over. I'd never received an IRS refund before and I had no idea I was going to get one, but often it seems like if you don't give up in hard times, if you keep your spirits up and relentlessly keep after it, sooner or later blessings will come your way.

Many of us eliminate possibilities for ourselves by giving up too early in the fight. Our biggest challenge is to overcome self-defeating thoughts, and to keep going. When someone tells me that they tried to reach a goal but couldn't, I always ask, "What was it that you weren't willing to handle?" In order to reach your dream, you have to be willing to do what is required. I believe that if you are willing to do the work, to devote the energy, to explore every avenue, that you can accomplish nearly anything you set out to do. I believe if you keep on coming back again and again—and if you are willing to ask for help and to keep asking until you get it—then life will give you what you want.

Are you willing to burn the midnight oil, scrub floors, wash cars, work weekends, take on a second job, get there early and stay late, go back to school? Most people who claim they couldn't reach their goals are people who, in truth, weren't willing to do whatever it took to do it. Most people take the escape route, they look for something to justify why they haven't done what they wanted to do. I believe that if you knock on the door of opportunity long enough and hard enough, somebody is going to answer. Knowing that and feeling that throws the doors open for you. You have to understand that you are always more powerful than the circumstances that surround you as long as you do not accept *momentary* defeats, hard times, or losses as a *permanent* condition.

When I lost my radio job, I kept on pushing and fighting to get back on top, and eventually life got tired of hearing me knock. Finally, it opened the door. The same thing happened when I was struggling to get my public speaking career going. I'd been barely getting by until my homemade audiotapes of my speeches, which I had been selling out of the trunk of my car, caught the attention of some independent film producers in Chicago. They offered to make videotapes of my speeches for sale to the growing home video market. Those professionally made videos landed me an appearance on public television in Detroit. The Detroit appearance, during a public television fund-raising program, brought in an unprecedented number of donations. That response brought requests for my tapes from public television stations around the country. Soon, I was considered one of the top fund-raisers for public television stations around the nation.

My popularity on public television helped land me a contract for my first book, and that led to the series of events that you will read about in the following chapters. Some of those events were highly public, some were very private. Some were great victories. Some were humiliating losses. Some were joyous. Some were incredibly painful. All, however, are part of the ebb and flow of life. The joy, you know, is in the journey.

- *Taking risks*
- *Facing fears*
- *Being willing to fail as a learning experience*

CHAPTER 2

Anything Worth Doing Is Worth Doing Badly

In the fall of 1991, my motivational specials aired nationwide on public television stations and brought me unprecedented attention in the television industry. Within a few months, representatives from Hearst, Disney, Warner Brothers, Fox Broadcasting, King World, and the networks approached me about doing a television talk show. At times, it seemed as though Mrs. Mamie Brown's baby boy was the main course in a feeding frenzy.

Not that it was a bad thing, mind you. Multimedia genius Quincy Jones, who also has joint productions with Warner Brothers television, invited me to his home overlooking Los Angeles to discuss working with him on infomercials and other projects. Disney's Buena Vista television division sent a producer to meet me on Long Island. Other television executives wined and dined me. Still, when this pack of television production companies came courting me, I had my fears. Who wouldn't? Television looks easy, but believe me, it isn't. And it doesn't come with a long-term contract guarantee. There is not a lot of security in television.

That was a big part of my problem. I had worked many years to develop my public speaking career. After a lot of sacrifice and some very lean times, I had established my position in the market. My wide client base ranged from church congregations to Fortune 500 corporations. As a public speaker, I was making a *good* living and deriving a great deal of pleasure from it. I was speaking to as many as eighty thousand people in some venues, and if you've never stood on a stage and listened to an ovation from that many people, believe me, that is a nice way to finish a day's work.

Of course, a television audience of some 20 million people has its appeal too. But I was concerned also about the trend in television talk shows. First *Donahue* and then *The Oprah Winfrey Show* had thrived on formats that had originally offered information and entertainment, usually in equal measures. They had been intelligent and informative programs, hosted by sharp-witted and charismatic people. And they had been hugely successful. Oprah Winfrey, in particular, had succeeded on an unprecedented scale. *Forbes* magazine lists her fortune at more than $340 million. After ten years on the air, she had become the wealthiest and most powerful woman in the television industry. That sort of success invites imitators and, in the case of the television talk show genre, imitation has not been flattering, nor has the competition elevated the quality of programming.

Nothing Is Too Low to Get Ratings

As the talk show genre became more successful and more crowded, the topics of the shows had degenerated into decadence, voyeurism, and worse. Even Donahue, who had established himself as a thoughtful television host, plunged into the pits with strippers, pornographers, transvestites, and the like. It would only get worse with Geraldo, Jerry Springer, Jenny Jones, Ricki Lake, Carnie Wilson, and others competing to see how low they could go. Increasingly, critics such as former FCC chairman Newton Minow were saying that these people and the television executives who put them on the air have confused their right to be on television with their responsibility to do what is right on television.

I believe that those who have so much power also have a greater responsibility than to cater to the lowest in us. I like a big paycheck as much as anyone, but I had no desire to get down into the garbage pile in order to get it. My decision to go into television on my own terms, then, was a significant gamble for me. I had no intention of joining the others in parading out the dysfunctional and demented simply to get ratings. I did not want to send the message that these segments of our society constitute the norm.

I believe we live in the greatest country in the world. We have the responsibility to maintain a high moral standard and a sense of social consciousness in our television programming. I did not want to join the bottom feeders. My goal was to elevate lives and television provided the greatest audience for doing that, but I knew there would be forces trying to pull me down to the lower levels. Still, I thought television was worth the gamble. I may have been naive, but my philosophy is "Do not go where the path may lead, go where there is no path and leave a trail."

Fear of Failure Will Guarantee Failure

I think you have to take risks and challenge life in order to live fully. Often, that requires sacrifice. In spite of all the legs that it has, the caterpillar cannot crawl fast enough to fly. It has to give up those legs during its metamorphosis in order to fly. I was willing to give up the relative security of my speaking career in order to reach a greater audience in the risky arena of television. What do you have to give up in order to fly?

Write down five goals for your life and next to each write down what you might have to give up or risk in order to achieve each goal.

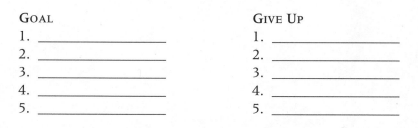

GOAL	GIVE UP
1. _____	1. _____
2. _____	2. _____
3. _____	3. _____
4. _____	4. _____
5. _____	5. _____

Going at Life Keeps You Alive

If you spend your life clinging to what is comfortable and secure, you may one day regret not testing your talents against the world. When you take shelter from life, you risk numbing yourself to it or even deadening your heart and mind. You cannot allow hard times or misfortune to permanently disable you. I can't tell you how many times I have come across old friends from Liberty City and Columbus and not recognized them because their life forces, once vital, have been drained and diminished.

My boyhood friend Lefty is one of those people, I'm saddened to say. He was from the neighborhood, a great basketball player and a very smart guy. I used to look up to him because he was such a gifted athlete, fun to be around, and a sharp dresser. He told wonderful stories and he seemed so worldly. It was Lefty who introduced me to the music of Miles Davis and other jazz greats. Shortly after high school Lefty was shot in the leg while committing a burglary and that ended his athletic dreams. I'm afraid he allowed that bullet to end any other dreams he might have had too.

When I was back in the neighborhood shooting promotional spots for *The Les Brown Show*, I saw Lefty on his old corner, the same one where he held court when I was in high school. Thirty years later, Lefty was still in the neighborhood hanging out. We talked for a while that day. He congratulated me on getting the show and he asked me when I might be back. I told him I come back regularly to see family, and he said, "Whenever you come I'll be right here." Lefty is like a lot of people who never leave their comfort zones because they have no vision of themselves beyond there. They allow life to wash over them. If something bad happens to them, they cave in to it totally. Lefty was only shot in the leg, but he allowed it to effectively stop his life from developing. It is such an unnecessary waste of talent.

Surviving Failure

Write down a fear of failure that you had at some point in life, whether as a child or adult. Example: *I was afraid that I would never escape the stigma of being in special education class.*

_____

_____

_____

Did you freeze up, or did you take steps to eliminate those fears? Example: *I mainstreamed myself by going after Mr. Washington as my mentor.*

_____

_____

_____

Dancing Up Life

We have a choice to let fear and hard times dominate us, or we can allow ourselves to see them merely as temporary setbacks. When my mother talked about her childhood, she never said she was "poor," or that she felt deprived of anything. In fact, her eyes always lit up when she talked about her girlhood in the swamps, and how much fun she had with her ponies and her pet alligator. "When I was young, I danced up this world," she'd say. And she continued dancing up the world for most of her life, in spite of all of the problems she faced as a poor single mother. I believe we all make the conscious choice to either sit life out, as Lefty has done, or to dance up the world, as my Mama did. Lefty taught himself to be a wallflower while my Mama taught herself to dance even when the band was playing.

It doesn't take much to keep people like Lefty down because

they carry defeat in their hearts. I know hundreds of people who have overcome more serious problems than a bum leg to live highly productive lives, and I am sure you do too. So what is the difference between Lefty and them, or Lefty and my mother? He sees defeat as a finality, rather than as merely part of the ebb and flow of life, while more positive people such as my Mama view defeat as only a temporary setback. Mama and people like her believe that they can always get their lives back on track because, like the children in that South African school, they believe that no condition is permanent.

Like Lefty and me, Wayne Bowe was a product of Booker T. Washington High School. In fact, Wayne was the president of the student council in 1964. He was a skinny little guy with a bubbly energetic personality who graduated at the top of his class. Shortly after graduation, Wayne was in a car accident. He was thrown through the windshield and suffered injuries that left him paralyzed and confined to a wheelchair. Unlike Lefty, who only had a wound in one leg, Wayne did not fold up. He never even complained. He maintained his energetic and upbeat attitude. True to his positive approach to life, Wayne eventually became a national advocate for people confined to wheelchairs.

Wayne and Lefty approached life from the same starting point at approximately the same times, but they took entirely different routes. When Lefty got shot, he allowed that wound to infect his entire life. He not only accepted it as a permanent setback, he allowed it to dominate the course of his life from that point on.

It is far healthier to take negative things that happen and isolate them. You can't let something bad in one aspect of your life affect all of your affairs. If tragedy strikes you, whatever it is, a physical accident or losing your job, you can't let it ruin your relationships or stifle the possibilities for your life. We all have the power to choose our responses to hard times, to failure and defeat. You have to take life on, you can't just let it have its way with you. Fear death if you want, but don't fear life.

Do You Dance with Life? Or Do You Sit It Out?

Take a minute or two to reflect on your attitude and approach to life by completing this exercise. Do you believe that when something bad happens to you it is a permanent defeat, or do you look at it as a temporary setback? Ask yourself these questions to help you define your approach. In hard times are you more inclined to say:

A DANCER
- I'm too tired to handle this right now.
- I'm not going to argue when you are in this mood.
- I'm having a rough time with the boss.
- I haven't heard from you lately.

A WALLFLOWER
- I'm never going to get this.
- I've had enough.
- I always fight with my boss.
- I thought you'd given up on me.

People who give in to life generally perceive bad things in terms of *always* and *never*—they are habitually pessimistic in their approach to life, while those who see bad things as temporary conditions are generally optimistic and positive. Interestingly, the opposite holds for their perceptions of good times. The optimistic person sees good times in terms of permanence while the pessimistic person sees them as fleeting.

A DANCER
- I have such good luck.
- This is wonderful.
- I earned this reward.

A WALLFLOWER
- I'm just lucky today.
- It seems unreal.
- What a fluke.

Do you see yourself in these responses? Differing views and approaches to life can have a definite impact on the individual's quality of life, even on matters of health. Studies indicate that people who are more optimistic live longer and spend less time in the hospital than people who are pessimistic. The optimists have better relationships. The person who sees life in optimistic terms is much more willing to take life on in a dynamic way.

Accepting Change as a Challenge

One of the aspects of life that the wallflowers seem to fear most is change, but change is an undeniable and often energizing part of life. When I travel around the country speaking to corporate employees, I find fear of change running rampant, even as this nation and the world are undergoing incredible change. If you cannot embrace change, you don't see life as a process of continued self-education. Author and social philosopher Peter Drucker writes that we are now in "The Age of Social Transformation." In this age, the dominant group will be the "knowledge workers" who have replaced the industrial workers and the agricultural workers who dominated in previous generations.

The great majority of jobs in coming decades will require a new approach to work, and a new mind-set. More formal education and the ability to acquire and to apply theoretical and analytical knowledge will be vital. Most importantly, he notes, the top jobs in coming decades will require "a habit of continuous learning."

The shift to a society based on knowledge and knowledge workers means a change in the way we will live. No longer will the majority of people earn their living by the sweat of their brow. Knowledge workers will gain access to jobs and social position through their formal education, but more and more knowledge, especially advanced knowledge beyond that of today's formal schooling, will be demanded.

Drucker is not alone in noting that the whole structure of our workforce is changing. The 40 40 Era is over—where we worked for 40 hours a week for 40 years to retire on 40% of what we made that wasn't enough in the first place. It is wise now to think of yourself as an independent contractor, whose value is constantly being measured. In this environment, the only security you have is your ability to adapt to change and to master as many talents and skills and as much knowledge as possible.

In this environment, you don't hold on to a job, you prepare yourself for a wide range of opportunities. The person who welcomes change and continuous learning leads a dynamic life, while those who back away from it, or fear it, are more likely to find themselves on the human scrap heap. You either expand, or you become expendable.

Examine your own attitudes toward change and learning in your life. Think about a change you would like to make, whether it would be a move to a new house, a change in jobs, a change in your marital status, or anything you would like to have happen. Write down what change you'd like to make and then note what steps you have to take to enact that change, and also note what is holding you back.

I'd like to change:

_____

_____

To bring about that change, I need to:

_____

_____

The thing holding me back is:

_____

_____

Now, look at what is holding you back. Is it really an obstacle, or is it something you could overcome if you could just eliminate your fear of change? How would this change make your life better:

_____

_____

Would it not be worth it to improve your life, or are you waiting for the next life?

Being on, But Not in, Television

From the start, I let the television executives who were courting me know that I didn't want to be part of the sleaze trend in television. Most claimed earnestly that they too were looking for higher ground and I took them at their word. In a way, I was blinded by their attention to me. They seemed to come out of the woodwork all at once, all of them telling me what an impact our show would have, all of them waving lucrative contracts. I'm as susceptible to that sort of thing as anyone else. And, like anyone else, I want to make a living. It was difficult not to be seduced by the compliments and the huge numbers they were throwing around. I had come a long way from Liberty City, but this was a whole new level. This was living a dream that I had not even dreamt yet. And maybe for good reasons.

At one point early in the recruitment process, I agreed to make a pilot show for Hearst Broadcasting. We went to a Boston television studio owned by Hearst and did a series of interviews with people involved in disasters and personal tragedies. It was a strange experience for me, working in this unfamiliar setting. As a public speaker, I was accustomed to delivering the message, but here I was expected to let the guest take the lead. My job was to draw them out about their experiences, and then to try to help them work through it.

One of the guests in the Hearst tryout was a woman who didn't want to get over a terrible tragedy, the death of a child. I kept saying, "You have to get beyond this," and she let me know she wasn't at all interested in moving on. It was painful trying to help her find resolution with the television cameras going. In another trial run, my guest was a chef who wanted to talk about the proper way to cook, serve, and eat lobster. I kept thinking, "What am I supposed to do, motivate the lobster to throw itself into the boiling water?" Have you ever tried to look dignified while eating lobster on television?

It was fun to make those pilot shows, but I was feeling like that lobster—something like a fish out of water. It was difficult for me to feel comfortable as the interviewer. As a speaker, I was so accustomed to being the primary source of information. It would prove to be one of my biggest problems in adapting to the talk show format.

In the Kings' Clutches

As it turned out, I signed with a partnership formed by Hearst and King World Productions, which is the nation's number one syndicator of television shows. Their biggest success story is *The Oprah Winfrey Show,* which they have syndicated since 1985. King World helped it grow from a local talk show in Chicago into a global phenomenon. King World also syndicates several other highly lucrative programs such as *Jeopardy!, Wheel of Fortune, Inside Edition,* and *American Journal.* The syndication powerhouse, which has annual revenues of more than $400 million, began as a small family-run business founded by Charles King of New Jersey in 1964. It is now run by his sons, Michael, based in Los Angeles, and Roger, who is headquartered in New York City.

The King brothers are a colorful Irish pair, particularly Roger, who lives life on a *large* scale. He is big and brawny and strong. I once grabbed Roger and playfully tried to lift him off the ground. He took it as a challenge. He wrapped his arms around me and lifted me as if I were a child. And I'm not a small person. This guy is as strong as a bear, and every bit as wily. Michael was almost as much of a character. He was a few years younger than Roger and more cerebral. It was always said that the reason King World became the syndicator of *Jeopardy!* was that Michael had once been a contestant and loved the show.

No Mickey Mouse

Initially, my business manager, Mike Williams, and I were wary of the Kings; in fact, we had been leaning strongly toward the Disney organization because we liked what they stood for, and they seemed to be honorable and interested in doing programs that helped people. I had even given some thought to finding a house in Orlando. But then, the street-smart King brothers came on strong. They kept saying, "We're going to make you the male Oprah." More interesting to me was the point that with an audience of 20 million, I could motivate and inspire a lot more people.

It was a strong argument, from our point of view. We had many discussions about the positives and negatives of television as a vehicle for my motivational messages and one of the biggest positives was the size of the audience, and the nature of the medium. Television had developed such a negative and cynical attitude overall. There seemed to be a great need for positive programming that inspired people to lead productive and successful lives. We wanted to do a show in which we explored the possibilities for people's lives rather than exploit their pain.

We agonized over whether or not commercial television was the proper arena for my message. We were extremely wary of the trend in talk television that was anchored in sensationalism and conflict, with people screaming and yelling, eyeball-to-eyeball. We didn't want anything to do with neck-jerking, tantrum-throwing, three-hundred-pound strippers. We told the Kings that up front. And they seemed to agree.

With assurances from them that I would have creative input on the content of the show—and with a sizable signing bonus to compensate for giving up my public speaking career—I decided to sign with King World. Though the brothers were a little rough around the edges, they are widely known as master salesmen. What I really did not understand at that point was that King World's experience and strength was mostly in syndicating existing television shows and selling them to stations around the country. They had very little experience in the actual production of television shows. And, of course, I had none.

By late summer of 1992, we were in New York to meet with the King brothers and to negotiate a contract. Mike Williams didn't want me at the bargaining table. I am terrible at hiding my emotions. That is a good thing when you are a motivational speaker trying to communicate with a large audience, but it can be deadly in a poker game or contract negotiations with savvy television executives. Mike made me rehearse what he wanted me to say at the beginning of the meeting, which was pretty much limited to

"Hello, so nice to see you. I've got a toothache, so I'm leaving. Mike will handle it from here."

At one point during negotiations, they broke up the meeting because they were at an impasse and I begged Mike to give me Roger King's phone number so I could call him and ask if we were still friends! I had been skeptical about becoming a talk show host, I was still skeptical, but these guys had me excited. I kept saying "Let's not be greedy. Let's not make them mad, they might go home." Mike wouldn't give me the phone number because he knew I'd cave in and tell them I'd take whatever they wanted to give me and that I'd probably throw in my children too.

It's funny how you can go from being wary of making a decision, even a little frightened, and then suddenly you find yourself throwing all you have into it. Have you ever done that when buying a car? You start out walking around the car on the lot as if it might explode at any minute. You dance with the sales person like boxers in the ring. And then, all of a sudden you find yourself practically begging for credit approval and the keys! I guess that's why they say you should be careful what you ask for, you may get it. Or it may get you!

Make a list of the things you have chased after in life only to have them cause you grief. Review this list whenever you feel the need to remind yourself about making decisions wisely.

I wanted _____

_____

It got me _____

_____

I wanted _____

_____

It got me _____

_____

Up-Front Negotiations

One of the more difficult areas of negotiations with the Kings had to do with how much input we would have into the show. Not control, just input. They had agreed, from the beginning, that I shouldn't be doing anything that would conflict with my work as a motivational and solution-oriented speaker, and they kept saying that they would stand by that, so we eventually decided to trust them. In late summer, we signed a contract to begin working on the show in the spring of 1993. In January of 1993, they introduced me and *The Les Brown Show* at the annual convention of the National Association of Television Programming Executives in San Francisco.

The King brothers hold a party every year at the convention, and it is generally considered a highlight of the event that draws more than nine thousand television programming executives from all over the country. In fact, nearly half of those registered for the convention are invited to the King World party. The gathering, like the Kings themselves, was larger than life. To give you an idea of the sort of party it was, the entertainment was a command performance by Elton John, who sang for more than two hours. I wanted to hear this exceptionally talented performer, but I fell asleep. I was worn out. I'd been working the convention, not attending it. I was already trying to build my audience.

The Kings had me selling the program to buyers from stations around the country and those station programming executives assured me, one after the other, that they wanted positive programming that would be helpful to their viewers. That's what they told me, and I told them that was the only reason I was there, to do positive programs. And they told me, Montel Williams said that. Jerry Springer said that. But they are all doing sleaze. So, I made a vow to them and myself that I would not sell out, even during the ratings periods when many talk show hosts will do anything to get ratings.

Walking Tall Before the Fall

I was walking in tall cotton. I didn't have any misgivings at that point because they kept saying the show had to reflect the host. After signing in February with King World, things moved rapidly. They wanted to get the show on the air by September, which gave us less than seven months to put it all together. The first step was to put me through television talk show host training. We had decided that because of my limited formal education, I needed some tutoring in three areas; American history, European history, and language. Although I have devoted most of my adult life to catching up on my education, my early schooling was weak. And even the things I learned, I've discovered, I sometimes "mislearned." My advisors were fearful that some of those "Brownisms" would slip out. I'm too embarrassed to reveal here what they are, so you know they must be bad!

Part of this talk show host training took place in a rather unlikely place, the small town of Marion, Iowa, where nationally known broadcasting consultant Frank N. Magid Associates Inc. has a corporate office. Magid's company also has offices all over the world, but it is based there because it originally grew out of his work and research at the University of Iowa, nearby in Cedar Rapids. The training involved interviewing techniques, how to ask questions and how to find more questions within the answers in order to keep the interview progressing. They were trying to teach me—someone who had always made a living by speaking—how to communicate by listening instead. This was something people had been trying to drum into my head since grade school. My mother always used to say, "Why do you think the Lord gave you one mouth and two ears?"

Whenever I'd ask someone a question, I'd always want to give the answer. It was difficult for me to turn the discussion over to others. My trainers were forever telling me that I should let the guest experts offer their knowledge, rather than jumping in with my opinions. I never really adjusted to that, and the producers of the show resisted changing the format to fit my skills. We pushed for an opening monologue and a closing talk in which I could do the sort of speaking that worked so successfully for me, but they felt it came across as too preachy in a talk show format. We could not convince them otherwise, and we ended up doing it their way, following the old path, rather than trying to blaze a trail that was cut for my strengths as a speaker.

It was more challenging than I had expected to convert from being a speaker to being a talk show host. I felt like I was turning myself inside out. Public speaking has always been fun for me. This was not fun, at least in the early trial shows. Trying to fit into the cookie cutter image of a television talk show host was stressing me out. Oh, I had some fun, especially during breaks when I could talk to people and make them laugh, but when the camera came on I had to be straight. It went against the grain of my personality. Remember what I said earlier, you have to be careful for what you wish for in life, because you may get it and it may beat you up!

Getting It Wrong to Get It Right

When we began taping trial shows and then real shows that summer of 1993, I had all kinds of problems because I had so much difficulty adjusting to the format. You have just five to seven minutes to bring a person out and introduce his or her story. In that brief time, you have to try and draw the audience into the story by creating "moments" that make the viewer turn up the volume and put down the remote control. And that opening segment has to flow naturally so that it just seems perfectly okay to interrupt the guest telling some intimate story and say "We'll be right back after this commercial message." That was difficult for me, to fast-forward the conversations with guests without appearing to rush them. My problem was that I empathize with people who have problems, and I'd get engrossed in their stories and forget where I was. In television, you can't do that. After all, the advertisers pay the bills.

We all find ourselves in these uncomfortable situations, particularly early in our careers, but now with people changing jobs much more often, it can happen anytime. You find yourself thrashing around in a job that you just can't get comfortable in, and panic sets in. My approach to these situations is to try and understand that there is always going to be a learning curve, and at first that curve is going to be a steep climb. Otherwise, it wouldn't be a curve, right? You've got to believe that anything worth doing is worth doing well. But you also have to understand that if you don't know how to do something, it is worth doing it badly until you learn to do it well. In other words, you have to think of failure as part of the process, not the end of the process.

Remember when you learned to ride a bicycle? Or how about when you taught your own child to ride? All of that crashing into curbs, mailboxes, and parked cars sure looked like failure, didn't it? But in the end, we all learn to ride. We all want to get on and ride off right away, but few things in life happen that way. You don't become the master of something simply by attempting it. But you never become master of anything if you don't try. You have to have patience and persistence and when you crash into the garbage truck you cannot simply say, "Well, I tried, and all I got was garbage, so I quit."

I have a friend, Chuck, who used to say cynically, "Nothing ventured. Nothing lost." He was kidding of course, but that attitude is carried by many people who are afraid to fail and as a result they never achieve anything. Cootie used to call himself "Captain Mediocrity." In high school, if he got a B in a class his philosophy was not to try and get an A because he might fail and then his B, which was a good grade, would seem diminished. That is an intriguing way of looking at it, but it is also self-defeating. In today's job market, for example, you can't afford to say "I have a good job, why should I try for anything else and risk failing?" The answer is that there are no longer any guarantees of job security, and if you don't do all that you can to make yourself invaluable and multifaceted then you are not preparing yourself adequately. In truth, the only way to succeed is to risk failure. Consider two young guys standing in an office plaza in New York City. Both of them are interested in finding a woman to date. The first one goes about this by approaching every attractive woman he sees. His theory is that by talking to so many of them he is bound to eventually find one who will respond to his charms. The second man scoffs at his friend's plan, saying that he would never risk being turned down like that. Of course, by refusing to take the risk, the second young man will never succeed. You can always avoid embarrassment by doing nothing. And if that is your measure of success, you'll be successful. But if you want acceptance—or whatever your goal—you have to be willing to face a lot of rejection.

When my friend Chuck was in the seventh grade, he was one of the top ten spellers in his class so he qualified for his junior high school's spelling bee. Now, Chuck believed he was not the best speller in the school, although he felt he was probably in the top three. Always analytical, he decided that he would not try to win because he felt he wouldn't win. He also did not want to be the first person to miss and be eliminated, so he waited for another student to drop out before he purposely misspelled the word "distribution."

"I lost on purpose," he told me in recounting the story. "I didn't want to stay in the competition because I didn't want to be disappointed. I knew there was a guy who was a better speller and that he would probably win it. So then it became a question of how to get off the stage without looking like a fool."

Chuck said he thinks often of how he threw that spelling bee, because he has caught himself in that same "I can't win, so I won't try" attitude as an adult. "There is some kind of angst causing this, but I don't know where it comes from," he said. Many people take on that self-defeating attitude and as a result they never challenge themselves. I think our society's corrupted "winning is everything" mentality is responsible to some degree. That mentality has been fostered more by the lust for money than any desire for a quality life. Winning may be everything if your life is centered on money, but if you are more interested in living a rewarding and active life, it is the striving that is everything. If you believe the chase is the reward, then you learn to see failure as only a part of the game, not as a disaster. You have to be willing to go the last mile because that is where the reward is.

Lost in Talk Show Land

Overall, it was exciting for me to be doing a television talk show but there was this nagging voice in the back of my mind saying "I have no idea what I am doing! Help me, I'm lost! I can't do this!" I knew failure was a distinct possibility, but the thrill of chasing after a dream overrode my misgivings. It was impossible for me to admit my fears to anyone openly. We were all swept up in the excitement. Nearly every day we'd get fresh news of a new television station that had signed up for the program. King World told us that in spite of the high price they were demanding for the show, we were signing stations faster than any other program they'd syndicated. They were already planning a companion show to run with mine, a talk show hosted by Rolonda Watts, who had worked as a reporter and guest anchor for King World on *Inside Edition.*

I was living large but feeling small on the inside. I remember riding to work one day in the limousine thinking, "My God, I'm in New York and I have a television talk show." I remember when we started to tape the first show. One of the producers said "Good Luck, Mr. Brown" and then they started the countdown, "5, 4, 3, 2, 1 . . ." and I said, "Hi, this is Les Brown," and I messed up. They had to stop taping and let me start over, but I messed up again. They took a little break to let me collect my thoughts. I was grateful, because I also needed to use the rest room. I asked the crew and the audience to excuse me for a second. I ran backstage, went to the rest room, and jogged back out, only to find everyone roaring with laughter. The crew. The audience. Everyone. Then I realized what all the laughter was about. Oh Lord, I had been in such a hurry, I'd forgotten to take off my cordless microphone! My rest room visit had been broadcast to the entire studio audience.

- Dealing with conflict by staying within your values and principles
- Making wise decisions in difficult times
- Accepting and offering criticism in a constructive manner

CHAPTER 3

Rantings and Ratings

The title of one of the more frustrating segments of *The Les Brown Show* was "Battle of the Sexes." It was supposed to be an informative show discussing how men and women communicate in different ways. The goal was to reach greater understanding. But it led mostly to mayhem and it proved to be an omen of things to come.

While I was backstage preparing for that show, my producers, who were employees of King World, were working the audience into a lather. They went into the studio before the show began and ordered the men to move to one section of the studio and the women to another. Then they began pitting them against each other. They goaded them into name-calling and finger-pointing. By the time I walked out for the start of the show, the audience was ready to rumble. I began the show by asking members of the audience to express questions they had about the opposite sex. The first question from a young man in the audience wasn't exactly on point. "Why do women think all men are boys?" he asked.

"'Cause a lot of men act like boys so we treat them that way," fired back a tough-talking woman. She was followed by an even more combative young lady who was neither asking a question nor responding, she was just firing wildly into the crowd. She glared at the men and snarled, "They sleep with you and don't call you back." Next came this reasoned response from an enlightened young man: "Most of the time it's a one-night thing and hey, you don't need to call them back!" he said. And so it went. Down, down, down.

A sneering thug stood up and proclaimed that "Most men have sex [with a number of women] because one woman ain't enough for most men." When the women jeered at his remark, he raised his hands over his head like a fighter who'd scored a knockout. The show disintegrated into women disparaging men for their bad breath and body odor, and men blasting women for "fake breasts" and "saggy underwear." When one articulate young lady, Wendy, stood up and said that she liked men who were good-humored, sensitive to her feelings, and intelligent, the audience chided her so much that I couldn't help myself. "Hey Wendy, don't worry, they're not in this studio," I said.

This was supposed to be *my* audience. But it wasn't my audience. And it wasn't my show. At least, it wasn't the type of show I had wanted to do. I had not been aware that my producers were stoking the fires in the audience before the show began, but I was not surprised when I found out. I had hoped that this show would involve a serious discussion of conflicting points of view between men and women, but it disintegrated into confrontation. And confrontation is what the King brothers wanted, because they thought you couldn't get good ratings with intelligent and positive programming.

On the Air and Out of Control

What do you do when you cannot control an important aspect of your life? How do you respond when your carefully laid plans turn to chaos? How do you stay in control of your life and your emotions in times of crisis? Often, your only recourse is to check your value system, and to anchor yourself to those values that guide your life while the storm swirls around you. By staying true to your value system, you may inspire those around you to follow your leadership as some of the greatest figures in our history have done, people such as the Reverend Martin Luther King and Nelson Mandela. But even if others don't follow you, even if you are cast out, you will still be living within the guidelines that *you* and no one else have established for your life. You may not always win—few people lead such charmed lives—but in the end you will be a winner because you will not have sold out the values and beliefs that make you who you are.

Your values are not set by government or church leaders. Your boss doesn't assign them to you. They are formed by your life experiences, by the way in which your family lives, and by the paths you instinctively have chosen or rejected. My mother gave me many of my values, sometimes she had to beat them into my bottom. But she showed me the path away from gangs and drugs. She showed me the way out of poverty. She showed me that you don't have to accept the labels that others place on you.

Your values give you consistency in the way you approach life. They exist within all of us, although we don't always pay enough attention to them. It's been said that such values or principles are laws that cannot be broken; you can only break yourself against them. Fundamental human values include faith, persistence, integrity, decency, and patience. By centering our lives on these beliefs, we ensure that we can always find our balance and our way, no matter what life throws at us. By holding to your beliefs, you can always stay on track toward your dream.

A Global Dream Based on Belief

When I write of facing your fears and pursuing your dreams, of course, I am not restricting the topic to dreams of financial or career success. We all have our own unique goals and dreams, and there are many who, by their nature and circumstances, are compelled to dream beyond the personal realm. These people have dreams that affect entire nations and the world's population. Perhaps one of the most courageous dreamers of modern times is the great Nelson Mandela, the living legend who faced down incredible resistance and even the threat of death to become the first elected black leader of South Africa.

In 1964, during his trial for sabotage against the racist South African white rulers, Mandela, then forty-four, said, "During my lifetime I have dedicated myself to this struggle of the African people. I have fought against white domination, and I have fought against black domination. I have cherished the ideal of a democratic and free society in which all persons live together in harmony and with equal opportunities. It is an ideal which I hope to live for and to achieve. But, if need be, it is an ideal for which I am prepared to die."

He displayed remarkable courage in giving that speech. Mandela defied the government that had arrested him and he continued to defy them when they imprisoned him in a former leper colony after convicting him in that trial. But his defiance was so courageous and so undeniably selfless that his opponents could not kill him. When a man's spirit is that powerful, there is no killing him or his cause. In 1985, the white prime minister of South Africa offered Mandela his freedom and the freedom of his followers if they would agree to give up their armed resistance to apartheid and quit the African National Congress resistance group. In fact, on several other occasions, his foes offered Mandela his freedom. He had already sacrificed greatly. Nobody would have called him a sellout if he chose to take his freedom. He would have traveled the world and dined with kings and queens as a hero. Mandela refused, saying that he could not be free until all black South Africans were free. "Your freedom and mine cannot be separated," he said to his followers.

His courage from a prison cell inspired admiration and support around the world. The leaders of governments and even the Pope called for his release. Finally, in February of 1990, Mandela was released from prison and four years later, at the age of seventy-five, he was elected the first black president of South Africa. In his inaugural address he said, "Let there be justice for all. Let there be peace for all. Let there be work, bread, water, and salt for all. Let each know that for each the body, the mind and the soul have been freed to fulfill themselves."

To fulfill our lives, we have to live as Mandela has lived, committed to our values and willing to take a stand with our lives. There will always be defeats and failures. There will always be temptations to sell out. Some people sell out to fear, some sell out to laziness and a life of mediocrity. Some sell out to drugs and alcohol. Some of us sell out to remain in our comfort zone, unwilling to change and learn. Others sell out their own principles in order to move ahead. The price of selling out is always too high. Whenever you think the odds against you are overpowering, think about Nelson Mandela. If he can go from prisoner to president by staying within his value system in the face of his powerful enemies, surely we can stand by the things we believe in during difficult and challenging times in our lives.

When Mandela refused to sell out to apartheid, he defeated it. He may never have been released from prison. He may have died there. But he would have gone to his grave as a man who did not sell out, and therefore he would have been remembered forever as a man who could not be defeated. When you establish standards or values for your life, you locate the center of your wheel, the point at which all other aspects of your life are held in focus. By holding to those values or beliefs, you maintain balance in your life. You find the strength to endure and persevere.

What Is Your Life Built Around?

Determine what you value most in life. Examine your life and how you live it. What drives and motivates you the most? Rank the following items according to their importance to you:

1. _____ Your career

2. _____ Your family

3. _____ Your financial security

4. _____ Your reputation

5. _____ Your possessions

6. _____ Your friends

7. _____ Your loved one(s)

8. ____ Your faith

9. ____ Your community

10. ____ Your values

Now, write a statement about each area of your life that is important to you. *Example: My* values *are important to me because if I stay true to my beliefs such as faith, persistence, integrity, decency, and patience, I will remain balanced in my life.*

1. _____

_____

2. _____

_____

3. _____

_____

4. _____

_____

5. _____

_____

6. _____

_____

7. _____

_____

8. _____

_____

9. _____

_____

10. _____

_____

In truth, most of us build our lives around all of these things, with the emphasis varying from time to time. But a life built around a value system encompasses all of these things, all of the time. Your life can get out of balance easily if you emphasize career over every other aspect, the same with financial security, or your possessions. But if you build everything else on the foundation of your value system of faith, persistence, integrity, decency, and patience, you will rarely get thrown off balance. Your job, your family, your possessions, even your partner might change, but your value system remains firmly entrenched. It is always there as a point of reference, a foundation, and a center of balance.

Each of us has our own unique value system. With the help of my friend Mike Williams, I established these Nine Principles for Dynamic Living based on the values that guide my life. You may find them helpful in creating your own guidelines for living through hard times. Copy them and keep them handy in your workplace or home for inspiration.

Nine Principles for Dynamic Living

1. *Each of us can achieve far beyond our horizons and in avenues of life we have never explored.* Many people never really know the full range of their potential, and too often they limit themselves to what they have seen others accomplish rather than assuming that they have unlimited potential. Sometimes it is best to live life with persistence and patience, with the unlimited vision of a child who thinks everything is possible unless shown otherwise. After all, you can't expect to reach beyond your horizons if your vision is limited to your own backyard. You have to be committed to growth, to expanding your life by pushing your talents and constantly testing them to discover new outlets and sources of energy. Set goals without limits.

2. *Each of us has some basic goodness which is the foundation for the greatness we can ultimately achieve.* Through the ages, great thinkers have debated the nature of men and women. Are we inherently

good, or evil? I believe each of us has elements of good and decency, even the worst of us. And I believe that what we achieve in life is related to how much faith and goodness we bring to the table. I am convinced that all great people, whether they are artists, teachers, athletes, parents, or housepainters, all of us need to find and nurture our goodness in order to achieve our greatest potential.

3. Each of us must take responsibility for our actions, our well-being, and the attainment of our maximum potential. One of the least enjoyable aspects of adulthood is the burden of responsibility that it brings down upon our shoulders. Having fun is no longer the priority. Being carefree is a rare state of mind. But integrity and personal responsibility are not burdensome. They prepare you for growth. When we show integrity by accepting responsibility for our actions and inactions and for our mental, physical, spiritual, and material well-being, we are becoming the catalyst for our own lives. No one else can pilot your ship.

4. Self-awareness, self-approval, and self-commitment are essential for self-fulfillment. These are the four stages of personal growth. You begin to grow when you achieve self-awareness by asking who you are, and establishing what your frame of reference is for looking at the world. You have to understand yourself before you can understand the rest of the world around you. And you have to have self-approval, or self-love, before you can expect others to see your goodness and love you too. You've seen people who "radiate confidence." Those are people who have accepted themselves and so are accepting of others.

Once you know yourself and accept yourself, you then can commit to the life and goals that most appeal to you. Champions and winners in life do not have to be rolled out of bed in the morning. They go at life because they know who they are, they are comfortable with themselves, and they have identified goals that are in line with their self-image. They manage their time, resources, emotions, and relationships to be in synch with their goals.

Self-fulfillment comes from achieving those goals that you have committed to. And to continue to achieve is to lead a fulfilling life. By constantly assessing where you are in life and measuring it against where you want to go, you will lead a fulfilling life. It is a cycle that will move you through life so that, in life's final weeks, days, and hours, you can look back and say, "I took life on!"

5. Building and maintaining relationships is critical to social development, both within the family and within the community. For a species that is supposed to be highly social, we devote very little time to studying relationships or ways to make them work. So much is trial and error, with the emphasis on error. Too many of us arrive at adulthood without a general sense of how to nurture and maintain relationships that grow as we grow. Communication is vital in relationships, yet men in particular are often without a clue as to the value of communication with loved ones. We all could do well to open the lines of communication in our relationships, to pay attention to those relationships as avidly as we watch the stock market, the sports page, or the fashion trends. Relationships that are carefully maintained are less likely to become stale, hostile, or to wither and die.

6. Mutual respect is the fundamental element of human relations. We often assume that it is our differences that get in the way in our relationships with others. Actually, differences do not matter, it is your tolerance or intolerance of others that matters. You cannot expect everyone else to share your point of view because we all come from unique ranges of experience. You do have the right to expect others to respect your point of view. By acknowledging the value of our differences, you open yourself to the greater experience through diversity. What matters most is respecting each other. When mutual respect is established, relationships flourish.

7. We elevate our own lives by helping others rise. The only way to push someone up a ladder is to climb with them, and so when you help others, your own life benefits. When we tune into the needs of others, we fulfill a vital spiritual need to be of service to others, and we also serve as an example for others to follow. When we teach by example that helping is good, we create more helpers and the good within us grows around us.

8. *Planning, measuring, and executing are the critical tools in the manifestation of our beliefs.* You can tell what a person believes by watching his or her actions. Beliefs are acted out. By observing how a person spends time, energy, and money, you can learn a great deal. That is why it is not enough to simply sharpen the language that describes your beliefs or to say you are sincere in them. You have to live them and that means planning your life, measuring your actions, and carrying out your goals with those beliefs in mind. The gifts we are given in life require the best of us, not merely our best intentions. Doing great work requires that we become great people, and all of us can become great people. What we must remember is to gauge the impact of our beliefs on ourselves and on those around us. We need tools to match our passions.

9. *Each of us must model integrity in the making and keeping of our commitments.* To model integrity is to have no gaps between what we promise and what we perform. Some of the worst emotional damage in others is created by those who promise what they cannot, will not, or do not deliver. We cannot avoid making commitments merely to avoid disappointments. You have to consider the consequences of broken promises, the loss of faith and trust. If you are guided by your sense of integrity, your word will have meaning and value and you will serve as a model for others.

Living a Valuable Life by Living Your Values

When you live within a system of values, no one can throw you off because you will always understand within yourself what the true value of any decision is to you. Your tempters may try to manipulate you by dangling one of your other interests in front of your eyes. "By fudging these figures, you will make *a lot* of money." "If you just tell the boss about this guy's past, you will get the promotion instead of him." But you understand the real power of those temptations is extremely limited because they go against your value system. Your values are principles that guide your life. When the distractions of fame, wealth, lust, or other temptations arise, your beliefs serve as road signs to lead you back. By checking your value system, you can find your way back. It doesn't have to be some momentous matter. It can be as simple as this: "What is more important to the value of my life and what will mean more down the road—hanging out with my friends, or spending time with the family?" By checking your value system, you find the strength and self-assurance to disregard chiding from your friends, peer pressure, or temptation. Your values give you a sense of yourself that goes beyond material possession or social position.

Check your decisions against your value system. Here are a few guiding rules.

A Value System Checkup

1. Check yourself. A proper basis for decision-making prepares you to make your decision based on the facts rather than fleeting emotions or prejudices. How do you evaluate your position? Here are a few suggestions:

• Are you looking at the facts clearly, or are you in a poor state of mind for decision-making?
• Evaluate your motivation. Are you in debt so that money concerns are taking precedence over your values? Are you feeling insecure so that you may be acting out of a need for security?

2. Check your ego. Have you let vanity lead you? Lust? What do you have to prove to anyone else? If you are secure within yourself why take an action that is not really reflective of who you are or who you want to be?

3. Check your emotions. Could anger or sorrow be influencing you? It is always important to monitor your thoughts and your emotions, to understand the influences at work on your actions. Be guided by your values, not by fleeting emotions.

4. Check your bearings. Develop the habit of regularly stopping to think before making decisions, "Is this consistent with who I am and where I want to go in life?" This habit will help you stay on course.

5. *Check your reference points.* An adage in the newspaper business is "Always check the clips." This means that whenever a reporter prepares to do a story on a subject, he or she should always check to see what has been written previously about that subject. There are scores of examples of inexperienced reporters writing glowing profiles of a businessman or community leader, only to discover that a few months or years earlier that same individual was caught in a crime or some morally reprehensible act. Too often, we assume that everything we encounter has materialized at that second and at that place. Without looking for points of reference and perspective when making a decision, you risk making mistakes. By checking with someone who has already gone through a similar decision-making process, you gain the benefit of that person's experience and a greater frame of reference.

Where do you find reference points? Here are a few suggestions:

- Co-workers
- Former employers
- Family members
- Friends
- Professional groups and journals
- Consumer groups
- Newspaper and magazine articles
- Educators
- Consultants and counselors

6. *Check your valuables.* You don't leave your car at the airport with the doors unlocked. You don't leave your children home without supervision. You don't leave cash sitting out at work. Why would you make a decision without mentally checking how it will impact the most valuable aspects of your life? If you face a decision about changing jobs, you should make a list of pros and cons and how each aspect will affect your life and the lives of family members. Will the increased hours be worth the increased pay if they take you away from family matters? How many people

have gone to their graves wishing they'd spent more time in the office? If you face a decision about your marriage or your relationship, you should ask the same questions.

Here is a checklist for your valuables. Feel free to add your own to the list. If I decide to do this, it will affect:

My family by _____

My friends by _____

My career by _____

My finances by _____

My social life by _____

My spiritual life by _____

Tearing at Your Value System

King World had hired six producers, six associate producers, and three assistant producers for the show. Many of them were young people eager to make their mark in television talk shows, but they only knew how to duplicate what they had already seen, which was exactly what I wanted to avoid. It wasn't their fault really. They were only doing what they'd been told to do. But it was sad to watch a new generation of television producers fall into the tar pit. They were trained to go for flash, not substance.

They were delighted if they could get two people in conflict to go at each other on camera. But they had very little sensitivity to whether or not that public venting served any useful purpose other than to fill airtime. They had not been trained to think about what happened to these people once the cameras went off. They would say things to me like, "This person will cry for you on the air, she will show a lot of pain and get real emotional." They were always talking about which buttons to push with the guests, rather than how to help these people find solutions and resolution.

For some of the producers, but not all, there were no boundaries. They would stoop to any level to exploit these people. It wasn't really that they were immoral or uncaring people; they were simply responding to what their superiors wanted from them. That was the talk show environment, so they busted their butts to do productive things but if it didn't have sparks they were criticized. So, they did what worked for their bosses—sex, drugs, and rock and roll. And they had to answer ultimately to executives who were answering to the Kings. I was cast as the party pooper, even though it was supposed to be my party. I stood by my belief in television as a healing tool, and I paid a price. I took some hits personally and professionally because I refused to abandon my values.

My value system was sorely tested in my dealings with King World on the set of my television talk show. As I'd suspected, the Kings and their producers were not committed to producing a show that sought answers to societal problems. Our differing visions for the show clashed often. My advisors and I would plan a show in which we would talk about a problem for the first third, and then discuss resolutions during the rest of the show. But the Kings' people would want to spend the whole show on the problem and then provide answers as the credits rolled for the last thirty seconds!

Like their role models on other shows, certain members of our staff were like the people who call for blood in boxing matches. They would beat the bushes for the wildest guests and audience members they could find. They'd reel them in with a free trip to New York, a limo, a free hotel room, and their fifteen minutes of fame. They'd get them pumped up and then try to rush them on the air as quickly as possible. In promotions for the show, they'd use language that would get people all worked up to respond emotionally rather than thoughtfully. In one show dealing with families and forgiveness, they set me up for an incredible shock, but fortunately I discovered the ambush before we began taping.

The Ambushed Talk Show Host

This show was entitled "Family Means Forgiveness" and it was supposed to be a healing show, but it very nearly was a disaster. The show brought together two brothers, one of whom had AIDS and was involved in a long-running feud with his brother's wife. We were going to try and address the family conflict on the show so that he did not go to his grave embittered by it. In my briefing, the production staff said the brother with AIDS, who was thirty-seven, had announced to the family twenty-three years earlier that he was a homosexual. I can't give all the details even now, but the story they told me about the brother with AIDS just didn't ring true. So, before the show, I went to talk to him backstage. He told me then that he had not told his family of his homosexuality, they had discovered it when his mother found him with someone in a sexual act. In addition, he told me other potentially embarrassing things that undoubtedly would have caused the family even more turmoil.

I'm sure some, or most, other talk show hosts would have reveled in the sordid truth of what had gone on in this highly dysfunctional family, but I was shocked. And I surely did not want this dirty laundry hanging all over my show. At the last minute, we had to restructure the entire show because I was not about to have these revelations come out. As it developed, we were able to heal some wounds in this family. But I felt after that I could not completely trust my staff.

During the earliest days of the show, I was presented one day with the list of program topics that my producers were planning and I could not believe my eyes. From my perspective, nearly every one of them was negative in orientation. Even when I would suggest a topic and get them to agree to it, somewhere down the line it would get twisted. It was like telling someone an innocent joke one minute, and then having it come back to you as a dirty joke an hour later. The method in earlier shows was for them to plan shows without consulting me at all. This was *The Les Brown Show,* and they weren't giving me input. They had courted me as a male Oprah, but they were programming me as a darker shade of Geraldo!

Used, Abused, and Televised

In another show, this one on reuniting lost loves, they brought in a guy who, unknown to me, had abused the woman who was the other guest. A producer I had hired because of her experience as a social services counselor, Karen Boyd, picked up on this man's emotional instability early in the taping, and during a break she told me to be careful. At one point, I had to physically put myself between him and the woman because his body language hinted to me that at any point he might snap. He had initially presented himself as under control, but as the show progressed it became obvious that he didn't have much control at all. We had hoped to bring the two people together as a surprise, but during the show we realized we were exposing this woman to a dangerous man. After the show, we arranged for the woman to go to another hotel and Karen spent the night with her. Even then, the ex-boyfriend managed to track her down and make threatening telephone calls to her. In the end, we assisted the woman in moving to another town and we helped her get therapy.

In reviewing what had happened, it was obvious that the staff had not adequately researched this relationship before inviting the two people on the show. They had not asked the right kind of questions because they weren't looking for depth. They just knew the guy was trying to get back with the lady and they were going to have him make his plea. They had no idea that the reason the woman had walked away was because he had beaten her.

You have heard of "ambush" talk show segments in which a guest is invited under false pretenses and then bushwhacked with someone or something from the past. Well, I had the opposite problem. I was the ambushee. Me, the host! Regularly some of my producers would give me a mistaken or superficial impression of what a guest was going to say, only to have the guest ambush me with some trash talk material while we were taping the show. Not that we didn't do some shows that I was quite proud of, but in the end the conflict between what I wanted to do with the show and what King World wanted was too great to overcome.

In the final analysis, they didn't believe enough in my concept to allow *The Les Brown Show* to find its audience and *then* to see if there was money in it. They believed in following the money trail, wherever it led. I am all for making money, but wasn't interested in chasing it into the garbage dump.

What do you do when many of those around you do not share your vision? What happens when you stick your neck out, take a risk, and then encounter this sort of problem? You have to remain focused on your value system. You have to have a greater vision that allows you to see beyond them to your dream. When I was working on my dream to become a public speaker, my brother Wesley appointed himself as my dream-buster. "You're gonna make a living doing *what?* Talking? Motivating people in Fortune 500 companies? *You?* The refugee from the Dodo Ward? You'd better go back to that job at Sears. The guy there liked you, maybe he'd take you back."

Don't Let Anybody Steal Your Dreams

If I had listened to my brother's advice, I'd probably still be hawking lethal carving knives in the appliance section. When you come from a background of poverty, especially, you hear those comments from those around you. They may come from the heart, or they may come out of jealousy and ignorance. I talked about this recently with my friend Dexter Yager of Charlotte, North Carolina, who also had to overcome the limited perceptions of others in order to pursue his dreams.

Dexter once drove a Utica Club Beer delivery truck for a living. The son and grandson of plumbers, he worked for years too as a salesman at Sears and later as a car salesman. He recalls that in those early days, his customers often talked down to him. They treated him as an inferior. But he also notes that "I was not intimidated by them. I did not react either with defensive anger or with passive self-pity." What did Dexter draw upon when he encountered this treatment? He focused on his own talent, abilities, and on his vision of what he wanted to become in life. "None of them, not one, could compare to my dream," he writes in his book, *Don't Let Anybody Steal Your Dream.*

Nobody stole Dexter's dream. Today, this down-to-earth, gutsy businessman makes millions upon millions a year and wields considerable political influence in this country. His vast business interests include more than one million Amway distributors around the world who sell more than $2 billion in products each year. His organization accounts for more than 50 percent of Amway's sales volume.

Dexter has invited me to speak to members of his organization all over the country, groups as large as eighty thousand people. I've spent a great deal of time with him and his wife, Birdie. We share backgrounds of relative poverty—not to mention our sales experience at Sears—and we share the belief that anyone can overcome his circumstances. Dexter is a common man with uncommon drive. He believes that if you want to make something out of yourself, you have to be determined to do it and that you can't allow the dream-busters to get in your way. He believes that anybody can come up with excuses to not make it, but those who want it bad enough don't make excuses. He believes that the people who excel in life are those who produce results, not reasons. He believes in the power of a dream and in the power of friendship and trust and service.

For every one of those beliefs Dexter is also an example. He has created an army of common everyday people who, by following his guidance, have achieved beyond their wildest dreams as entrepreneurs. This is a man who truly turned himself into what he needed to become in order to get where he wanted to be. And he did not listen to those who did not share his vision or his dreams. He says, "If the dream is big enough, the odds don't matter."

You are going to encounter people who don't share your vision, and all you can do is to step around them and keep fixed on your goals and be true to the beliefs that you've built your life upon. Wesley did not share my vision, but he was easy to ignore. I only had to see him during family gatherings. My producers and the powers behind them posed a much greater challenge.

When you believe strongly in something you have to fight to defend it. And I was in a royal battle with the Kings. That was made obvious one day when Roger King pulled me aside and said, "Look Les, you can do good shows about mothers who kill their children. You can motivate them. You can motivate them not to kill the little bastards. Those kind of shows get good numbers!"

Obviously, I was banging my head against a wall. I still believe you can get good ratings and do quality television, while the Kings believed you had to choose between the two. In my speeches, I've often told my audiences that you cannot expect all of those around you to share your vision and your dreams. Roger King's mantra was "If it ain't broke don't fix it." Mine is "If it ain't perfect keep working at it. Don't try to reinvent the wheel." He wanted us to do what every other talk show was doing, but at that point even *The Oprah Winfrey Show,* which was the standard by which all other talk shows were measured, had begun to drift into the lower levels of talk television in order to compete. And it hadn't even begun to get as down and dirty as it would eventually get before Oprah, to her credit, pulled out of the dogfight. She proved that you could get good ratings with quality television and, eventually, she forced others to acknowledge it. Of course, Oprah was established and she had a lot more clout with King World than I did. But, in the end, we both won because we did not sell out.

Standing Your Ground

Think about a time in your life, whether in your family, community, church, or club, where you should have taken a stance and didn't. Write it down. Do you feel badly about not taking a stance?

_____

_____

_____

Now, think about a situation where you did take action. How did it make you feel? Write down what you did and how you now feel about it:

_____

_____

_____

Is there anything you are currently facing or soon will face that you need to take a stand on? Are you going to operate based on your values, or are you going to give in to outside pressures? Write your responses:

_____

_____

_____

You are always going to run into people who want to bend you to their will, their vision, their way of doing things. That is why it is so important to be centered on your value system. If you hold to what you believe in you can't really fail, even though others may see you as a failure. You can stand back from the reactions of others and feel secure. That is a powerful way to live. It enables you to look at the big picture and to weigh all of your needs and desires and to come up with the best solution for the situation, the one that leaves your values and beliefs intact.

Sticking to your values offers these advantages:

- You feel confident to make your own decisions.
- You make the decision from a standpoint of strength.
- Your decisions always contribute to your growth.
- Your comfort with your decision-making process allows you to include those close to you in the process.
- You can enjoy the process because it is empowering rather than disabling.

Playing to Your Strengths

There is a lot of security and empowerment in sticking to your beliefs and values, and to what works for you. Very early into production on *The Les Brown Show,* it became apparent that the show was not designed for my strengths based on my experiences. As a regular performer on public television, I had great success by speaking directly to the audience and offering them solutions for their lives. But whenever we suggested a solution-oriented exploration of a topic, the show's producers would take it and run— down to the mud hole. For one show, which serves as one of the worst instances of this, we suggested bringing in an expert to talk about the problems of teenagers and peer pressure regarding sex and drugs, but King World's people prepared a show that focused on promiscuous teens boasting about their conquests. It wasn't always that bad, but early on it became clear that the show wasn't designed around my particular strengths. After one of our first shows, I telephoned my fiancée, Gladys Knight, and asked her what she had thought of it and she said, "I think you need to listen to some of your own tapes and watch some of your videos too." Leave it to the woman who loves you to remind you to be true to yourself and your talents.

Gladys was telling me that I had allowed myself to wander too far afield from my strengths. What are your talents and strengths? List below the things that you feel you are good at, the things that give you pleasure. I'm good at:

_____

_____

_____

Now, what do you feel the best use of that talent would be?

_____

_____

_____

I asked you to write this down because I want you to think about using your talents in the most positive manner. Don't let anyone else dictate the use of your talents. Guard them zealously because they are life's gifts to you. There are people out there willing to corrupt your talent for their purposes, so you always have to be on the alert and maintain your bearings.

Doing Good Television for the Good of All

There were some shows that fell together beautifully. We did one with the Pointer Sisters and in it they gave insights into their lives. People who knew them said I'd brought out things they hadn't seen before. There was great interaction and they were all very comfortable. We had a wonderful interview on the show with James Earl Jones and he told moving stories from his life about his problems with stuttering and how he overcame them. One of my favorite shows was one entitled "They Said I'd Never Amount to Anything." The guests were Olympic diver Greg Louganis, television writer and producer Stephen Cannell, and the editor of *Parade* magazine, Walter Anderson. All three of these guests had been counted out earlier in life and had made something of themselves.

This show proved to be one of the most requested on videotape and it was exactly the type of show I had hoped to be doing all the time. But the Kings argued that we couldn't do this sort of uplifting material all the time and keep our station programmers happy. I had hoped they would see the success of this show and use it as the standard, but they weren't buying it as the model for the program. They remained convinced the only way to keep viewers and attract advertisers was to do what all the other talk shows were doing.

Early in the production of my show, King World would take a show that we'd done to focus groups for evaluation and often they would come back with criticisms that were confusing and hard for me to take. Some of it was valid, without a doubt, because this was a new experience for me. But it was difficult for me to accept what was legitimate criticism about my performance, and what was based in our very different approaches to television.

I came to distrust the source of the criticism. I knew I needed to learn more but I didn't trust them enough to listen. I needed a way to critique the criticism. I needed to effectively evaluate their criticism in general and get out of it what I could use to get better. I attribute my success as a public speaker to my willingness to accept criticism. But I always could trust those critics. In this case I couldn't trust the King World people, and my closest advisors were not experienced in television either, so those conditions made the issue of accepting criticism much more difficult.

Seeking Criticism

I'm not a saint, mind you, but I've learned that taking criticism is vital to my continued growth not only as a speaker but as a father and a husband. I'm willing to take it in all areas of life. I'm willing to let my wife tell me about things I don't know. My children too. Your children will call you on your behavior, won't they? We have to make the people in all areas of our lives feel comfortable enough to tell us what we need to hear. We can't take it personally, or try to justify our behavior or blame someone else for our mistakes.

An airplane reaches its destination because it gets feedback along the way from radar and the control tower. But too often people ignore feedback from those around them, or the people around them don't tell them what they need to hear so that they can measure up to their true greatness. They don't want to hurt their feelings. We have to make people feel comfortable so we can grow with their help. In corporations, teamwork is very important and you can't be a good team member if those around you can't communicate with you openly. All of us have shortcomings and those around us have to be comfortable.

I once discovered someone on my staff was lying to clients. I blasted him in front of the entire staff, and told him he would be fired if he did it again. But one of my top-level employees came in behind me and said the fellow was wrong for what he did, but that I was wrong in how I dealt with it. She said I hurt his feelings and embarrassed him in front of his co-workers. I said I was not running a day care center. She did not back down: *"You praise in public, you criticize in private,"* she said before giving me one last shot: "We expect more from you as our leader." And then she walked out.

That night I could not sleep. Winston Churchill said, "The truth is incontrovertible. Malice may attack it. Ignorance may deride it, but at the end, there it is." William Cullen Bryant said, "Truth, crushed to earth, shall rise again." And Scripture said, "Ye shall know the truth and the truth shall make you free."

And so, the truth gave Leslie Calvin Brown a slap in the face. I was wrong and I needed to acknowledge it. I called a staff meeting the next day and I apologized to the employee in front of the staff.

I had been reminded of the difference between *con*structive and *de*structive criticism. When I was in the Ohio legislature, I wanted to attack a legislator for something he was doing. I went to a veteran legislator, C.J. McLin, to discuss the problem and he asked if I had approached the other fellow privately. "If you can tap a man on the shoulder and get his attention, why publicly knock him in the mouth?" He noted that if I confronted him in public, the fellow would have no choice but to fight me, but if I talked to him privately we might reach an agreement. And that is what happened.

Functioning Under Fire

At some point in our careers, all of us come under criticism. It is often difficult to keep going when you feel as though your every action is being second-guessed, criticized, or perceived as just another piece of evidence in your incompetency hearing. Being centered on strong principles will help you deal with criticism in a positive and self-assured manner, but there are also other tactics that can help you deflect and depersonalize the heat of criticism. Handling criticism is relatively easy to do if you train yourself to do it properly, by not taking a defensive posture.

Why does criticism bother some of us so much? Many people accept criticism uncritically by:

- Taking it personally as a criticism of them rather than their action.
- Reacting to the criticizer rather than analyzing the criticism.
- Assuming the criticized behavior or characteristic is uncorrectable.
- Shunting the blame onto someone else.

It almost seems silly when you look at how we allow exterior criticism to knock us off track, but we all do it. We fall apart. We roll up into a ball. Or, occasionally, we lash out at people who love and care for us. And yet we all know people who understand the value of helpful criticism. They take it, evaluate it, learn from it— and move on. I think one of my best attributes is that I take criticism well. It's painful, it's uncomfortable, but I know I can't grow without it. Mike Williams, my co-producer for *The Les Brown Show,* has always told me what I needed to hear, not what I wanted to hear. There have been times when I have avoided him because it hurt, but I've always gone back because I know he is good for me. You can't grow with people catering to you and stroking your ego. You have to have people who will tell you what you really need to know.

Have you ever noticed that someone had offensive breath but you did not tell them? Would you rather walk around with bad breath all day or have someone tell you? Would you rather get helpful information or have people wish you'd gargle with ammonia? When was the last time you heard a comment about some behavior of yours that made you upset? Write down the comment:

_____

_____

_____

Did you take time to evaluate if the observation was correct? Did you try to justify it or blame it on circumstances? Are you still speaking to the person? Write down your reaction to the criticism:

_____

_____

_____

How might you have handled the criticism better?

Taking Criticism

1. Critique the criticism. Do your best to subjectively evaluate the criticism you received. Was it accurate or inaccurate? Was it accurate only from the point of view of the person who said it because of that person's own bias? Or was it generally on target? Was it way off base? Run the criticism by someone you know will be honest. Does it sound fair or unfair to them?

If the criticism is flat-out wrong, you have nothing more to concern you. Why waste any more time on it? Too often, we take inaccurate and unjustified criticism to heart, which is a huge waste of time and energy. Now, some people may have your interests at heart but others' criticism may come from their own consciousness, their own experience, their own biases, anger, and vision of the world. You cannot be responsible for everyone's perceptions of you and your actions. The person who accuses you unfairly of being two-faced may have just come out of a relationship of mistrust and alienation, so you cannot always assume that what someone says to you is based solely on your actions regarding that person.

I once worked with a woman who was generally nasty to everyone she worked with except for one young man. When it came to him, she was warm, flattering, and even loving. What did he do to deserve the treatment? How was he different from the other people in the workplace? I asked him one day what he did to charm this woman and he told me that he had often wondered the same, until the woman told him that he reminded her of an old boyfriend that she had never gotten over. That's all it took for her to decide she liked this guy! And it takes even less for some people to decide they dislike others. That is why you should not throw yourself off a ledge because someone chooses to criticize your actions.

2. Don't fear criticism. Are you afraid of compliments? Odds are you get as many of them as you get criticisms, yet so many people respond in fear when criticized. You may fear criticism because you put too much emphasis on being loved or having the approval of others. You have to love yourself and approve of yourself first, and then what comes from others, whether love or criticism, can be placed in its proper perspective. You simply don't have time in this life to devote yourself to either pleasing other people or to living up to their expectations of you. The only master you have is yourself, and your guidelines are the core beliefs that you establish.

3. Think about your thoughts when criticized. In other words, when you are criticized, listen to your own inner dialogue. Do you automatically take the criticism to heart? Or do you say "Bull"? Are your immediate thoughts negative? Defensive? Is your thinking process logical or emotional?

Think about the last time someone criticized you and write down your responses and the process you went through and then note what the result of the criticism was. Did it result in positive growth or negative thoughts?

Criticism:

_____

_____

My response was:

_____

_____

_____

And the result was:

_____

_____

_____

Once you learn a process of evaluating criticism critically, you take control of it rather than allowing it to control you. You no longer waste time and energy focused and stuck on negative thoughts. Instead, you move forward and use the criticism to better yourself whether it was intended that way or not.

Taking Heat Without Getting Burned

Just as there are techniques useful for debating, there are also methods you can apply to situations in which you are being criticized. These step-by-step techniques allow you to accept criticism gracefully and tactfully without losing your temper or your pride.

FIRST STEP: GET IN THE SHOES OF YOUR CRITIC

Rather than be hurt or angry when criticized, attempt first to understand where the criticism is coming from. Don't prejudge or go on the defensive; instead, calmly ask for more specific information. Exactly what was it that brought on the criticism? Was it one instance or an ongoing pattern of behavior? Can the critic think of anything else you have done to upset him or her? If the person becomes insulting, you can probably write it off to a personality conflict or a personal problem the critic has with you. Listen to what the critic is saying and let the critic see that you are trying to get to the heart of the criticism rather than going on the attack or being defensive. The goal here is to get at the source of the criticism and to steer the interaction away from an attack mode into one of mutual respect and collaboration.

SECOND STEP: TAKE THE CRITIC'S WEAPONS AWAY

When a critic comes at you with guns blazing, you can run for cover, fire back, or attempt to disarm the criticism. At least in this form of verbal warfare, the third option seems to be the best. If you run for cover, you'll never find out the source of the criticism and therefore never benefit from it. And if you fire back, the only thing you'll likely get is anger and frustration and maybe a black eye or sore knuckles. How do you take a critic's weapons away? Agree. You don't have to buy the entire criticism, or any of the criticism at all, but by finding at least one small point of agreement, you will probably at least take some of the emotion out of the criticism.

Sample criticism: *Les, you aren't doing the job as the host.*

Sample response: *I agree that I'm not completely comfortable out there. Tell me specifically where you think I need to improve.*

Do you see how this response takes most of the "you against me" antagonism out of the discussion and turns it into more of a collaborative effort to work toward a common goal—a better show? I could have responded defensively by denying that there was any problem with my performance. Or I could have counter-attacked or placed the blame somewhere else. It is difficult to fight the impulse to defend yourself when criticized, but the strategy of disarming a critic can be so intriguing that you find yourself enjoying it like a good game of chess, or a tennis match. Try not to smile, however. It might not sit well with your critic. You need to practice the techniques for disarming critics just as you would your chess or tennis strategies so that you don't fall into the trap of anger or defensiveness. Some psychologists suggest practicing with a friend, a good friend, or you can do these writing exercises.

Re-create a recent argument with someone who criticized you, or make up one that applies to your life. In response to the criticism, write what you might have typically said in the past. And then try a disarmament strategy.

Criticism:

_____

_____

Old Response:

_____

_____

New Response:

_____

_____

THIRD STEP: FIND A POSITIVE RESOLUTION

After you have carefully evaluated the criticism and the critic's position, and then established some common ground with the critic, it should be safe to put forth your own point of view in a nondefensive, nonthreatening way. You can now explain your point of view and work with the critic to determine just what it is that separates you. If you think the criticism is flat out wrong, you can say so but take the sting out of it by acknowledging that *you too* could be flat-out wrong from the critic's point of view. Depersonalize the difference by noting that it may just come from differing perspectives rather than out of any personal animosity.

By admitting that you are capable of making mistakes, you give your critic room to gracefully admit that perhaps his or her criticism might also have been wrong. If it becomes clear that the criticism stems not from the facts but from differing points of view, you can then attempt to negotiate an agreement to work out your differences. You may have to settle for something that is not entirely to your satisfaction, but it will certainly beat total surrender, and the entire process will be more rewarding and fulfilling than heated argument or walking away in anger.

There will be times, probably more than you'd like to admit, in which the critic will be entirely right and the criticism of you entirely justified. In this case, the healing process for both you and the situation will be vastly speeded up if you lay down your defenses and admit that you were wrong. Nobody is right all the time. No one is above criticism all the time. And so, there is no shame in admitting that the critic is right. Take the criticism, apologize for what went wrong, and thank the critic for setting you straight. It may hurt for a little while, but you will feel like such an *adult* later.

It's not that you don't have a right to defend yourself or a right to even be angry when criticized. There is no doubt that sometimes it's better to get angry than to become depressed. At least anger can be channeled into a positive use. I have a workout partner who visualizes his critics when he lifts weights so that he uses his anger to build strength. Some psychoanalysts, including Freud, have described depression as anger turned inward and they argue that it is more healthy to direct it outward. But we are looking at the long term here, and while displaying anger outwardly may allow you to temporarily vent your feelings, once you've vented, you still must face the criticism and the critic. It hasn't gone away. By disarming the critic and creating a collaborative approach, you are building something rather than merely letting go of feelings.

The choice, and the solution, is very simple really. When the boss tells you that you are not cutting the mustard, you have three options. You can accept the criticism without evaluating it and become depressed and despondent and get stuck in your self-pity. You can get defensive and angry and decide that the boss is out of his mind. (But he is *still* the boss and you are still stuck.) Or you can accept the challenge of examining the criticism, using it as a learning experience, and working toward a common goal—improved performance and a better relationship with the boss.

Brotherly Advice

When you are in a new venture with unfamiliar people, all you really have is the people you trust and the values and beliefs that you carry as your foundation. Those values help you distinguish and not retreat from them in the midst of pressures and emotionally charged issues. During my television trials, my beloved brother, twin, and self-appointed critic, Wesley, read a newspaper story saying that if talk show host Les Brown was only willing to do what Phil and Geraldo and Sally and Ricki and Jenny and Montel and Jerry were doing with their shows, he could be making millions upon millions. Wesley, bless him, telephoned to tell me about the newspaper story and to inquire whether or not I'd lost my sanity. Knowing that my brother is a devout Christian, who drives eighty miles each way to church—twice a week—I said, "Wesley, what if a man gains the whole world but loses his soul?"

Wesley pondered that a moment and came up with this devout response: "For twenty-five million dollars you can buy a new soul. Better still, you can make twenty-five million, give ten percent to the church, and ask God for forgiveness. If he forgave the thief on the cross, he'll forgive you for being a sleazy talk show host!"

- Losing a career gamble
- Dealing with workplace problems and termination
- Handling career-related stress
- Bouncing back from a career defeat

CHAPTER 4

Canceled

In the fall of 1993, *The Les Brown Show* was the nation's number-one-rated new talk show. In New York, the most important television market in the world, we had the best time slot you could ask for; right after *Regis and Kathie Lee at* 10 A.M. We were winning our time slot in New York. But it wasn't enough.

The television ratings game is a complicated one, but the only thing that really counts is whether or not a show is making money. King World is known for charging a high price for the shows they syndicate. They can demand a premium rate because their shows have generally done extremely well. They were charging up to $15,000 for each of my shows, even though *The Les Brown Show* had not been tested in local markets before it was syndicated. Unlike *Oprah*, which began as a local morning show in Chicago, found its stride, and then went into syndication, it was sink or swim for us—in more than 90 percent of the nation's television markets.

Television programming executives bought *The Les Brown Show* eagerly, but only because they thought it would quickly pay for itself. At its premium price, they were not going to give it much of a grace period to find its market. In our earliest conversations with the Kings, they had told us that their goal for the show was a 3 percent rating, but when the show pulled that figure, they said it was not good enough because we were losing too much of the audience from the lead-in programming. And they also said that we were "skewing higher or older" which meant that we weren't attracting as many young viewers as the advertisers wanted. My advisors and I thought we had exceeded expectations, but then, we hadn't understood what the expectations really were.

We had decent ratings numbers in national syndication and we were extremely strong in the two top markets, New York and Chicago. The biggest problem was the drop-off in viewers. In New York, we weren't retaining enough of those who tuned into *Regis and Kathie Lee.* That drop-off was ominous. Television stations don't like to see viewers switch channels, for obvious reasons.

Tension on the Set

The showdown approached in the form of the November ratings sweepstakes. This is the period in which ratings are recorded and decisions are made whether or not to continue a show or to move it from its time slot in each market. It is the only time you get an official rating for every market the show is aired in. This was crunch time. As we neared the November sweeps we discovered that the Kings and their people had been cooking up show topics for this critical period without consulting us. We were concerned about them going totally off the deep end with topics like "Wardens Who Date Their Convicts' Wives."

We wanted ratings. We understood the game. But we wanted to maintain our values too. The Kings were impatient. Because of the costs involved and pressure from their client stations, they were not willing to give our show much time to find its audience. From the very beginning, they'd made that clear. Other talk shows such as Jerry Springer and Bertice Berry, whose ratings were not nearly as strong, were given a whole television season to find their audiences.

In New York, as in most major markets, station managers get ratings figures overnight, which means constant fretting and constant evaluation. This was a new development that many of the talk shows that started earlier had not had to deal with. Each of our shows was immediately judged solely on its ratings. We may have done a really strong program that saved a thousand people from committing suicide or that stopped them from buying an unsafe product, but if the ratings numbers weren't good, that show was judged a loser, and so was I.

It was a tense time. We were doing five shows a week and getting harsh critiques after nearly every one of them. It was draining me. Under these conditions, and in the television environment in general, it can quickly disintegrate into every man and woman for himself and herself. When veteran staff and crew members sense that a show is in trouble, they begin looking for the next job.

In stressful situations such as this, communications break down and tensions escalate. Only a few weeks into the show, there were mini-feuds erupting everywhere. One of my top producers simply stopped talking to me, having apparently decided she didn't have to communicate with Les Brown even while doing *The Les Brown Show*. It was becoming increasingly difficult for me to hold it all together.

Mastering Resistance

One of the outstanding traits frequently attributed to General Colin Powell, who is among the most admired figures of our time, was his ability to navigate his way to the very top of the perilous and often treacherous channels of the military bureaucracy without making scores of enemies. He did this by always working to form consensus where there was conflict.

Obviously, I was no Colin Powell, but the experience of locking horns with the King World producers has made me aware of the importance of handling conflict well. I've done a lot of research on the topic of conflict resolution in recent months, and here are a few tips I've come up with for resolving conflict in your work-place and professional life:

1. *Don't be afraid of conflict.* Too many of us become agitated when we encounter conflict or disagreement out of concern and fear. It's odd when you think about it, because conflict is a part of na-ture, a part of life. Unless you are a hermit, odds are that conflict is inescapable. And so, you need to approach conflict calmly, as an expected part of dealing with others. Consider conflict a way of learning to see things more clearly.

2. *Abandon the concept of winning and losing when faced with conflict.* Instead, adopt a strategy of resolution. Unless you are on a battle-field, chances are the person you come into conflict with is not The Enemy, but instead is probably someone whose goals are generally the same as yours, or at least interrelated with yours.

3. *Be flexible.* When the other side senses that you are interested in finding a solution, you likely will have created an ally where a potential adversary once stood. Rather than confrontation and conflict, you can work together in cooperation to find a solution that suits both sides.

4. *Avoid negative or confrontational language.* Rather than "buts" and "you're wrongs" try using positive language that disarms rather than confronts, such as "I understand your position and . . ." or "I can see your point and here is where I'm coming from . . ."

5. *Talk through the situation with a neutral party to gain perspective and clarity from that person, and also to better understand the conflict through talking it out.* It is always helpful to get a problem out in the open and to get input from people you trust and people who under-stand your frame of reference so that they can help you better un-derstand what you are going through and tell you, for better or worse, whether they think you have properly judged or handled the situation.

6. *Rather than approaching the conflict with the attitude of stopping it or overcoming it, think of redirecting the energy toward a common target.*

Look for similarities in your positions rather than focusing on your differences. Although war is part of our nature, most successful societies have been built on cooperation. Common goals are great unifiers. How many stories have you heard of strangers acting together in times of emergency? When a common goal is made obvious the natural reaction is to put differences aside.

7. *Make a mutual commitment to the greater good.* Whether it is to a successful television show that will employ both sides, or the manufacture of a product of a good or the offering of a service that is the source of your mutual wealth, there is undoubtedly a common focus in your lives that should be the center of your attentions.

8. *Find something to distract you from the conflict.* Take off on a vacation or weekend getaway, a new project, or a family outing—so that you can clear your mind, reevaluate your position, and perhaps come back to it with a fresh vision of what needs to be done to resolve the matter.

Running with the Choke On

Late in the second month of the show, I took my youngest son, John Leslie, to see the movie *Cool Runnings,* which is a funny movie about a group of unlikely winter Olympians—the Jamaican bobsled team—persevering because of their determination and dedication. Mostly, it is a light comedy, not to be taken too seriously, but considering my own battles at the time, I could identify with the Jamaicans trying to make it way outside of their normal element. In one scene late in the movie, during the Olympic competition, they run their sled off the bobsled track and get angry with themselves, talking about how they had choked under pressure. I turned to my son and said, "John Leslie, do you know why I am not as good on the show as I could be? *I've* been choking too."

The power and confidence that I had brought to my career as a public speaker were conspicuously absent because I choked. Even though they were trying to fit me to a format that wasn't right for me, even though they did not seem to know what I was really capable of, the bottom line was that I had to take responsibility for the show. If I believed in myself and my ability, I should have been capable of overcoming the obstacles in my path. I had lost my center of balance. I was no longer grounded in my values. I had become disoriented and thrown off my game, which shouldn't have happened if I had been strong within myself. But I had let other people tell me who I was.

What to Do When You Are Thrown Off Center

When you find yourself in the sort of situation I found myself in with *The Les Brown Show*, I'm not recommending you respond exactly as I did at the time. But I have had a lot of time to think about it. I have talked to a lot of people, and I have come up with a few suggestions to follow when you find yourself thrown off center.

1. *Accept responsibility for the things you are responsible for.* You can only do so much, and you can only be blamed for so much. When you find things spiraling out of control around you, take responsibility for the things you can control and do the best you can with the areas in which you have influence.

2. *Let go of those things that you cannot influence.* Think about water-skiing. When you are in perfect balance holding on to the tow rope behind the boat, all is well. You don't have any influence over the boat other than your communication with the pilot. If the pilot doesn't pay any attention to you, all you can do is hold on. But if holding on causes you to lose your balance, you don't continue to hold on and get dragged by the boat. You let go and swim on your own. That is what you have to do in life situations in which you find yourself being dragged by circumstances you can't control. Let go!

When you let go, you give yourself permission to fail and to recover from failure. You recognize the situation as a bad one and you get out as painlessly as you can, with your dignity intact. You are also letting go of embarrassment and self-doubt, so that you will be able to recover more quickly. When you let go properly, with the proper spirit, you can pursue the challenge of recovering because it is a reflection of your enduring spirit, your dynamic life. In letting go of bad circumstances outside your control, you reassert control. You are no longer being dragged, now you are moving on your own power.

3. Tell the truth, to yourself and to anyone who asks. When faced with hard times, some people feel they have to manipulate the truth to save face. *The Les Brown Show is failing because there is a conspiracy against me.* No. It failed because of two seriously conflicting philosophies. Mine and theirs. No one wanted it to fail. We all wanted to do good television. We all wanted good ratings. We all wanted to make money. It's just that I thought I could do it by helping people, and they didn't see how that was possible. Looking back, I was just a few months ahead of my time because talk show television hit bottom about a year after my show was canceled. And even before that, Oprah, the star in the King World galaxy, rebelled against the trend and showed that quality television could get good ratings.

When you tell the truth to other people, they sense your honesty and they are more likely to tell you the truth in return, opening up lines of communication. Telling the truth is simply the best and easiest way to live. Lying defeats communication.

4. Be honest with yourself. Assess your performance in the light of the truth. Ask those you trust to discuss it with you. You will learn a great deal about yourself. Self-deception comes when you don't trust your own inner wisdom or your own essential goodness. Once you have learned to be honest and to trust yourself and your goodness, you can feel free to focus on the goodness inside other people.

Letting Go, Charging On, Dropping Out

After some evaluation, I decided that if this show was going to fail, it was not going to be because I didn't give it my best shot. I recommitted myself to doing everything I possibly could to produce a good television show in spite of the fact that my approach and goals were at odds with those of King World. I decided to ignore the distractions and the directions of the people who didn't know me, and to do the show my way. And when I did that, the show took on a greater vibrancy. Ratings climbed. I was starting to feel really *good* about the show.

Unfortunately, the executioners had already made up their minds. The ratings still weren't as strong as the Kings and the television programmers wanted them to be. And they could all see that even though I had become more confident, I still was not about to invite three-hundred-pound strippers on the show. I was the star quarterback who insisted on calling his own plays, and that was not going to cut it with the Kings, who owned the playing field. I think they had hoped that I would give in, that I would be seduced by all of the media attention, the limousine rides, and the celebrity. Others have sold their souls to stay on the air, and I'll admit that I enjoyed the trappings of it all, but I wasn't prepared to let my reputation go down the drain just so I wouldn't have to take a cab anymore.

During the November sweeps, rumors of our imminent demise began to fly. When the King brothers signed Rolonda, who had been a reporter for one of their other shows, to do a talk show, the gloom over my show thickened. The Kings insisted that her signing had nothing to do with my show, that she was not being groomed as my replacement—even though they were building her set in *my* studio on East 75th Street.

I believed them.

We were scheduled to take a break from taping the show during the Thanksgiving holiday, and before we all went off to our families Roger King called everyone to a telephone conference. While thirty of us gathered around a speakerphone, he told us we were going on hiatus, meaning that we wouldn't be taping any more shows for a while. He said that did not mean that the show was going to be canceled. He also said, "Don't worry about the industry rumors, the Rolonda show has nothing to do with *The Les Brown Show*."

During Thanksgiving break, I went to Miami to visit Mama and to have Thanksgiving dinner with her. While I was there, I stayed in touch with our people in New York. There were rumors flying all over the city that our show was about to be canceled.

Anxious to find out what was going on, I decided to fly to the Bahamas. Roger King was there visiting the casinos. I was tired of hearing rumors, I wanted to hear it from one of the Kings. I found Roger at a craps table on Paradise Island. He was on a big roll and there was a crowd around his table. Roger always attracts a crowd. He looks and talks like Rodney Dangerfield, but he commands a great deal more respect. He is a master salesman and certainly someone who is not afraid to take risks. I don't gamble, but I could tell that the huge pile of chips in front of Roger was not small change. He doesn't deal in small change.

He saw me, waved, and yelled out, "Hey Les, how you doing?" I was wondering the same thing. When someone else took a turn at the table, I asked him what was happening with the show, but all he would say was "Once we get the ratings we'll know."

He went back to shooting craps, and I went back to pondering which way the dice would roll for *The Les Brown Show*. I'm certain now that he had already made up his mind but he wasn't about to tip his hand to me in a gambling joint.

I returned to New York still uncertain of the show's future. And so I decided to go to the studio to get a few things to work on during the remainder of the holiday break. Immediately, I realized that the end was nearer than I'd thought. The first thing I noticed was that my photograph had been taken off the wall. Then, I saw an article pinned up on the bulletin board. It was from one of the New York tabloids and the headline said "No More Les."

It wasn't exactly the handwriting on the wall, but it served the same purpose. When I went to the dressing room, I noticed my suits weren't there. I went into the main office and none of the staff members there would look me in the eye. The door to my personal office was closed, though I never closed it myself. I went inside and found that all my things had been cleared off the desk and put in boxes. My tailored suits for the show, nearly forty of them, were there, all boxed up. Shocked, I turned and a bunch of the King World staffers had formed a line like mourners in a funeral parlor.

They'd gotten word that my show had been canceled by the Kings. It was the first time they admitted it to me. Nobody had much to say. Finally one of them shook her head and offered her assessment of what had prompted the premature decision to end a new talk show. "Your show was too decent for television," she said, providing an appropriate epitaph for *The Les Brown Show.*

Keeping Your Head Up in Hard Times

It is difficult to step back from your emotions under such trying circumstances, but that is what you have to do to function properly. You can't let yourself be tied in knots. You have to subjugate your ego and your anger, get a vision of the larger picture, and then lift your head and march forward on your path. Not that I exactly walked out of there humming "We shall overcome." Even though I'd long suspected it would come to this, I was stunned.

More and more we see job-related stress ignite into violent and destructive actions. As I write this, there is a news story of a Miami restaurant worker and struggling entrepreneur who became so distraught over a $15,000 tax bill that he hijacked a busload of handicapped youngsters and then got himself shot to death by police. I'd love to have had a chance to talk to this man because I've had much worse tax bills than his. *That* is not the way to handle stressful situations. This poor man was not killed by the police or by taxes, or by pressure; he was killed because he became overwhelmed by the challenge he faced. By all accounts that I saw, his problems were not insurmountable. In fact, it appears that his problems were similar to those faced by many businessmen who take risks in order to grow. Life is about change, change means growth, and with any growth—physical or personal—there is the stress caused by *growing pains.*

Stress and anxiety not only cause emotional strain, they have been conclusively shown to trigger physical illness and to inhibit the body's resistance to disease. Anxiety is a natural condition that nature designed as a sort of red alert system in times of danger. But in the modern world, stress and anxiety are too often out of proportion to any real danger we face. Instead of being triggered by actual physical threats, these red alert systems are now often set off by mental triggers. Researchers have shown that stress can speed the spread of cancer, make you more vulnerable to viruses, bring on asthma attacks, ulcers, colitis, colds, the flu, and herpes. Stress has also been found to increase the likelihood of blood clots and blocked arteries.

I've become something of an authority on stress over the last few years, and I'd like to share with you some of the methods I've learned for disarming this potentially dangerous problem.

Methods for Dealing with Stress

1. *Unload the stress*. Talk to someone who cares about you. Women with advanced breast cancer who partake in regular discussion groups with fellow patients have been found to survive twice as long as those who isolate themselves. Or simply take a few minutes a day to reflect on what is causing you stress and what you can do about it. People who do this have been shown to improve their health, miss fewer days of work, and better fight off infections and viruses. Researchers advise that the best way to go about this is to first write down how you are feeling, expressing your anxiety or sadness or anger, and then to write about the causes of your feelings.

How are you feeling stressed emotionally or physically?

_____

_____

_____

What is the cause of this emotional and physical stress?

_____

_____

_____

2. Distract yourself. When you focus on stressful things constantly, you only heighten the stress and give whatever is stressing you more importance than it deserves. Get away from the stress by exercising, reading something that absorbs you, watching a funny movie, or taking part in any activity that demands all of your attention.

List five things you can do to escape the stress and relax your mind:

1._____

2._____

3._____

4._____

5._____

3. Control the stress. Don't allow yourself to focus on whatever is stressing you until you feel up to it. That means keeping it out of your mind except for a specific period when you feel confident that you can deal with the issue without heightening your anxiety. For most people, this means avoiding it in the evening or late at night when the mind is weary and your defenses are down. Early in the morning, when you are generally in a more energetic and optimistic mood, is probably the best time to confront stressful matters.

4. Focus on the positive. If you find yourself overemphasizing negative stressful matters, you need to do what the driver of a car does when he finds his car wandering off the roadway: oversteer in the other direction to get back on course. So when you are feeling stressed out, focus on the good things in your life. Take your children to the playground or treat yourself to a night on the town.

Remind yourself of all the good things in your life and in your relationships.

Facing Challenges by Living Dynamically

Have you ever experienced any sort of growth that didn't come
with challenges? Life is fairly even-handed in its no-pain, no-gain
pattern. You can avoid the pain by finding a comfort zone and lying low. That's the safe way to go. But in this case, playing it safe
generally means an early death. I'm not referring to a physical
death. I believe that we carry a life force in us that fires and feeds
our desire for spiritual and mental growth. Call it your inner
drive, your zest for life. Whatever name you put on it, this life
force is what makes for *dynamic living.* I can spot a dynamic-living
person in seconds. This is the person people search out at social
functions and at work. Dynamic people always have something
going on in their lives. Ask them "What's going on?" and most
people say, "Oh, not much." Dynamic people knock you down
when they answer that question because they are so full of life
that opportunity chases them around begging for their attention.
Every day presents them with a new way to grow and a new challenge. They are unafraid to face their fears or the pain of growth.
They don't live out of their memories, they live out of their imag-
inations. They have learned to live dynamically. How can you
start living more dynamically? What do you do when you go to
your car and the battery is dead and the engine won't turn over?
You jump-start it.

Here are a few suggestions to be followed step by step:

Jump-Starting Your Life

1. *Make a vow to go after what you want in life.* It shocks me how
many people tell me that they'd like to do something more with
their lives—if they could only decide what they wanted to do. To
tell you the truth, often I want to shake these people! I tell them

to get off their "buts" and make a list of their "wants" and then go after them.

2. Get up on the roof and kick the ladder away. I once knew a roofing contractor who used this form of motivation to keep his crews on the job. Once they got up on the roof, there was no going back until the work was done and the trucks came to pick them up. Too many people lack motivation, so my advice is to make it impossible to do anything but go after your goals. If you really want to go back to college to get that advanced degree, quit your job and do it. If you really want to apply for a better position, walk in to your boss's office and do it. What is holding you back? Don't talk about it. Don't look for reasons why you can't do it. Kick the ladder away and get to it.

3. Develop more than one strategy. Even people who set goals and go after them make mistakes and a common one is to limit yourself to one strategy. There are many ways to get where you want to go, and sometimes the direct path is not the best path. It may be blocked or overcrowded or simply not suitable to you. So devise a number of strategies and scenarios that will take you where you want to go in life and be open to changing your approach if your path is blocked.

Undynamic Approaches

I once was asked to speak to a group of engineers in the automotive design center of a major American automaker. They were in need of motivation at the time because the Japanese automotive industry was kicking their doors in. I was amazed when I walked into their headquarters and found only a few computers. When I inquired, I was told that the employees had resisted using computer technology in their design work because they feared it would cost them too many jobs. What incredibly stunted thinking! Had they embraced computer technology from the beginning, these employees would have made themselves invaluable.

I'll wager that by now they've embraced it, or they've embraced the unemployment line.

Walk into any high school in this country and you may find classes in reading, writing, arithmetic, social studies, and history, even home economics and wood shop. But rarely will you find classes that teach you how to live a dynamic life, how to overcome your fears and deal with challenges, how to best use your talents so that the world will open up to you. I don't doubt the importance of those other classes, but I can't believe that we neglect such an important aspect of living. Then again, it has resulted in a huge demand for the work I do, so I guess I should thank the school system for staying out of my market.

Far too many people today are intimidated by change, and as a result they are eliminated by change. They spend way too much time on their seats, rather than on their toes. They do just enough to get by, and then it's bye-bye. No wonder so many employers now hold personal development seminars to teach their people to do their best, develop their skills, and increase their value in the marketplace. You'd think people would want to do this for themselves, but so many are happy just to warm a seat. You can't get away with that attitude anymore. Company strategies change so rapidly, and, sadly, the days of the "family" work environment are rapidly in decline. Some futurists, including Carolyn Corbin, predict that by the year 2010, 65 percent of the jobs in this country will be "permanent part-time" slots and the competition for work will be so intense that people will be bidding for jobs.

Recently I heard of two executives discussing a downsizing in their company. One of them asked the other why he had terminated an employee who had been a friend of his. "I didn't even realize I'd fired him, I was only looking at eliminating his position," said the other. That is the management mentality today. Middle managers in particular are an endangered species. The more money you make, the bigger the target you are for the people who get bonuses for cutting back. So playing it safe is playing it stupid as far as I can see.

A Pat on the Back or a Push out the Door?

A speaker I know was asked to address employees at the regional headquarters of one of the big telecommunications corporations. In his briefing with executives, he asked if there were any particular points they wanted him to emphasize for their workers. Now, this happened to be a division of the company that was experiencing tremendous growth. Just prior to his speech, the employees would be receiving awards and bonuses for record-setting performance.

They had been working seventy-hour weeks. They were nearly fanatic in their devotion to additional growth. And the executives wanted him to inspire them to do even more. They wanted them to be obsessed with expansion and innovation and company pride. They wanted these employees to eat, sleep, and breathe within the corporate culture. They asked the speaker to do this because they were going to raise their work quotas to unprecedented levels.

The speaker followed their directions, but on his next stop for the same company, he was asked to take an entirely different approach in his speech. Again, he was addressing a group that was to receive achievement awards prior to his taking the stage. But in this case, the executives in charge did not want him to emphasize company loyalty or to motivate the employees to work harder and harder to lead the company's growth.

Unknown to this audience, the axe was looming over their heads on this festive night. The company had decided to shut down their office and to relocate it to another state where the business climate was more favorable. The executives told the speaker not to inspire them to be loyal. "Encourage them to think not in terms of corporate loyalty, but in terms of entrepreneurship," the executives said.

The speaker was asked to tell them there was no such thing as job security anymore and that they had to be open to change. And so, in his speech, he told them to always be willing to learn new skills, to be versatile and open to change as opportunity. He said this while looking into their eyes, and he felt badly for them.

The speaker knew the good times were about to end for them, that another challenge awaited.

It was not easy for him to be inspiring that night, but he must have met the challenge. In fact, the executives for the company later told him that he had been *too good*. Two weeks after his speech, they announced the relocation of the plant, and 80 percent of the staff said they would welcome the opportunity for a change—by moving to the new location with the company!

The Great Experiment of Life

I had no fear of making the change to go into television as long as I had a chance to do it on my terms. That doesn't mean I was sure the experiment would work. I knew I couldn't control all the factors involved. I knew only that I could control how I responded, and no matter what they said or how they pressured me, I was not going to sell out in order to stay on the tube under their terms. I knew that if I stuck with my principles, I might fail to do television the way the King brothers wanted me to do it, but I would not fail myself. Ralph Waldo Emerson said, "Do not be too timid and squeamish about your actions, all life is an experiment."

Still, I'd be lying if I claimed that it didn't hurt to fail in my experiment with television. When the axe fell, I bled profusely. "This is not supposed to happen to me, I'm the motivator," I moaned. I had gotten into a groove and a way of life. We had developed a sense of family around the show and I'd lost that family.

I had an overpowering sense of loss. I had worked and trained for something and I'd finally gotten it and then it was taken away from me. In many ways, though, I was relieved when it was over and that relief may have masked some of the deeper hurts.

The Hit That Hurts

To the people who knew me best, the show had been a great disappointment except for a few episodes. Those who were not familiar with my work as a public speaker were more positive about the show because they had not seen me doing my real life's work, but all in all, I was disappointed in my inability to make the transition to television talk show host.

The King brothers had failed me by going back on their promise to allow me to do an uplifting show, but I had failed myself too. Until the very last few shows, I had been unable to make the conversion from speaking with power and authority as a public speaker to the more conversational and journalistic style of a talk show host. Still, I couldn't believe it had happened to me. I said that out loud one day, and one of my less sympathetic friends replied, "Who would you suggest? Oprah?"

I knew I had failed, and so did millions of other people. Failing privately is one thing, failing in public is another altogether. In the first few weeks after the show was canceled, at least a half-dozen people came up to me and said, "Didn't you used to be on *The Les Brown Show*?"

I know they meant well, but Lord, that hurt.

Most people do not suffer such a public defeat, but that doesn't make it any less devastating for them. And when they come back from their quiet losses, they often do it in heroic and dynamic ways.

There was a fellow who was among the millions of mid-level managers who lost their jobs during the downsizing mania in corporate America in which 43 million people lost their jobs from 1979 to 1996. Many of those who were fired from their jobs became despondent. Many gave up on life. This fellow walked out into the middle of rush hour traffic in Philadelphia, but with an indomitable spirit, rather than a broken one.

In search of a way to support his family, he devised an insulated tank that could be strapped to his back and he filled the tank with hot coffee. Then, he walked out into the rush hour traffic to sell it, car to car. He is known as Mister Coffee, and he has become a celebrity, as much for his spirit as for his innovative business.

How do you motivate yourself to get up and get back into the flow of life after getting knocked down? Mister Coffee had the right idea. He took a positive action. Even the smallest step out of the briar patch of depression is a positive move. It brings hope closer in what has seemed hopeless. If nothing else, taking some small positive action turns your mind away from the negative and self-defeating thoughts that have you pinned down. When he strapped the coffee tank on his back, Mister Coffee freed himself of some of his self-doubt. He was slowly moving from lethargy and inactivity toward a dynamic life again.

Here are a few tips on how to bounce back from hard times in your career.

Making a Career Comeback

1. *Find some good company.* Don't isolate yourself from life. We all need assistance or at least someone to talk to in hard times. Sit down with those you trust and ask for help.

Talking about what happened will help you put it in perspective. It also helps just to be with other people and to see their lives are on track. A key here, though, is to avoid other people going through hard times and depression. You don't need to take on their burdens at this point, nor do you need to constantly unload on the people you are with. The first time you are back with them, it is okay to discuss your problems, but after that concentrate on their positive energy and work to draw strength from it.

I have a whole list of positive friends I look to when I'm feeling down because I know they will lift me up.

Make a list of those people who can give you a boost when you are down. My boosters include:

_____

_____

_____

_____

2. Restore your positive power. To recharge your batteries build up a storage of positive thoughts. This is important particularly as you get ready to go to bed so that your mind is tuned for self-empowering thoughts. I keep inspiring books and motivational tapes and music that I read or listen to if I find myself feeling low before I go to bed. Believe me, the morning sun seems even brighter when you take a positive outlook to bed.

3. Give yourself an A in failure. Go to school on your mistakes. Understand how you contributed to your own defeat. Analyze what you did wrong, consider the effect it had on you, and accept it as a learning experience by devoting yourself to correcting the behavior that might have led to it, and then forgive yourself. Keep a record of your negative thoughts so that you can analyze the self-defeating thought processes that are holding you back.

4. Walk away from the dragon. No defeat is permanent. There are other victories to be won. Defeat will stay with you only if you hang on to it. Each night before going to bed, and again in the morning, thank God for the good things in your life, and ask for the strength to handle the challenges you will be facing. It may help to visualize yourself rising from the defeat and returning to the path you were on before it happened. Make it as elaborate as you want. You might even develop a shorter scenario to use during the day. Just a mental picture of yourself back on track, moving confidently forward will help. Or see yourself running up a set of steps confidently and easily.

5. Draw up a daily comeback plan. Perhaps most importantly, draw up a plan of action. Should you keep the same goals? Maybe now is the time to go after that secret dream? Perhaps a return to college for a degree that interests you more? This may be your chance to chase after that wild dream you've always had to do something else.

Draw up a daily activity sheet. Write out a detailed plan, hour by hour, of what you would like to accomplish each day. They don't have to be major accomplishments, just getting dressed and going out to the store, reading an informative or motivational book, watching a funny and upbeat movie, or getting in thirty minutes of exercise is good enough.

You don't have to do everything you write down, but just doing a few small things will get you going in the direction of more dynamic living. Then, at the end of the day, write down the things you accomplished and how those accomplishments made you feel. If nothing else, this takes your mind off negative feelings. Keep this daily schedule for at least a week and you will see your level of activity increasing with each day as the positive action creates a more dynamic approach to life, pulling you out of lethargy and the doldrums of depression.

6. *Eat the elephant in small bites.* If you find yourself facing a big task that causes you to waver back toward your negative feelings, don't throw your arms up or go into hiding. Instead, do what the ants do, eat the elephant one little bite at a time. Break down the task into the smallest possible bits and pieces. That's what I do when I face the daunting task of writing a book. I break it down into chapters and then sections and subsections until I feel that I can handle it comfortably. It's amazing how it all comes together quickly when you take that approach. Taking even the smallest steps is helpful because if you are moving forward you are no longer falling backward.

Just thinking about positive action stops you from obsessing over negative events and sinking further into depression. It is particularly helpful to do things that give you pleasure. They don't have to be work- or goal-related. Laughter is a powerful antidote to depression and even if it isn't as easy to laugh now as it may once have been, any lift in your mood helps break up the dark cloud overhead. It becomes increasingly difficult to maintain any of the negative attitudes outlined above when you find yourself laughing and taking positive steps again.

7. *Clean up your language!* In some of the negative attitudes outlined earlier, one of the most damaging factors was self-defeating, negative, or coercive language. Get rid of *can't, should, must, ought to,* and *but.* Don't go for a jog because you *should* or because you *ought to.* Go for it because you *want* to get your blood flowing. Do

it because it *will* make you feel better. Don't go to work because you *have to*. Go to work because you are going to bring new energy to the job.

Suited for Firing

I like to think of myself as a dynamic person most of the time, but I will confess that when I first learned that *The Les Brown Show* was going down the tubes, I went into motivational autopilot, which is a little less than dynamic. That's when you pump yourself up with inspirational thoughts in order to keep from falling on the floor and sobbing. People were walking up to console me, and I was saying things like "Hey, as long as you wake up in the morning without a chalked outline around your body, you're okay!"

Oddly, when I ran into some of the higher-ups with King World, they still denied the show had been canceled. They wouldn't look me in the eye, but they insisted that the fact that all of my suits had been packed up meant nothing. And so, later in the day that the show officially ended, when they finally admitted that it was over, the first thing I blurted out was "Do I still get paid?"

They said I did.

"Thank you, Lord," I said.

"And do I get to keep the suits and the shirt and the ties too?"

Yes, they said, looking at me as if I'd lost my mind.

I hadn't. It's just that I have a philosophy. Sometimes, you have to face the pain, acknowledge it, and then head for the door to the next opportunity. *But it certainly doesn't hurt to be well dressed when you go!*

- *The value of finding the one you really love and respect*
- *Understanding your partner and improving communication*
- *How to have disagreements without being hurtful*
- *Building a foundation to support a long-term relationship*
- *Tuning up a relationship*

CHAPTER 5

Letting Love Have the Last Word

One of the most popular and highest-rated programs we did on *The Les Brown Show* featured my favorite all-time favorite guest, the legendary singer and performer Gladys Knight.

Of course, I have reason to be proud of that show and its guest. As you may know, Gladys and I were engaged at the time that program aired and, three years later, we were married in a private ceremony. People tell me they could see our chemistry in that program, and when they tell me that, I have to laugh.

Not that it wasn't a great show, very warm and funny. But the truth is, Gladys and I had a *huge* argument just prior to taping that show. And I'm surprised we weren't doing a *Geraldo* during it, you know, throwing chairs at each other, screaming, yelling, and alley-fighting.

I was always tense and edgy before taping began on a show, and it was my fault that we argued, but it's funny how one of the finest moments in my television show followed one of the more volatile moments in our relationship.

Fortunately, Gladys and I were able to put our anger with each other aside before they started rolling the cameras. We came together and did a very loving show by letting our love rather than our anger have the last word. It isn't always easy to do that. Nor do couples generally have to cool down in front of several million people.

Gladys and I share a deep love, but, like most couples, we have our conflicts too. She lets me know about it when I don't hang up my clothes, or if I spend too much time on the telephone when she thinks I should be talking to *her*. She tells me my feet smell too, even through my shoes!

I give her grief about being slow to get ready when we are going out, being hardheaded and playing rough when we argue. It may be difficult to believe, but this sweet, loving woman can hold her own against anyone when she thinks she's been wronged.

In truth, we are both hardheads and, occasionally, we butt them together. We each entered the relationship with plenty of war wounds from the romance front. We each have baggage of failed marriages, past relationships, and extended families.

But certainly, we are not unique. Disagreements, misunderstandings, and anger occur in every relationship, whether you are married, dating or just friends.

Keeping Love Alive in a Relationship

In this chapter on dealing with hard times in relationships, Gladys and I would like to impart to you some insights into how relationships can work, the value of supporting each other, and how to overcome some of the major challenges you will encounter.

We don't claim to have any magic formulas. We surely can't prevent you, or us, from having rocky times in relationships. But we can get a dialogue going, and all the experts say that communication is the most important aspect of relationships—and often, the missing link in them too.

Having strong personal relationships is vital. I've found that when your personal relationships are strong they make you stronger in all other aspects of your life. A strong relationship provides the steel reinforcement that braces you against life's hard times the way in which steel beams hold up a bridge or support the floors of a building. But when your personal relationships are troubled, your life strength weakens like a bridge with a cracked infrastructure.

Look to people you know who are doing well in life, people who seem confident and well rounded, and then look at their personal lives. In most cases, you'll see that they have a strong foundation from which to operate. Those who fall in the face of adversity often do so because when they reach back there is no one to take their hand.

Celebrity Challenges

There are some special challenges, however, when you have a relationship with someone as famous and beloved by the public as Gladys Knight. Wherever I go, guys young and old come up and say, "Hey, you married *my* woman." When I travel with Gladys, there are usually roses sent by her admirers waiting for her in the hotel room or dressing room. During her performances, starry-eyed men approach the stage with gifts for her.

Many men have to deal with rivals for their woman's affections, but how many have to deal with a nationally syndicated radio show host who makes it a point to declare his undying love for their woman on the air every day? Tom Joyner, one of the best known radio personalities in the country, has broadcast his feelings toward Gladys for years. He has been one of her greatest and most powerful supporters over the years. Long before I came into Gladys's life, Joyner was wooing her on the radio, telling his millions of listeners how he was going to marry her someday. He even kept a picture of her on the ceiling of his studio. And you know *that* wasn't for his listeners' benefit.

I know Gladys is a popular lady. But Joyner is something else. He once invited Gladys to come to his studio for an interview, and when she went there were a half-dozen guys serenading her on violins and singing songs to her. Joyner got down on his knees and proposed, on the air!

Gladys said it is all just in good fun, but you should hear Joyner talk about me on the radio. He says I've got big teeth and a big mouth and I'd better protect my kneecaps if he sees me in the parking lot. He has announced that Gladys should kick me to the curb and come and marry him.

I'd like to think Gladys is right, that Joyner is just kidding, so I am friendly to him. You know the saying *Keep your friends near, but your rivals closer.* I think Tom has it *bad* for Gladys.

Before I met her, I'd always thought highly of Gladys as a performer, and I'd wondered what she was like personally. Then, a year or so before the television syndicators began pursuing me about doing a talk show, a public relations woman from Chicago called and said she wanted to do business with me. To get an idea of her experience, I asked who she represented and she noted that Gladys Knight was a client. That got my attention.

I told her that I had always wanted to meet Gladys, and, to my surprise, she invited me to attend one of Gladys's concerts in Chicago sponsored by Jory Luster and Luster Hair Products. (There, Jory, I finally gave you credit for being our matchmaker.)

I was particularly excited about going to the concert because I'd just seen a television interview in which Gladys mentioned she was single. That sounded good to me.

Love on the Run

I'd chased love a long time, catching it occasionally, losing hold of it more times than I care to recount. It is difficult to build something lasting on a foundation that moves constantly. My career as a public speaker takes me from city to city, all over the country, every week. For most of my speaking career, I have kept an apartment but I've stayed there only during rare breaks in my schedule. I've been in more hotels than Gideon's Bible. I'd worked hard to build my clientele and it had paid off for my career, but my personal life had often been victim to my gypsy existence.

Looking back, that was one thing that attracted me to Gladys. She seemed so rooted, even though she too had spent a good deal of her life on the road. She seemed to be such a solid person, secure in herself and in her talents. I had come to a point in my life when I wanted to be rooted in a relationship with someone who understood the challenges of pursuing a great dream that requires constant travel.

It was beginning to bother me that although I had children and a large extended family, I really had no one to go home to at the end of the day; in fact, I didn't even have a home to go home to. In reflecting on that time, I think that was another reason I was drawn to Gladys. And so I went to see her perform in Chicago, and after the show the public relations woman took me backstage to meet her. My heart was pounding.

I had often heard that she was a down-to-earth and warm person. And I found out just how warm she could be. When we were introduced, we gave each other a hug and I felt a little shock go through me. A red-hot jolt. Gladys must have felt it too because after we talked awhile she told me that next time I wanted to come see her I should just call her direct. Then she gave me her private telephone number. I was cooking!

Later, she confessed that when I walked out she looked into the makeup mirror to watch me walk out, and she liked what she saw. But it took a long time to get her to admit that she liked me at all. Gladys and I had a courtship that lasted more than four years before we finally took the leap and eloped in the summer of 1995. We are very happy together, but I'm not going to tell you it has always been smooth either in our courtship or our married life.

We each have attended Hard Knocks University in coming up with our philosophy on relationships. As I mentioned earlier, both of us have been married before. Gladys has three children and I have seven by previous marriages. We each brought our share of baggage into the relationship, our share of set ways, our share of suspicions and old hurts.

In this chapter, I'd like to offer a little of what we have learned in putting our relationship together and to offer you some of the things we have discovered and come up with in committing ourselves to a loving and lasting relationship.

Rules of the Road

Although Gladys and I care for each other a great deal, I doubt that we ever would have taken the final step and gotten married if we hadn't had many discussions that went deeply into our individual beliefs of what makes relationships worthwhile. Passion is a part of any relationship, but it generally is not the part that sustains a relationship. If the relationship is to endure when passion subsides and matures, you have to establish a broader basis for it. Earlier in our lives, neither of us probably had such strong views and values concerning relationships, but we have both had a lot of experiences, good and bad, in past relationships. We've talked about those experiences, and about how we view this as a great opportunity to avoid the mistakes of the past. Our long and deep discussions helped us form a strong shared concept of what our relationship should be built upon.

Here are a few ingredients that we think are vital to the success of our relationship and, probably, any relationship.

1. *Total commitment to the relationship and to our mutual growth, mentally, emotionally, and spiritually.* Even when we argue, there is no talk of ending our relationship. That is off limits, out of the question. We regard this as our best and last chance to share our lives with someone. And so we are committed to staying together and to growing together.

If you aren't growing as a couple, you will grow apart. It's as simple as that. One partner can't sit back and idle away the day while the other does all the heavy lifting in a relationship. Gladys and I are fairly relentless in our continuous search for mutual growth. We work out together. We read books to each other. We accompany each other on road trips. We pray together. When we are on the road, we hang out in the room all day. When we are home, we hole up like a couple of hermits, refusing to go out.

Are we making you sick yet? Don't worry. We haven't started wearing matching sweaters. Of course, we have our individual interests, and we don't hold ourselves up as the ideal couple. But we each have spent so much time alone and on the road that we want to savor each other when we can.

The point is, we try to stay actively committed to taking life on *together.* Think about that. What can you and your partner do to grow closer?

List five things that you can do to become closer mentally, emotionally, and spiritually:

1. _____

2. _____

3. _____

4. _____

5. _____

2. Communication. Gladys and I probably have an unfair advantage here. After all, we make our livings as communicators. We both have a black belt in talking, but talking is only one aspect of communication. In relationships, in particular, *listening* is the key component. Even though we are both natural-born talkers, we work hard at really communicating more fully by listening as intently as we talk. And we talk about the relationship, our feelings, our hopes, our fears—all aspects of it.

It can be painful, this communication business. It's hard to sit there with your lips sealed sometimes and hear that your partner has doubts and fears and serious problems with some aspect of the relationship. But if you think of the relationship as a collaboration, a partnership that each of you has a vital interest in, you can put ego and pride aside. After all, you do have a self-interest in preserving your relationship too.

Communication in a relationship includes listening attentively, expressing your thoughts, expectations, and concerns effectively, and defining and dealing with problems in a cooperative manner. You often hear of couples who have grown so close they can practically read each other's minds and complete each other's thoughts and sentences. I got a sense of that with Gladys recently when she helped me out at a speaking engagement in Atlanta.

I had to address the National Speakers Association convention in St. Paul, Minnesota, on the day before the Atlanta engagement. The weather in Minnesota was bad, big surprise there, and I was concerned that I might not be able to get to Atlanta. Gladys had gone ahead to visit family and friends, so I called and asked her to be prepared to fill in for me if I couldn't arrive on time.

Gladys had been working on her public speaking. I'd been coaching her and it was obvious she had natural talent in this area too. I didn't realize how much talent until I arrived late for the Atlanta event, just as she was preparing to take the podium on my behalf. The audience was enthused about hearing her, so I decided to let her speak for ten minutes or so. My mistake!

She was *hungry* for this opportunity. She got up there and wrapped that audience around her little finger, her big finger, her thumbs, and her toes. And she spoke for thirty-five minutes before I finally dragged her away from the podium. *She's leaving now,* I announced. She wiped that audience out, there wasn't much left for me to work with.

I was proud of her, and I was touched by how hard she had worked to become part of my career. And now, let the world know. At the very next opportunity, I plan to step in and sing for her. Look out Luther Vandross!

3. Total trust and mutual support. Gladys and I try to always be there for each other. When we are traveling apart, we talk on the phone for hours and hours, which can be bad when both of you have to be careful about abusing your vocal cords. If we're facing a challenge, we are there for each other, to support and watch each other's backs.

Total trust means that we can count on each other always in times of need. It means we will protect each other from outside influences. And it means we would never knowingly hurt each other. I know that if something bad happens in my life Gladys will be there by my side as quickly as she can get there—as she was for me when my Mama was first diagnosed with breast cancer. And Gladys knows the same is true for me.

With those assurances, then, Gladys and I can always assume that even when it may appear otherwise, we each always have the other's best interests at heart.

Total trust also means that we know neither of us would do anything to harm the other one or to betray a confidence. Even highly public figures are vulnerable. But in any relationship, each partner has to be able to place total trust in the other.

4. *Absolute loyalty.* It is key to any relationship that you know your partner will be on your side, looking out for your best interests in any situation. It is also vital that both of you put each other above all others. No relationship can survive disloyalty. And Gladys and I will take on all comers in this category. Absolute loyalty can be important particularly in dealing with family problems. We each have large extended families and there are always going to be times of conflict, so it is important in those times that Gladys and I know that no matter who is in conflict, she and I are always on the same side.

5. *Togetherness.* As difficult as it may be with two professionals who travel incessantly, we get together wherever we can, whenever we can, however we can. If Gladys has a free day on the road, she flies to me. If I have a free day, I fly to her. And if we are both off, watch out for a midair collision! We try to coordinate our schedules and to work together whenever we can with our "Music and Motivation" program, which has been amazingly well received, even if *I* don't get to do any singing. We also do our best to make important career and personal decisions together.

6. *Dedication.* Some people joke that marriage is the first step toward divorce. We don't go at it that way. We are committed to this relationship and we are willing to do everything we can to make it work. That includes always seeking to dwell on the positive rather than the negative things that come up. We try to always seek solutions rather than retribution. And there is never any question that this marriage will not last for the rest of our lives together.

Gladys is a sweet person with very feminine charms. She is also a strong-willed woman whose strength has been forged in a lifetime of working in the male-dominated music industry. She traveled for years on the road with the Pips, the only woman among males. She saw the ways of men firsthand, the good and the bad. She learned to be hard-nosed in business situations, and sometimes she brings that mind-set home with her. That is understandable, of course, but it is not always easy to deal with, particularly if you are a bull-headed man like me.

She acknowledges that occasionally she brings her work attitude into the house. With so many women working outside the home today that is fairly common. And it is also a fairly common point of conflict in relationships because men do not adjust well to their women being forceful and direct with them. Like most men, I sometimes carry the mind-set that *If I back down, she will think I'm a wimp.* Her answer to that is *There is no place for ego or pride in a relationship.*

Ah, women. They always have an answer. And in this case, a good point. It's said that marriage is a humbling experience, and I am here to testify that it is indeed. Since Gladys is a strong-willed woman, I've had to learn to bend more than I have in other relationships. It hasn't killed me yet. We have found that most arguments, whatever they deal with, are triggered by ego and pride. The key is to let love and commitment override ego and pride but that is easier said than done.

Relationships 101

Gladys and I learned early on that we each had a lot of work cut out for us in overcoming our egos and pride for the good of our relationship. We have often talked too about what people can do when hard times hit a relationship or when it is dead in the water, or falling apart. It is a question many couples face. What can you do if you are dying together rather than living and growing together as a couple? What are the keys to having a successful and loving relationship? In studying this topic for our popular relationship seminars, as well as for our own interests, we have identified a few of the reasons relationships fail:

- Lack of communication
- Lack of trust
- Differing expectations for the relationship
- Lack of self-awareness
- Lack of knowledge of the other person
- Lack of time spent together
- Differing values
- Mental and physical abuse
- Problems with sex
- Drugs and alcohol
- Difficulties with children or other family members
- A lack of counseling to learn methods for solving conflicts
- Personal baggage from old relationships
- Money problems

Look at that list and identify the problem or potential problem areas in your relationship. Write below what those areas might be, and, as we go along, make notes on how you might resolve those problems.

The problems or potential problems in my relationship include:

_____

_____

_____

_____

Here are some ideas on what I can do to prevent or resolve those problems:

_____

_____

_____

_____

Distinct Differences

Every couple has their differences. If you don't have frustrations and occasional anger and disagreements, then there is cause to think that maybe you aren't dealing realistically with your relationship. There are quite natural differences that spring simply from the differing ways men and women approach their lives.

As a couple of people accustomed to communicating with large audiences, Gladys and I are both excellent at *projecting* our voices, and so we don't have quiet, polite little arguments. We shake the roof. In general conversation, Gladys speaks in this gentle, womanly voice, but when we get to arguing, she lets fly like she's arguing with someone way up in the cheap seats at Madison Square Garden. And it's deep too. She can rumble down there like Barry White. She *scares* me sometimes.

In truth, I have learned to back down from Gladys, rather than launching a counterattack when we argue. In the past, I had a problem with being vindictive in arguments. If the other person went ballistic, I went nuclear. *You started it, I'll finish it!* That was my motto. But I realize now that it does no good to be vengeful in arguing with a loved one. No one wins when one of you hurts the other. It is far better to let love, rather than anger, have the last word.

Love Conquers, Anger Destroys

You can argue without causing damage when you operate from the position of letting love have the last word. What this really means is that when you have disagreements, you keep in mind what is most important—the preservation of the love and trust and mutual respect that bond you together in this chaotic world where everyone and everything seem determined to pull you apart. If you can train yourself to hold the high ground when you disagree, to always keep in mind what is most important, you don't endanger your most valuable resource in hard times—your partnership.

Most couples have to deal with problems that come up because of their different points of view as individuals, their different life experiences, and their own individual taste, biases, and emotional baggage. Often, there are factors influencing their behavior that they are not conscious of.

My ability to build relationships was hindered for a long time by subconscious feelings of unworthiness that sprang from the fact that I'd been abandoned by my birth mother. I had this sense that if my own mother had not wanted me, how could any woman be trusted to want me? As a result, nearly any relationship I got involved in was doomed because, deep down, I had no trust of women. I felt it would be just a matter of time before I'd be rejected and abandoned, so I'd cut the ties before I could be hurt. And often, I'd keep a secondary relationship going as a backup because I always felt the primary relationship would not last.

For years, many of my relationships self-destructed because of the baggage I brought to them. It took me a long time to work out those subconscious feelings and to deal with them. I'm sure there are others that I still haven't gotten a handle on. We all have baggage from past relationships. A lot of people can't enjoy a relationship because of past experiences.

My longtime friend Lenore had a father who cheated on her mother. As an adult, she had no trust of men. She thought all men were like her cheating father. Another friend of mine never will trust guys because she used to listen to her brothers talking on the telephone to girls and lying to them. This is understandable, but tragic. You can't let past experiences drive your present relationships. Not all men are insincere or dishonest. Not all women are unreliable.

Losing Your Balance

Take a few minutes to think about your own life and your approach to relationships. What baggage might be affecting your relationships adversely? Write down factors from your past that you think may work against your ability to maintain a relationship:

Just being aware of these factors can help you short-circuit destructive behavior. Now write what you can do to eliminate or counter damaging behavior in your relationships:

When you look at all the influences that come into play in relationships, it's amazing any two people stay together for any prolonged period of time. But the fact is they do, and they always have, in spite of gender-related differences, personal baggage, past histories, and fragile feelings. Why? Because it is worth it to have someone as your partner in life, someone who can share all of the good times and bad times and help you live life to the fullest. If you learn to accept each other and understand each other, even problems can become sources for growth and deeper understanding rather than pushing you apart.

An Ounce of Prevention

Too many people enter into relationships based on physical attraction, without thinking about the other aspects of a relationship. This may come as a shock, but everything that feels good isn't good for you. You can't allow emotions to guide your good sense. Too many people become trapped in relationships that are destructive and negative. You have to approach relationships with both your mind and your heart fully engaged.

A boyfriend's possessiveness and jealousy may be cute and endearing in the early stages of a romance, but later that insecurity could trigger serious problems. I know a woman who was beaten by her jealous boyfriend. She told me that she'd been flattered by his possessiveness early in their relationship, and that she had pretended to herself that it would not be a problem down the road. It was.

Now, it is true, people do grow up and mature. Some wild party animals do become responsible adults, business professionals, and pillars of the community, but it is better to be cautious and aware of what you are entering into, because your relationships are critical. Some dogs don't change. In fact, my friend Chavonne once introduced me to a boyfriend known as "Dawg." I asked him how he'd gotten such a flattering nickname, and he said, "My friends say I'm a dirty dude, always dawgin' after women." He then proceeded to tell me about some of his doglike activities.

I took Chavonne aside and said, "Look, do you need a translator? This Dawg is a hound. Do not get involved with him!" But she said he was really good to her. Two months later, I saw Chavonne and I asked her how she and Dawg were doing. She started crying like she'd been to somebody's funeral. I knew she'd been mauled by Dawg but I asked what was wrong anyway. She told me he'd lied to her. He was married.

"Dawg? No! I'm shocked!" I said. "Surely you are kidding about being surprised that Dawg was no good. Those must be tears of joy you are shedding! You were in serious Dawg denial when you hooked up with that guy."

If you go into a relationship blind, believe me, you are going to walk into more than the furniture. The best way to handle hard times in a relationship is to stay away from the Dawgs out there in the first place. Here are a few advisory points and preventive measures you and your partner might take early in your relationship, in order to avoid serious problems down the road.

Matching Up

1. *You have to accept yourself before you can be acceptable to others.* This is a key in all relationships. You can only be loved if you feel worthy of love; otherwise, you will sabotage the relationship. Self-acceptance is the basis of all interaction with other people. How you feel about yourself affects how you treat other people. It affects the signals you send out, the perceptions you have, the treatment your behavior invites. If you feel unworthy, you will act under that mentality.

Peter was a participant in a motivational seminar I was conducting for a church congregation, and he stood out as one of those people who others are naturally drawn to. He was just a very warm person, handsome but not at all egotistical, and interested in other people. I learned later that Peter had a troubled relationship with his wife, who believed the way to hold on to him was to make him feel inadequate. She put him down constantly and, as a result, he felt insecure about his relationships with other people.

I became aware of this only after something odd happened during the seminar. Part of the program called for giving feedback to people on how they came across to others. When it came time to give Peter feedback, people lavished him with compliments and praise. They told him how wonderful they thought he was. And, to our surprise, he broke down and cried. Later, he told me that he felt so unloved in his closest relationship, he was overwhelmed when he got such positive feedback from relative strangers.

He contacted me months after the seminar to tell me that he'd gone home with a renewed sense of self-love and appreciation. He explained to his wife what had happened and how it had affected him. And he told her that he felt she had hurt their relationship in her treatment of him. She refused to accept that, or to change her attitude toward him. And Peter found the courage to leave her.

If you feel good about yourself, you take care of yourself and you don't allow your partner to tear you down by being toxic. If you smoke and drink and eat yourself into poor health and an unattractive appearance, it is because you have no respect for yourself. And if you don't respect yourself, you can't expect to attract the respect or love of someone else.

Check yourself on this, and check the person you are involved with. You don't want to get into a relationship with someone who has self-hatred, anger, and bitterness. These people hurt not only themselves but anybody around them. Not only do they dislike themselves, they have contempt and disdain for people who *like* them.

I once invested a great deal of time and money into a talented singer and piano player named Johnny. I befriended him after hearing him perform. He was a charming guy. But I would later learn that he had spent most of his adult life charming people with his talent and his personality, only to run out on them as soon as they got too close.

Although he hid it well, Johnny was an alcoholic beset by great insecurities and self-loathing. He has left a trail of hurt and disappointed people across the country. He has wasted his gifts, and he has wasted his relationships because he has no self-love.

2. *Make sure you know your partner.* Too many people put the cart before the horse: They move in together or get married *before* they have a serious relationship. They never look beyond the first impression or physical attraction to make sure they really know the person. First impressions or physical attraction certainly don't hurt a relationship, but they're not what you want to build a lasting relationship on.

In this era of instant food, instant credit, instant banking, instant communication, too many people dive into instant relationships and then one day they wake up to *instant realization.* I'm married to the wrong person!

I call this "delayed enlightenment." Remember the movie *The Candidate* with Robert Redford? The movie focuses on his incredible drive to get elected to public office. It concludes with him winning that office, taking over, turning to his advisors and saying "Now what?"

In relationships, the answer is too frequently "Divorce Court." You can't be so involved in the chase that you don't think about what you are going to do with the catch. And it doesn't pay to have the attitude that you can change the person later. Throw that idea out the window. There are no "fixer-uppers" in relationships.

Kate was divorced and lonely when Curt called her. He was an old friend from high school. A star athlete, handsome, fun to be with, but seriously troubled. He'd come from a troubled family and he'd led a troubled life as a result. Curt had a lot of anger in him, and a lot of insecurities. He'd been married a couple times and although he had worked hard to keep himself on track, he had demons that were difficult to control.

Kate knew all this, but she had always liked Curt, in spite of his problems. She thought she could help him. And besides, she was lonely too. They dated for several months before trouble set in. Curt had been affectionate and loving and attentive in the beginning, but suddenly nothing Kate did was good enough. He turned cruel and cold toward her. But when she tried to break off the relationship, he begged her to take him back. Kate stood her ground, to her credit. She refused to get back with him, though she offered to remain friends. Within just a few months, she heard that Curt had married someone else, and that he had beaten her severely.

The only reason you'd buy a house in need of repair is because you might get it cheap. But believe me, you can't afford to become involved with someone whose psyche is damaged. Kate knew what she was getting into with Curt, and so she was not all that surprised at how their relationship ended. But she still paid for it emotionally.

Often it is difficult to listen to your head, particularly when you are lonely, but a good defense is the best offense in cultivating relationships. You need to be guarded about who you allow into your life. You can tell how someone feels about himself or herself by the way he or she treats others.

Our actions toward others reflect our feelings about ourselves. If your partner is angry and hurtful to family members, friends, and strangers, my advice is for you to run for cover. That anger and hurtfulness will be turned on you one day.

When I was a teenager, I had a girlfriend who was loving toward me, but one day I saw her turn on her little sister in a fit of rage over a very small matter. I knew then that this was not the girl for me, because I knew that my turn would come. It did, and when it came, I saw it for what it was: the true picture of this girl's personality. I did not waste time on a long goodbye.

3. *Check your perception of relationships.* Often we carry antiquated or set ideas about how relationships should work. The truth is, you have to shape your relationship according to the personalities of those involved. Although some women want to nurture and take care of others, to stay home and raise the children and manage the house, there are more and more who prefer focusing their lives on careers outside the home.

In other words, men, don't assume the woman in your life will want to iron your shirt, wash your clothes, and cook you dinner. You hand some women a dirty shirt and they'll ask if you know where the cleaners is. And there are some women who have their homes designed with no kitchens.

Not all men think working around the house is the best way to spend their time either. The point here is that before you invest your heart and soul in a relationship with someone, make sure you are in agreement on your lifestyles and philosophies, or at least make sure that you can deal with each other on fundamental issues. (By the way, if you have someone who will iron your clothes for you, hold on to them.)

4. *Make sure you have similar values.* This is critical in relationships. What this is really about is checking your values against those of the person you are involved with. I believe that shared spiritual values hold a relationship together in the hard times. I'm not talking, necessarily, about being religious, but if you both believe in a power greater than yourselves, that faith can get you through the storms of life. I call that power God, you may have another name for it.

Having different values can be highly destructive to a relationship. If the man expects the woman to stay home and raise the children, he'd better find a woman who agrees with that philosophy, because it won't do anyone—the man, the woman, or the children—any good to force this issue.

I know of relationships in which the children suffer because the mother stays home against her wishes. And I know of relationships in which the husband resents his wife's refusal to stay home. Both are unhealthy environments for raising children, and the way to avoid this is to reach an agreement and mutually compatible philosophy before children come on the scene.

This applies to other aspects of the relationship as well. I had a friend who resented that his wife earned more money than him. A lot of men feel insecure with high-achieving women. Others welcome and support wives who are career-minded.

It's a matter of finding someone with compatible values. If you aren't into drinking or smoking or doing drugs, don't develop a relationship with someone who is because you think you can change them. If you are into personal growth don't get involved with somebody who could care less about it. If you transform or grow, you could make your partner feel threatened.

5. Determine what you want out of a relationship. I asked a friend recently to tell me what it was that she wanted out of her relationship with her boyfriend. "I just want to be happy," she answered. But she could not define what that meant. She really had not worked out in her mind what it would take to make her happy in a relationship. She didn't know what her bottom line was.

You need to know what you want out of a relationship. You can't expect to figure it out as you go. That will only lead to confusion and conflict.

What is your bottom line? Gladys and I exchanged lists of what we expected out of our relationship. We think it is important to do that because there are periods of adjustment to any marriage and relationship. The minister may talk about "two becoming one," but that doesn't happen overnight. You have to learn each other's ways, what habits are annoying, what you can share, and what you can't.

It is one thing when you are courting each other and holding hands. It's something else altogether when you are snoring in each other's faces. When you get married there are a lot of things you learn that you didn't know before. I call it "delayed enlightenment."

And so it is helpful to establish what your bottom line is as far as what you will or will not tolerate in the relationship. List fifteen things that you want out of the relationship.

Example 1: My partner has to share my belief in a monogamous relationship.

Example 2: I am an affectionate person and I expect affection in return.

1. _____
2. _____
3. _____
4. _____
5. _____
6. _____
7. _____
8. _____
9. _____
10. _____
11. _____
12. _____
13. _____
14. _____
15. _____

Now, highlight those points above that you consider to be your bottom line.

1. _____
2. _____
3. _____
4. _____
5. _____

If you and your partner can't come to an agreement on your bottom line, then your relationship is probably in for some rocky times, so you may want to forget being intimate and settle for a social or business relationship, unless it's already too late. In that case, you may want to sit down and hammer out compromises in order to avoid head-butting down the road. A lot of people blow relationships because they expect people to change for them. People don't change unless they want to change. Make sure you establish what your bottom line is up front.

6. *Know that without trust, you have no basis for a relationship.* You have to have trust. If you can't believe what someone says you can't live in harmony. I was once involved with a terribly insecure woman. I was faithful to her. But she didn't trust me.

It became an impossible situation. I did everything I could to assure her that she was the focus of my life. It got crazy. Every time the phone rang she assumed it was a woman calling to steal me away. At one point, I had the phone taken out of the house. It didn't matter. One day she turned to me and said "I'm tired of those women calling us." We didn't even have a telephone.

Of course the phone wasn't the problem, her irrational jealousy was. I was in the Ohio legislature at this time, and one day while I was at the office, she saw a television soap opera in which an elected official was having an affair. She asked where I'd been. "I've been in a committee hearing," I replied. "What's her name?" she demanded.

7. *Guard your identity and self-image.* You can't forget yourself and your life in a relationship. You need to maintain your interests and your talents as the foundation of your sense of who you are. If you lose your sense of who you are as a person it can throw the entire relationship off.

I have come to admire the relationship of motivational speaker Tracy Lynn and her husband, C.B., who is a flight attendant and entrepreneur. Tracy is a very dynamic and attractive woman. She travels around the country speaking to business executives, but C.B. is not intimidated or insecure about it.

He knows who he is, and he trusts their relationship. Tracy Lynn's previous husband was not so secure. He lost his sense of identity, and as a result, he lost trust in their relationship. He demanded that Tracy Lynn give up her career. She gave him up instead, and found a man who was secure in himself.

You have to feel equal in the relationship. Now it might be that your partner has a better-paying job or a higher profile; often there is no way to avoid that. But you should find ways to develop your own interests and to assert your own personality so that you don't feel undervalued or unappreciated. Those feelings can undermine a relationship.

8. *Take responsibility for your own feelings and actions.* Your happiness is not guaranteed by anyone else. If you are feeling insecure or unhappy, check yourself before immediately placing the blame on your partner. Be honest with yourself, and you may save disrupting the relationship. Often, our insecurities and frustrations come from within rather than from anything our partner is responsible for.

9. *Monitor and work always to improve the relationship.* Sometimes you have to ask tough questions of your partner. Are you happy? What can I do to improve? These are tough because the answers might hurt a bit, but if you want to make the relationship work, you have to work at it. You can't take your relationship for granted. There have been many relationships that fail while one of the partners says, "I didn't know there was anything wrong." Some relationships sail upon launch, others require hard rowing.

I believe in establishing My Week and Your Week. On my week, Gladys does things to make me happy. On her week I do things for her. On my week, she will cook my favorite foods, have my bath ready for me, give me a massage. On her week, I'll take her dancing, surprise her with little gifts, and take her to one of those old movies she likes.

Make up a wish list for Your Week and have your partner do the same. You might want to keep this where no one else will find it.

Your Week

During my week I would like to do the following:

Sunday _____

Monday _____

Tuesday _____

Wednesday _____

Thursday _____

Friday _____

Saturday _____

Your Partner's Week

During my week I would like to do the following:

Sunday _____

Monday _____

Tuesday _____

Wednesday _____

Thursday _____

Friday _____

Saturday _____

10. Be alert for things you can share together. Make it a point to develop common interests. If your partner enjoys golf, learn the game. If it's horseback riding, mount up. Gladys had never explored the whole motivational and self-awareness field until I opened it up to her and now she is intensely interested in it. I've taken up tennis because she loves it.

A key to relationships is being open to growth and exploration. Sometimes you may resist sharing an interest, but you can be surprised at how enjoyable something becomes when you share it with someone you love. When we bought our first house, Gladys asked me to go to High Point, North Carolina, with her to buy furniture. Generally, I would rather shower in ice water than go shopping for furniture. It bores me to tears. But Gladys was so enthused about doing it together, I went along. And I have to admit we had a great time. I learned a great deal, and we had fun.

Gladys now says that the trip was something she will never forget. It meant more to her than I ever could have guessed. It reinforced to her that I was committed to the relationship.

For her part, Gladys has shown her commitment to me by taking a serious interest in public speaking. I've worked with her, and we now do appearances together, which gives us more time than we might have had if we had simply gone separate ways in our careers.

She has refused, however, to take this togetherness to the next logical step. I've been trying to get her to teach me to sing so that I can become a Pip, but she claims I'm tone-deaf. I know I've got a singing voice in there somewhere, just dying to come out, but she says if it does come out, people may die as a result!

Ownership Versus Partnership

You know, you might think that old-fashioned, sexist concepts of relationships had passed out of existence, but they haven't. Some men still think that women are the weaker sex. Obviously, they've never tangled with my wife.

It's very important to know the difference between ownership and partnership. Very few relationships will work if one partner totally dominates the other. You have to balance your needs and desires with those of your partner.

Often, this means that sometimes you get what you want, and sometimes you give in to what your partner wants. That is how a partnership works. If you give willingly, chances are your partner will respond in kind.

People who stay together do it because they've made a commitment to stay together. My friend Sarah says that you have to know how to "fill each other's bucket." This means that you have to be attentive to your partner's emotional needs. I recently saw an example of this when a fellow I know, Brad, lost his business. He was terribly despondent, he felt like a failure in his career and in his life.

But the woman in his life sensed his down spirit, and she filled his bucket. She took him in her arms, held him and said, "Baby, we have each other. I'll never need any more than you can give me." Brad never got the business back but he was happier than if it succeeded because he knew she loved him in spite of his business problems. His woman was committed to the relationship, rather than to being married to a successful man.

Women sometimes forget that men need to feel loved and appreciated too. We may not be very skilled at letting you know it, but we do. When a man knows that a woman is totally into him and appreciates him fully, he naturally becomes more attentive and responsive to her. If he feels he is not respected or appreciated, however, he tends to draw back within himself and the relationship often suffers. Too often, women take for granted that the man knows that he is valued and appreciated, without working to make sure he feels that way, and vice versa: too often the man takes for granted that the woman knows she's valued.

I don't know whether Gladys did it purposely or not, but she got the message across to me shortly after we started dating. We rendezvoused in Las Vegas, where she has lived for nineteen years. It was a very special meeting because it was her birthday party, and since she is Gladys Knight, it wasn't held at the Elks Club. It was held at Caesars Palace, where she often performs.

I have to admit I was a little intimidated when I first walked in, but Gladys sensed it, and she made a very significant move to make me feel comfortable. In fact, looking back, I think of it as one of the first moments when I really knew that she felt as strongly about me as I felt about her. And it wasn't all that big a deal.

Everybody was gathered around after singing "Happy Birthday" to her, and Gladys started cutting her cake. She handed the big first slice to me and when I turned to hand it to a friend, he said, "No, she gave that to you because she wants to let you know you are special to her."

It may sound silly, but that small gesture meant a lot to me. It told me that I was number one with Gladys even in a room filled with people who had known her and loved her for a long time. In this case, I got my cake and married her too. All because she filled my bucket.

Filling Your Bucket

Here are some of our suggestions for filling each other's buckets, for doing little things that show your partner that you care for and respect them.

For Her Bucket, He Can:

- Let her know how much the marriage means to you even though sometimes you don't express it very well.
- Listen to her when she wants to talk about a problem or her feelings, without trying to solve her problems.
- Drop her off at the door and then park the car.
- Offer to take over a task that she dreads.
- Call her from the store to see if she needs anything else.
- Tell her when you feel she looks especially nice.
- Offer without being asked that she looks really slim in those pants.
- Go for walks with her.
- Write her love letters.
- Ask her out for a date at least once a month.

For His Bucket, She Can:

- Refrain from saying *I told you so.*
- Stock the refrigerator with his favorite foods and beverages.
- Mate his socks.
- Let him read the newspaper or watch his favorite television program in peace, and then talk to him about what is bothering you.
- Let him go off on his own when he needs to think through a problem.
- Encourage him to do things with his male friends now and then.
- Let him know you appreciate him.

Resolving Conflict

Relationships are a union of two imperfect individuals and both of you have to keep your commitment to the commitment to make it work. By working through the challenges you'll encounter, your relationship can grow. By staying committed *even when it doesn't feel all that good,* you make the relationship stronger. Sometimes walls have to come down, habits and priorities have to change. It takes courage, commitment, and character to work it out.

Gladys is a very neat person. She keeps a very clean house—until I come home. She says I'm junky. I say I'm merely *"tidy-impaired."* Rather than drive a Rock and Roll Hall of Famer into the insane asylum, I've been working on putting my things in their proper place. Gladys has even given me a *designated junky area* where I can mess up as much as I want.

Now, in the other corner, we have Gladys Knight, who is, you might say, *"punctuality-impaired."* She is not only often late, she is defiant about her right to be late without being hassled.

The Pips, including my brother-in-law Bubba Knight, learned this lesson on the road with her over the years. I learned it the hard way. One time I walked into her dressing room while everybody was waiting for her to go to an event. I went up and said, "Hey baby, how much longer will it be?"

She gave me a look that took ten years off my life and awakened six generations of dead ancestors. Then she followed up with a warning in her deepest baritone, "Don't you ever ask me that again!"

My junky ways and her lateness were problems early in our relationship so we targeted them as things to work on for the sake of getting along. We now offer "positive advice" instead of criticism in these areas of our lives. This means I try to be neater and she tells me to go on ahead without her if she is running late.

In the course of resolving your differences, you've got to be conscious of what you are saying and how you are saying it. You have to take the emotion out of criticism and fight the tendency to push each other's buttons. I know how to send Gladys off the deep end. She knows how to get to me. *(I thought I married a REAL man!)*

You can fight, or you can try to resolve differences. We've had some really passionate arguments only to discover, in the end, that we had been arguing about arguing. Because I was listening with my pride and ego, I found myself being defensive about *how* she was saying things as opposed to *what* she was saying.

It is true too, however, that you have to monitor how you express yourself in times of conflict because *how* you say something often determines to a large extent how people take what you are saying.

We must keep that in mind when we are communicating with each other because some people hear what they *want* to hear, some hear what they *think* they hear, and some hear what is really being said.

If you want a person to hear what you are really saying, you have to express yourself clearly and rationally. If your voice is charged with anger, the anger will carry more weight than your words. Nine times out of ten, your partner will respond to the emotion rather than the content of what is being said.

When you argue based on your ego, you don't really hear what is being said, you only hear *how* it is being said. To truly listen, you have to put aside both your ego and your anger.

A good rule to follow in deciding how to respond to challenges in your relationship is to always ask what really matters. Does this argument really matter more than all that we have together? What will be more important ten years from now, the relationship or who won the argument?

Here are Five Basic Rules for Couples in Conflict. Consider them when your relationship hits rocky times:

1. Most hard times in relationships stem from misunderstandings and misinterpretations rather than a lack of love and appreciation.
2. Most miscommunication occurs when we filter our partner's words through our own background, experience, and point of view.
3. Both of you are responsible for making the relationship work and for resolving problems. Think of the sociologist who looked down at his plate and saw bacon and eggs. He

turned to his breakfast companion and said, "You see, this breakfast reminds me of the different approaches people have in their relationships." The person with him did not get the point. "Well," the sociologist said, "you can see here that while the chicken was involved in this meal, the pig was fully committed." In relationships, you have to be fully committed.

4. Laying blame or finding fault are destructive practices and contribute nothing to resolving conflicts and getting past hard times.
5. More often than not, things that your loved one has done to upset you weren't intended to hurt you.

Ground Rules for Conflict

Many conflicts arise out of the power struggles that occur when two people live together. Couples have to work these out in a manner that does not tear at the foundations of their relationship. You can disagree without being disagreeable, hurtful, or abusive. You can even argue without becoming mean-spirited or violent. Under no circumstances should physical abuse be tolerated. Once is too much; if the abusive partner refuses to get serious help, get out of there.

1. You must agree that only one of you is allowed to go crazy at any one time. The other must stand there calmly with the life preserver, ready to throw it out and bring the other back in. One of you has to be responsible for holding the relationship together when the other one is exercising his or her impulse to go absolutely crazy.
2. Leave the gloves on. Too often, a small disagreement turns into an argument over the way you are disagreeing. The tendency when you are hurt is to be hurtful, and that leads only to greater pain in a relationship. You have to hold yourself to a higher standard when you are in a relationship that you value and want to keep. There is no room for being vindictive.

3. Give it time. Allow each side to make a case for his or her point of view, and then call the game, bring down the curtain, and retreat to a neutral corner. Repeating the same points over and over only leads to anger. Especially if you come at the argument with vastly different perspectives. So state your case and then rest. Let the other side have time to absorb your argument in deliberations. Let time provide a perspective.

4. Give the other side the benefit of the doubt. If your partner says the action that offends you was unintentional, what good does it do you to challenge that? None. If you love the person and the person has been loving to you, why assign a darker motive to his or her actions? You have to give your partner room to maneuver. Of course if the offensive action is part of a long-term pattern, then the benefit of the doubt becomes doubtful.

5. Understand that for men the process is usually to find out what was hurtful and then determine how to make it right. Women, on the other hand, want to express how much they were hurt. Sometimes those two strategies don't work well together. Work to help your partner deal with the hurt in his or her own way, and then ask them to do the same for you.

6. Ban the blame. Women have a tendency to blame their men for their unhappiness while not accepting their own responsibility for it. And men tend to blame women for being negative while often not paying enough attention to the problems they are citing or dealing with the issues they are raising. Either way, it does no good to cast blame. Seek instead to offer understanding, empathy, and support.

   Often, if a man helps a woman get past casting blame, he finds that she is really looking for love. And when a woman digs deeper, the man will acknowledge that he doesn't want to blame her, he wants to feel respected and appreciated by her.

7. Practice empathetic listening. Rather than simply listening to each other and interpreting through your own mind-sets, try to understand where your partner is coming from based on his or her mind-set.

This means men should listen to women without defending themselves or counterattacking. And women should allow men time to put their anger aside. It also means that when women talk about their problems, men should understand they are being asked to listen and empathize, not find solutions. And women need to understand that when men don't talk about their problems, it means that they are trying to work them out on their own, which men feel is their role.

8. Keep the family and friends out of it. Too often one side or the other takes a complaint or a problem to others in the family, a father or mother or sibling, or to a friend. The problem is that when the couple patches things up, that family member or friend is still upset and may hold a grudge. It's not fair to either one to bring in family members or friends unless you know the individual supports the relationship and can be trusted to be impartial.

Take Time for a Tune-Up

Has your partner ever said to you in anger or frustration, "I forget what we ever saw in each other?" Or has your partner ever said in a moment of warmth, "Now I remember why I loved you"?

It's true that in the day-to-day mad rush of living, we sometimes lose track of the feelings that inspired us to love our partners in life. It may help your relationship if you and your partner take time to write answers to the questions below and then review them with each other. Make copies and fill out the answers at key points in the year, or on anniversaries of your first date, your engagement, or wedding, if you think it might help you tune up your relationship.

1. How did you first meet your partner?

_____

_____

2. What first attracted you to your partner?

_____

_____

_____

_____

3. When did you know it might be love?

_____

_____

_____

_____

4. What qualities did you admire most?

_____

_____

_____

_____

5. What activities did you most enjoy doing together?

_____

_____

_____

_____

Dealing with Changing Roles

While we may sometimes lose track of the reasons we fell in love with our partner, the truth is that all relationships undergo changes and shifts. Infatuation seasons into loving affection and deep caring, romance grows into empathy, understanding, and intimacy. The honeymoon is over in a few days, but the relationship can remain strong if you both tend to it and make adjustments.

Roles change. We change. The young beauty who caught the man's eye at a party will eventually become the more mature beauty who gives him children. The dashing young man who strutted across the dance floor will become the fatherly figure coaching the youth league basketball team.

We change, our lives change, but our commitment to a life together does not have to change if we always keep in mind the reasons we became partners.

Being in a relationship with a celebrity like Gladys has its unique challenges, as I mentioned earlier. She handles it well, but I had to learn to deal with it gracefully. Gladys did something early in our relationship that showed me who she really is, in spite of her fame.

We had gone to one of her favorite restaurants in L.A., a down-home place called Roscoe's. When we arrived, there was a long line of people waiting to be seated. The maître d' saw Gladys and recognized her and said he would seat us immediately. But Gladys politely declined.

"No," she said, "these people have been waiting. I'll be fine." She then took a place at the back of the line.

They had to come get me, because I had already started to follow the maître d' to our seat. Since I was not such a big celebrity, I was all too willing to get a taste of the sort of treatment that Gladys says no thanks to. But I was impressed with her demeanor that day, even if she wasn't so impressed with how I handled her fame.

And so, when I got my own television talk show, I was extremely interested to see how she would handle *my fame.*

Reality, and Ego, Check

When we were doing a practice talk show taping at my "boot camp" in Iowa, Gladys accompanied me to the local high school where we were using the auditorium.

As we were wrapping up, one of the production people told me that a crowd had gathered outside. He asked if I minded signing a few autographs. I said that would be fine, but I wondered how it would affect Gladys to suddenly be the one in the background. I hoped it would not bother her.

From the moment they opened the doors and we came out of the gym, I could hear the adoring voices. But when we walked out, I realized they weren't calling for Mrs. Mamie Brown's baby boy.

"Gladys! Gladys! How ya' doing? Hey Gladys, will you sign this for me? Gladys? Gladys!"

And these were young kids, high school and college.

Well, Gladys seemed to handle *my* fame very well. So well, in fact, people were apparently overlooking me in their enthusiasm for her humility!

Speaking of humility, after I had an ample dose of it that day, I finally heard my name called out as we approached our car. "Oh look, there's Les Brown too!" someone said.

It's true. It really happened that way. And I've been trying to live it down to Gladys ever since.

- Dealing with the depression, anger, and guilt that come with hard times and failure in career situations
- How to better understand your moods and yourself during such times
- A step-by-step process for handling bad times so that you learn from them, and then move on

CHAPTER 6

Lost and Looking for Direction

Shortly after *The Les Brown Show* was canceled, I began having flashbacks to other periods when I have struggled and lost. I think it was my subconscious mind's way of reminding me that I'd been in worse situations in my life. One of the flashbacks that came regularly was a vision of me running through the hallways of the Penobscot Building in downtown Detroit. In just my underwear. With a janitor chasing me.

This dream was very close to reality. Almost too close for comfort. When I was just starting out as a public speaker, I rented office space in that grand old building. It was more than I needed, or than I could afford, but I felt if I rented a nice office, I'd force myself to grow into it. Even a motivator needs motivation now and then. But it took me quite a while to get my speaking fees up to the same level as my office rent. I couldn't afford to pay the rent on my apartment and on the office too, so I lived in my office.

I worked there, ate there, slept there. And I wasn't alone. Two buddies who had been sharing my apartment moved into the office with me because without my help in paying the apartment rent, they couldn't raise enough to pay the bill either. They slept on little sleeping mats they bought at Woolworth's. They left the office couch for me, but I refused to sleep on it. I slept on the wood floor. I didn't want to be comfortable sleeping in the office. The discomfort and pain reminded me, even as I slept, that I had a lot more work to do and that I'd better not rest too long. (Okay, that old couch wasn't all that comfortable anyway.)

I woke up every morning aching. I'd be stiff and sore with bruises on my backside. But every ache reminded me that I had to get going and quickly. I didn't think I could hide my office apartment from the building managers forever. I had to get up at 4:30 A.M. so that I could go down the hall to the rest room, bathe in the sink, and get cleaned up before the people who lived in actual homes showed up for work.

One morning, I was walking down the hall to the rest room, wearing only my T-shirt and undershorts, when I spotted a janitor mopping the floor. I did a quick turnaround and raced back into the office, hoping he hadn't seen me. A few days later, the security guard, George, tried to hail me down when he saw me walking in the lobby. George was a nice guy, but I was afraid he had bad news for me, so I ducked him. He caught up with me later and handed me a letter from the building manager. It informed me that the office tower was not an apartment complex, and that if I was, as suspected, living in my office, I could soon be both homeless and officeless.

George the guard was sympathetic. "I feel badly for you. I know you are going through rough times," he said. I assured him that things were going to turn around soon and I'd find somewhere else to live. "Well, I'll just look the other way," he said, "but be careful when you go traipsin' down the hall in your Jockey shorts."

Healing Time

It's been said that you put the prosperous times in your pocket, but the lean times are stored in the heart. When I was struggling to establish myself as a public speaker, I had periods in which I had no car, no home, and barely enough money to get by. It was difficult, but I had a clear goal in mind and I knew I was working toward it. It was a little different to have been so high (eighteen feet tall, remember?) and then to get knocked down. It was a real blow and I needed to do some healing. I could hardly face my family and friends, and although I wouldn't admit it then, I went into hiding from the public. I was sad and embarrassed because I'd lost the show. I felt I'd never had the chance to do it my way. I was angry at the King brothers. I was angry with myself and guilt-ridden because when my show failed, others lost their jobs too.

I'll never forget hearing a radio deejay in Los Angeles announce that "apparently the great motivator Les Brown couldn't motivate people to watch his show." That hurt. I was tempted to pay an unfriendly visit to this guy, but then I considered that in risking failure in television I'd probably made more money than that deejay would ever make in radio. As I'll note later, that was a more healthy response than moping over what I'd lost. In adopting that attitude toward the deejay, I was showing signs of coming to my own defense.

All in all, though, I mostly served as a wonderful example of how *not* to respond to adversity. I mostly focused on what I had lost, rather than on the new opportunities that awaited. This philosophy toward life's hard times was exemplified by Helen Keller. Blind and deaf since birth, Keller became a dynamic source of inspiration as an adult. She noted that when one door closes in life, another usually opens but we are often not aware of it because we tend to be still tugging on the door that closed. We miss new opportunities when we devote our energies to regaining what was lost. The Apostle Paul noted the same thing when he wrote, "Forgetting those things which are behind, reaching forth unto those things which are before. I press toward the mark of my higher calling. . . ."

Oh Lord, It's Hard to Be Humbled

I'll admit it, I spent way too much time staring at the door that had been closed on *The Les Brown Show*. I'm only human: I *liked* being a television talk show host. I really enjoyed walking the streets of the country's most sophisticated city and having cab drivers, people in cars, and pedestrians greeting me, "Hey Les, great show!" It would have been wonderful for anyone, let alone someone who grew up with the stigma of poverty and mental retardation, someone who lived in Liberty City and Overtown in Miami's most impoverished neighborhoods. No matter what you accomplish in life, that poverty and its stigma never completely leave you, and when you have climbed so high, to get knocked back down triggers all sorts of deep-lying fears—fears that you may get sent back to those childhood places.

In his retirement years, Muhammad Ali has talked often about "the intoxications of life." He recalls getting off a plane for his "Thrilla in Manila" fight and finding thousands and thousands of people waiting for him. Here he was, in a foreign land he'd never seen, among people whose language he did not understand, and they were chanting his name: "Ali! Ali!" Fame, the fighter noted, is an unnatural thing, and yet it is difficult to accept the end of it.

What I had forgotten, temporarily, was that we have it within our power to overcome defeats and setbacks. In my emotional state, I'd lost my inner coach, the voice that says, "Look how poorly you're handling this. It is only temporary. There are greater things in store for you." I was letting my emotions guide my actions, which is a good way to waste your talents and ruin your life. In Eastern philosophy there is a story of an ancient wise man approached by a young warrior who demanded that the wise man give him a description of heaven and hell.

The wise man looked into the young warrior's eyes and said, "You are such a fool, why should I bother with you?"

The young warrior was outraged. "I should cut your throat for saying that!" he roared.

"That," said the wise man, "is hell."

The young warrior was taken aback. He dropped his sword, and sat down, weeping. "I am a fool. I allowed my anger and my hurt to take control of me."

"And that," said the wise man, "is heaven."

The Power of Your Thoughts

Self-realization and self-awareness are vital to our lives. You feel the way you feel because of the thoughts you are thinking. If you are feeling down and out, nearly every thought that comes into your head will be colored by negativity. Often when you have been knocked down by life, you tend to see only the worst in people, in situations, and in your options. You feel hopelessness. Notice that I have not said that your life *is* hopeless, only that you *feel* that way. You should not make the mistake of thinking that your feelings reflect the reality.

Psychologists have found that people going through hard times almost always feel hopelessness out of proportion to what is really going on and so their depression is based on inaccurate thoughts. I am referring to nonclinical depression that is rooted in emotions rather than any chemical imbalances or mental and medical problems. In hard times these dark moods can be treated by learning how to recognize the distortions in your thinking and correcting them. Modern-day psychologists are not the first to recognize this. It has been a tenet of ancient philosophers for centuries. The Buddha said, *"We are shaped by our thoughts; we become what we think. When the mind is pure, joy follows, like a shadow that never leaves."*

An old friend of mine exhibits this type of thinking. She has been diagnosed as HIV positive, and yet she has kept her mind generally clear of negative thoughts or bitterness. I am amazed at how vibrant and energetic she remains in spite of the threat to her life. She has concentrated on helping other people instead of focusing on her problems. I asked if she gets depressed and she says, "Sure I get depressed, I get down on myself. My friends don't come around anymore, or they treat me differently. Family members have isolated me. Sometimes it's very lonely, *but I can't afford to stay there in that mood of depression and powerlessness. I have to keep myself together."*

None of us can afford to let our lives be dominated by feelings of depression or powerlessness. It is natural to be emotionally down after taking a hit from life, but, as my old friend has shown with her courage, we all have the power to keep it together.

Staying in Control in Hard Times

We cannot always control the thoughts that come into our minds but we can control the thoughts that we dwell on. During the down times, we have to monitor our thoughts and eliminate those that drag us down while embracing those that elevate our moods.

In hard times, your life can get stalled or it can be propelled. It depends on whether you allow negative thoughts and emotions to dominate your actions, or whether you control your thoughts and actions in spite of your emotions. It is the difference between "I am angry so I am going to inflict pain" and "I am angry so I am going to calm myself."

If you master the ability to step back from your emotions and hold them in check, you assert a control over your life that opens great opportunity. Having an awareness of your emotions is highly important and that skill is one on which others, such as self-control and self-motivation, can be built. As Shakespeare said, "There is nothing either good or bad, but thinking makes it so." If your thinking is colored by sadness, you will feel sad. Learning to recognize distorted thinking is a key to controlling your mental state.

When I was fired for my social activism while working as a radio deejay in Columbus, I first responded angrily by locking myself in the radio control room in protest. I had to be removed by the police. It was silly, and self-defeating. Instead of thinking of the possibilities for my life, I acted as though it was the end of the world. There had been a failure, but I was not a failure. In such situations it is important to anchor yourself in hopefulness rather than hopelessness. Here are some common forms of negative thinking. Read them and see if you recognize any of them as similar to your own thought processes when you hit hard times.

1. I'm finished. In the weeks following the loss of my talk show, I had this feeling that I had peaked and that there was nothing to look forward to. This is particularly common to people who are perfectionists. This is thinking that allows no shades other than black and white; it reflects an "all or nothing" approach. It is seriously flawed thinking because the world is not like that. No failure is a total failure—I've already shown you examples of people who have overcome tremendous defeats and hard times.

You can't allow yourself to think in all-or-nothing terms because no one leads a perfect, unflawed life.

2. If it wasn't for bad luck, I'd have no luck at all. This is a form of thinking practiced by the person commonly depicted in cartoons with a dark cloud hanging overhead. Too bad Charlie Brown. (No relation.) This is the philosophy of the person who claims he *always* gets into the wrong line in the supermarket, he *always* gets taken advantage of, he *always* picks the wrong person to fall for.

This negative form of thinking assumes that life has it in for you, which is pretty silly when you think about it. It's also self-centered. Fate has better things to do than concentrate on you. Things go in cycles. You may get caught in a bad one from time to time, but the gods are not focused on destroying you. No one is *always* a victim or *always* unlucky in life or in love. But your thinking can make it appear that way.

3. I made a mistake so I can't do anything. This form of thinking is like negativity radar. It accentuates the negative. "I missed *one* question on the exam and it ruined my day." This pessimistic approach causes you to dwell on the least positive aspects of any situation. It does not make you much fun to be around, and it adds a whole lot of unnecessary problems to your life and to the lives of those who care about you. By focusing on the negative you become a negative person and people develop negative feelings toward you.

4. Look at the dark lining in that silver cloud. The person who thinks like this revels in taking even positive situations and shrouding them in gloom. I was at a concert in New Orleans recently, when the performer, whom I won't name—but it was *not* Gladys Knight—exemplified this sort of negative thinking. She was singing on stage. Thousands of people were cheering and singing along. But she noticed one person in front who wasn't clapping or responding.

For some reason, this performer chose to focus only on that person. Between songs, the singer walked to the edge of the stage and confronted her. "If you don't like the show, get up and leave," the singer said.

Those in the audience who heard the remark were shocked, and so was the poor woman in the audience. I talked to her as we walked out at the end of the show. She was still stunned. She said she had been enjoying herself but she just isn't an outwardly expressive person. She noted, however, that she had lost all respect for the performer. I didn't blame her.

Rather than enjoying the applause of thousands of fans, this singer chose to focus on what she mistakenly had taken as disapproval, and as a result she made herself look bad. How often have you done this?

I call this "snatching defeat from the jaws of victory." This type of thinking results in misery and the complete inability to enjoy life's best moments. If you follow this negative philosophy of life, you won't have to worry about a crowd at your funeral. By the time you die, your folks will have had enough gloom.

5. You act like I'm a total idiot. This is a sort of "negative clairvoyance" because it refers to people who automatically assume the worst in any situation, regardless of evidence to the contrary. You don't have to worry about insulting people like this because they take insult at nearly anything you do, intentional or otherwise. It stems from insecurity and a habit of negative thinking. It also involves a great degree of self-centeredness, since most of the time people hurt your feelings because they just aren't thinking about you, rather than because they are thinking about you. For example, I don't assume that the fellow snoring through my speech thinks I'm dull. I assume that he probably couldn't get to sleep the night before because he was so excited about hearing me speak! I knew a fellow who would return from every social gathering with a report on a slight or insult he'd received. The truth was, he went looking for slights or insults because, for some reason, he reveled in the outrage he would work up. Most of the time, the people who had supposedly insulted him had no idea that they'd said anything to offend him, or that they'd even made a reference to him.

Recently, I was at a gathering with a childhood friend who has a doctoral degree. When I introduced him by his first name, he took insult. "Call me 'Doctor,'" he insisted. I was shocked and so were the people I was introducing him to. I had not meant him any disrespect. In fact, I admired the fact that he had worked so hard to be an educated man. But it appears that he had let his new title go to his head, which in today's tough job market can be a mistake. There are a whole lot of Ph.D.'s out there looking for work. I know employment counselors who say a Ph.D. means only "Piled high and deep."

6. *I'm in over my head. I can't do it.* Sometimes called "emotional reasoning," this faulty thinking is exhibited by people who let their moods define their reality. If they *feel* overwhelmed by their job, then they assume their workload must be beyond human capacity. If they *feel* picked on by the boss, then the boss is a monster. This is a very self-defeating way to think because often if we give ourselves time to get over our initial fears, we find that few things are as difficult to do as they first appear.

How many times have you worked yourself into high anxiety by fretting over something coming up—an exam, a trip to the doctor, a job interview—but once it was over, you looked back and said, "Well, that wasn't so bad after all"? This happens to me every time I go to the dentist. I am petrified at the prospect, not only of the pain, but of being anesthetized. I have a real fear of losing consciousness. The last time I went to the dentist, he gave me some of that gas and told me to count to one hundred. The next thing I knew, they were telling me to wake up and go home. So my fear was greater than the actual operation.

7. *I would but . . .* This is a judgmental form of thinking in which the person is always second-guessing his or her own actions as well as the actions of others: "I should have applied for that job sooner." Or "Well, *I* would never have treated anyone the way she treated me! She should have been more thoughtful." Second-guessing yourself and others is of little healthy use, as opposed to thoughtfully reviewing your actions and vowing to do better next time. And being judgmental is terribly time-consuming. You waste so much time watching and evaluating and commenting on the actions of other people that you don't have enough time to work on the things that *you* need to improve about yourself.

8. *I screwed up and now I'm doomed.* This is another form of absolutism, in which the person sees himself and everyone else as the sum total of all the mistakes they've ever made. Every mistake spells doom. "I'm a total screw-up. I'm worthless and I'm weak." It is a self-destructive and irrational way of thinking about and viewing yourself because no one's character can be defined by any single act or mistake. We all make mistakes. We all have flops. But we also have moments of grace. If you wear a green shirt one day, that doesn't define your wardrobe, just as making a mistake does not define you as a loser. The same holds for defining others. Assigning labels to people because of one impression is irrational. A golfer who misses a key putt in a tournament should not be labeled a "choker" for the rest of his life.

9. *It's ALL my fault.* At one point in my pity party over the loss of the talk show, I blamed myself for everything that went wrong. It was *all* my fault. This is called personalization of guilt and it is a millstone around the neck of those who take it on. The problem is that people who do this take on guilt for things that they have no control over. They may have some influence, some role, but they should not be burdening themselves with full responsibility for everything that goes wrong.

I worked recently with a woman who does public speaking and she talks about how she once blamed herself for her husband's physical abuse of her. She said she blamed herself for being successful because it made her husband feel like less of a man. So he beat her to feel better about himself. That sort of thinking is highly dangerous. It's really faulty self-analysis to take on the blame for everything, because the truth is, you may have been responsible for some of the things that went wrong and by taking all the blame you relieve yourself of having to do a thoughtful evaluation of your actions and the result of them.

Just the Facts, Not the Feelings

Reflect on the categories listed above and write down any of those that fit your behavior or the behavior of someone you know. Write down those behaviors and note what can be done to correct them.

Negative Behaviors:
   Example: I blame myself entirely for the failure of my talk show.

_____

_____

_____

Corrective Measures:
   Example: I will take a more thoughtful look at what went wrong and consider all the factors that contributed to the show's cancellation.

_____

_____

_____

In all of the forms of negative behavior cited above the one consistent error made is that of *mistaking feelings for facts*. You feel overwhelmed so your job is overwhelming. You feel insecure so somebody must be picking on you. You feel inadequate, so you must be worthless and weak. You feel guilty so you must be guilty. No.

The fact is this: Your feelings are not always reflective of the reality. Your feelings do reinforce themselves, however, so that a continuous cycle of feeling insecure will only heighten your insecurity. Surely you've read that the way to win the trust of your bosses is to appear confident in yourself and your ability to get the job done. I've got a friend who every now and then starts a sentence with "You make me feel like . . ." Now what this person is really saying is "I'm feeling this way because *you* are making me feel this way." The truth is, this person was already feeling that way, and so she was looking for validation by blaming me.

How do you escape this cycle of wrong-thinking and false emotions? You must learn to look at your thoughts and your life realistically. You must learn to eliminate misperceptions that are created by your emotions and moods. You can do this by monitoring your inner thoughts and correcting the negative and self-destructive messages you create for yourself. It's like the old cartoons in which the angelic you and the devilish you sit on each shoulder and whisper in your ear at the same time. Here are a few positive responses to irrational negative thoughts you might have.

Negative Thought	Positive Response
• *I always screw up when I try something new.*	• *I'm still learning and getting better.*
• *I'm always late.*	• *I can be on time. I just need to start getting ready earlier.*
• *I'm such a fool.*	• *I may have been fooled this time, but I'll catch it next time.*
• *They'll all think I'm not educated.*	• *I have confidence in myself and my abilities.*

Writing down your negative thoughts and positive responses is more valuable than you may think at first. That is because you may still be working out of a negative and distorted self-image that is telling you that you cannot become master of your own feelings. By completing this exercise each day and recording your thoughts, you dispel that feeling; you are taking a positive step. So don't try to do this in your head, do it on paper. You will be surprised how it helps you resolve even complex feelings and troublesome situations. There are many negative forces trying to get in our heads, and it is increasingly important to structure quiet time in which you can get alone with your thoughts and become centered.

Another method is to put yourself on a Seven Day Mental Diet. For seven days make a conscious effort to think only positive thoughts and say positive things. Every time you catch yourself in negativity you have to start all over again. It's said that we typically have thousands of thoughts a day and the majority of those thoughts are negative. You only need to write down the recurring and most detrimental negative thoughts. Learning to discipline ourselves to think positive, upbeat thoughts will dramatically change the quality of our lives. Every day on television you see violence. Every day you see horrifying headlines. There are few places to hide from all the negativity bombarding you, so happiness has to become a do-it-yourself project. You have to be able to influence your own moods by finding those things that lift your spirits and inspire you and focusing on them.

Feeling Guilty

One of the greatest burdens I carried around after losing the show was guilt. I felt guilty for losing the show because it meant that other people lost their jobs. There were several people working on the show whom I'd brought in. They'd quit other jobs to come and work for me. And I felt I'd let them down. It is difficult to overcome guilt when someone attributes their problems to your actions.

The problem with guilt is that, unlike remorse, in which we feel bad about our *behavior,* guilt makes us feel bad about ourselves. When we feel bad about ourselves, we lose self-esteem and we get stuck in life just as I was stuck in a self-defeating cycle of irrational behavior after I lost my television show. I felt I had let people down. I wallowed in that guilt for several weeks. In hiring those people I was trying to bring them in on an experience that I thought would be *good*. I failed to make it good, as promised, so I felt guilty.

Again, this is a case of allowing feelings rather than facts to control your life. True, I lost the show, but I did not do it to hurt anyone; in fact, I did everything I could to keep the show going. Still, I felt guilty and it weighed me down. There was a short period when I wasn't doing anything positive with my life because of my guilt. This is a guilt cycle. And I was riding it like an eighteen-speed Exercycle, going nowhere fast. When you feel guilty, you tend to unconsciously punish yourself and when you punish yourself with self-destructive behavior, you only create more guilt and more unhealthy behavior. People who can't handle guilt properly tend to overeat, overdrink, overworry, and procrastinate. They are self-destructive in many ways because they feel badly about themselves.

Wallowing in guilt seems like a waste of emotional energy. Does it do you any good to feel guilty? How do you get rid of guilt? How long do you pay for what you did that is making you feel guilty? Cash or credit card? Feeling guilty didn't erase the embarrassment I felt, nor did it do any good for those people who lost their jobs. They'd have been much better served if I had spent the energy trying to find them new jobs somewhere else. Some people think they have to feel guilty in order to keep their bearings on their values. It is one thing to view yourself as human and capable of making mistakes, even bad ones. It's something else altogether to wallow in guilt—to decide that you are inherently bad and that you have to feel guilt in order to whip yourself in line. That is not healthy.

It is much healthier to recognize that damage was done, a mistake was made, and then take action to learn from the experience and keep moving. Rather than feel guilty, it is far more constructive to deal with the situation. The people who lost their jobs when I lost the talk show would have benefited a great deal more if I had directed my energy to being helpful to them and their situations rather than focusing on my own guilt. A lot of people feel guilt because they don't have the courage to deal with the situation.

Getting Beyond Guilt

How do you control whether you feel guilty or whether you take action to remedy the situation? Here are a few questions that you can ask yourself:

1. Did I do it on purpose? Did I do it to be mean or hurtful? Or did I just make a mistake? Am I feeling guilty because I don't allow myself to make mistakes?
2. Do I feel guilty because what I did means I am a bad person? Have I made my mistakes seem worse than they really are? Am I only seeing it from the worst possible angle?
3. Is my guilt in proportion to my responsibility for what happened? Or am I taking on more than is reasonable?
4. What positive actions am I taking? Am I doing something to make myself better or to improve the lives of those around me? Or am I moping around, acting irrationally, and only making things worse?

Guilt Makes for Dangerous Trips

If you have a tendency to wallow in guilt, you need to think about the fact that along with impeding your growth in life, guilt can make you a fat target for people looking to take advantage of you. How many times have you given money to relatives or a friend who made you feel guilty? Were you responsible for that person's condition? It's okay to be charitable for the right reasons, but guilt isn't one of them.

Children are great at laying the guilt trip on you. "Dad, all of the other kids have their own cars." Ouch. That is a very expensive guilt trip. My third oldest daughter told me she wanted a Jeep for her sixteenth birthday. She noted that many other kids have them. I told her she was not asking for a trinket from Toys R Us. She is a good kid, but I told her she didn't need to lay the guilt trip on me. So she tried a new approach: "I'm getting good grades, I'm not in trouble, I'm not into drugs."

As a wise, loving, and weak father, I came up with a powerful response to her persistent demand. I told her it was fine with me if she wanted a new Jeep because she was such a great kid. But, I added, "Your mother said no."

The truth is that when you allow someone to manipulate you because of guilt, no one wins. Your children should have a car only if they truly need it, if you can afford it—and if they understand the responsibility and value of a car. If you feel responsible for the happiness of all those around you, you had better be prepared to quit your day job. The demands on you will only increase. The uncontrolled and obsessive need to please everyone will leave you trapped and feeling miserable.

Here are a few things to think about when someone is laying a guilt trip on you, or when you are feeling overwhelmed by guilt.

1. In general, you are not responsible for other people's feelings or their actions, and you are not to shoulder the blame for every bad thing that happens in the world around you.

2. You have the right to say no to people who play upon your guilt.

3. Caring for someone does not mean always giving them what they want.

4. If you are prone to feeling guilty and falling prey to others' pressure, remember that you owe it to yourself to protect your own interests and those of your entire family.

5. Understand that not everybody is going to like you all the time; it is more important that people respect you.

6. Consider this: If you did something wrong, intentionally or otherwise, and if you had to do it over again and you would do it differently, then there is no longer a need to blame yourself or to beat yourself up because you would be condemning an innocent person. You have been reborn to a new state of consciousness.

Deep into the Blues

In the weeks following the cancellation of the show, I could have served as the poster child for guilt and despair. Not that I locked myself in a darkened room. No, I put on a happy face and said things like "I still have my health." In some ways, that wasn't such a silly thing to say. At least I was looking for the silver lining in the dark cloud rather than the dark lining in the silver cloud.

It is important in times of despair to focus on what you didn't lose more than on what you lost. I did have my health and I still had my talents. My family still loved me. My real friends and family members consoled me by saying things such as "Hey, that show wasn't you anyhow. I loved you but I hated the show. I'm glad you didn't do trash television like everybody else." Even though the show wasn't me and it was a fight every day, it was still energizing and challenging, and, I confess, the minute I walked out of that studio I missed it.

It always helps to know and recognize your own reaction during times of disappointment. If you train yourself to keep tabs on your own moods, you are less likely to do desperate or uncharacteristic things.

Recognizing Your Own State of Mind in Hard Times

Think about situations when you have been depressed and feeling defeated. Write down how you responded, and some of the things you did that, looking back, were not typical of you. Keep that list and keep in mind what is on it, so that next time you'll have a better perspective on what you are going through.

1. I felt guilty about:

_____

_____

My response was:

_____

_____

The next time I'll respond differently by:

_____

_____

2. I felt guilty about:

_____

_____

My response was:

_____

_____

The next time I'll respond differently by:

_____

_____

3. I felt guilty about:

_____

_____

My response was:

_____

_____

The next time I'll respond differently by:

_____

_____

Dazed and Confused

In my case, I was going through grief and I didn't recognize it. And so I didn't give myself permission to get over it. I have a friend who was once fired unexpectedly from a job. Like me, he had been riding high only to get knocked down. On the surface, he did the right things. He immediately put his energy to finding a new job, an even better one so that he would not feel as though he had taken a step back. He felt as though he was responding well to the shock of being fired until one day he ran into an acquaintance who was a psychologist and counselor. The fellow had heard about my friend being fired, so he casually asked how he was doing. Standing on a street corner, my friend went into a long and rambling explanation of what he felt had happened. When he finished, the psychologist put his hand on his shoulder and said, "Let's get a cup of coffee." He could see that my friend was in despair and that he was denying it. Trained to see these things, the psychologist knew that there is an emotional process that we need to let ourselves go through in these situations.

Without realizing it, I was doing the same thing. By denying that the cancellation of the show had hurt me deeply, I was not coming to grips with my true feelings. I knew I had let down all those people who were counting on me. I could see their faces at night. They knew if I was gone they were gone. That kept me awake. They had left other jobs to work for me. I had tried to assure them of the show's success even when some of them were really aware of what was going to happen. They saw the signs when I didn't. In the weeks after the cancellation, I was denying my own emotions, and you can't do that if you are going to overcome hard times.

As a result of my denial, I made a lot of mistakes in the subsequent weeks and months. It affected my relationships with friends and family, and my business decisions. I was hiding from my emotions and I was hiding from the world. My closest advisor, Mike, would later tell me that he could see that I hadn't accepted the loss of the show emotionally. I had asked him to help me get my career as a public speaker going again, but he couldn't get me to focus on any one thing for more than a few minutes. I was erratic. I thought I was using good sense, but I wasn't. I'd call people up and have them start projects that I hadn't thought out. I'd forget about projects that I had ordered people to begin.

One day I decided to move my entire office in Detroit to Orlando. I wanted to do more executive training and Orlando offered the best location because of all the corporate retreats there. I actually made a trip there with my office manager to look at potential office sites, and I'd made contacts with the chamber of commerce and other resources in the state and the city. But then, I just let it drop. I didn't decide against the move. I was too emotionally paralyzed to make a decision either way. So I just let it drop, to the exasperation of my staff in Detroit and their families.

I had also decided to record a new set of career training tapes, so my staff booked time in a recording studio, but when I got in there I couldn't get into it. I was paying $100 an hour for the studio, but I might as well have been standing on a street corner giving the money away. Come to think of it, that probably would have motivated more people than the work I did that day. I had people coming in from other cities to work in the sound studio and by the end of the day they were sitting around shaking their heads wondering where Les Brown's mind had gone on vacation. As another friend said about that day, I was there, but I was not checked in. The lights were on, but nobody was home. In addition to being brain-numb, the least little thing would send me off the deep end. I was very argumentative with my staff. I was hypersensitive. I was defensive. I'd have these haranguing and intense conversations with staff members, screaming at them over the phone. I even cursed at staff people on the phone—and I teach children that profanity is the strongest expression of a weak mind. Call me "Exhibit A."

Stuck in Neutral and Going Nowhere Fast

Grief robs people of their motivation to get on with life. Yet, one of the best ways to get over it is to get going with life. So, what I needed, what anyone needs in this situation, is a way to jump-start life again. To get back into the flow and out of neutral. To take on the world and experience some small victories that can help build your self-esteem and motivation.

I was so typical in this manner that it's embarrassing now to look back on my actions—or my inaction. I procrastinated. I hemmed and I hawed and I spun my tires like a junk car in a mud pit. It's amazing how feelings of depression work so effectively and how depression feeds on itself. By failing to accomplish anything, I became even more disgusted with myself. Other people became disgusted with me too. And pretty soon I had every right to feel badly because I had dug myself a real deep depression, a real hole to wallow in!

I had confused starting things with doing things. What I really needed to do was to go within and clear my head, to take a reading of where I was in life. I was erratic because I had not dealt with what had happened. I'd been knocked out on my feet but I was so dazed, I didn't know it. I was like Evander Holyfield in his most recent fight with Riddick Bowe. Bowe knocked him down and Holyfield managed to get up, but he couldn't even lift his arms, he was so out of it. Bowe had no choice but to hit him again, and that ended the fight.

When you are going through hard times, this "knocked out on your feet" lack of awareness can go on for weeks unless your friends and family pull you out of the haze. But even then, it does no good until you yourself recognize what is going on. Otherwise, you'll just slide back down into the pit. What do you do to stop this vicious cycle in which you feel so depressed that you convince yourself that you are worthless and your negative attitude and your behavior convinces your family and friends that you *are* worthless and so you conclude they must be right?

In hard times, you generally get down on yourself and begin to feel sorry for yourself and you become angry and bitter as well. You sink deeper and deeper. This is when self-destructive behavior can become truly dangerous as in the case of those who try to drown their sorrows with drugs or alcohol. This is the result of a cultivated self-hatred.

After I lost my talk show, I became unconsciously self-destructive, not with drugs or alcohol but in my work habits and in my personal life. It's difficult to halt this process, but one way to get a handle on it is to remember again that no condition in life is permanent, that there are cycles of change in human experience just as there are in the world of nature. Your feelings of low self-worth are just that, only feelings; they have nothing to do with the reality of who you are.

You can combat those feelings and get back on track by focusing on the open door in front of you that leads to growth and the possibilities for your life rather than on the door that has closed behind you.

Recognizing What Ails You

It is difficult to take positive action when you are burdened with self-defeating thoughts and behavior. You have to recognize what you are going through and what it is doing to you. Here are some descriptions of this wallowing-in-the-mud, self-pitying behavior that may trigger recognition when you are weighed down with life's difficulties.

1. *Oh poor pitiful me.* Melody is depressed and drained of energy on the job because of her parents, who are elderly and in poor health. She is struggling with the decision on whether or not to put them in a nursing home. She has forgotten what it feels like to live a dynamic life. She is stuck in a state of hopelessness and she can't see any reason or any way to get unstuck. The very idea of seeking help strikes her as beyond reason. Melody can't hear life calling her because she is tuned to hard times.

2. *I've fallen and I can't get up.* Fred has been knocked on his back by life, and he feels like life is still sitting on his chest, pinning him to the ground. He was laid off. A company man all his life, he is in

a state of shock. He doesn't think he has the capacity to get up and get going again. He blames his inactivity on outside factors that he sees as beyond his control. He is afraid to look inside his own heart to see that his own emotions, not some outside forces, are holding him back.

3. *I can't handle it.* Helen is divorced and has two children. She sees all her problems, even the small ones, as mountains blocking her path. She can't get her work done because when she sits down to do it she sees this massive pile of paperwork. She can't get her personal life together because she sees it as a battlefield teeming with enemies. Helen can't handle life because she has convinced herself that life is more than she can deal with. It's just too much. Helen has overwhelmed herself, and as a result she feels justified in remaining stuck. But the truth is, she is pinned down only by her own self-defeating thoughts.

4. *Nothing will work anyway.* Natalie is stuck. She has been over-weight most of her life. She is very sensitive if the issue of her weight is raised. She feels she lost her job because of it. She blames it for the lack of any meaningful relationships in her life. Her family is ashamed of her and she is ashamed of herself. Even before Natalie tries to get unstuck, she gives up. Diets and exercise won't work anyway, so why waste the energy? Natalie looks at her goals and sees red circles with a diagonal line drawn through them. She is not being rational because she is depressed, but the only way to climb out of the dark mood is to take positive action. One small step at a time.

5. *It's not worth it.* Wayne was a brilliant architect who lost his footing in life through alcoholism. He has been in and out of treatment programs. His family has spent a great amount of time and energy to help him. It has cost him contracts, his job, and his marriage. And now because of his self-destructive thought processes, Wayne is saying life is not worth living. He is unable to experience pleasure or satisfaction. "Why should I try to get my career back on track? It won't make me feel any better." Again, this is a self-destructive thought process that only plunges Wayne deeper and deeper into the mire.

6. Even if it works, I will screw it up. Sam built up his own video store business but it went bankrupt when Blockbuster moved in next door. Now he doesn't want to get his life going again because he knows he'll just screw it up again. Sam blames himself for not seeing it coming. He should have known he could not compete. And now he is afraid to get in the game again. This is fear of success, a common negative result of a failure or a defeat. It allows Sam to do nothing rather than risk succeeding and failing again. Sam feels that if he succeeds, there will be even greater demands made and failure will be the unavoidable result. He needs to be reminded that nearly all great achievements are preceded by many failures and that failure is part of the process of success.

7. I can't take the pressure. Ida had taken an early retirement package so she could go into business for herself without any training or coaching. She blew all of her money quickly in the mean world of business. With creditors on her back, a daughter in college about to be sent home for lack of tuition payments, an uncooperative ex-husband who felt no responsibility for the child's education, and the threat of losing her home, she is on the brink of a nervous breakdown. The sense of being pressured causes her to retreat from taking action, and again, results in self-defeating lethargy and inaction. The pressure felt is usually coming from within, and it comes from Ida's fear of taking on her problems. To relieve pressure, you have to take action.

8. Something's stopping me. Calvin was turned down for a promotion and he wants to quit. Impatience and a sense of being entitled to success result in Calvin's stuck attitude, which is typified by statements such as "For all the work I've put in, I should be much farther along. They are only going to let me go so far and then they are going to stop me." The implication here is that someone or something outside his control is holding Calvin back; otherwise, he would have accomplished his goals. The unseen obstacle is merely an excuse to give up rather than put forth more effort. Calvin tends to confuse reality with the goal and when the two don't line up, he gives in to the reality rather than adjusting the goal.

Healing Sadness

Too often, people dwell on their depressed feelings rather than on the opportunities in front of them. Even when your hard times and difficulties are very real, there is no such thing as a justifiable or realistic depression. It is true that sometimes depressed feelings can be the result of a chemical imbalance and you may need to take medication. It is wise to consult a doctor to make sure your depression is not the result of such an imbalance in the body. But most depression is the result of distorted thinking.

Sadness, on the other hand, is a justifiable and normal emotion that arises in response to loss, and failure or defeat. It is reasonable to be sad and have the thought "I lost my job. I'll miss the people. I'll miss the paycheck." But it is unreasonable and a sign of distorted thinking to think, "I lost my job. My life will never get back on track. It is just not right!" In the first reaction, the response is realistic and healing. You acknowledge the loss and what it means in realistic terms emotionally so that healing can begin. In the second reaction, there is only negativity, self-pity, and hopelessness.

Generally speaking, you can tell if depression has set in because there is a feeling of total hopelessness. You feel as though the hard times will never go away, while in experiencing sadness you have more of a sense of loss rather than hopelessness. With sadness, there is generally no sense that your life is not worth living anymore, with depression, there is. Although hard times can produce either sadness or depression, you should accept only the sadness. It is important to be able to distinguish between the two so that you can deal with depression either by getting medical help if necessary or by fighting your way out of it. Sadness is a healing emotion that comes and then fades with time. It cleanses your emotional reserve, washing out anger, hurt, embarrassment, disillusionment. It does not damage your sense of self unless it is allowed to get out of control. Depression only breeds and encourages those negative feelings and distorts them, tearing at your self-confidence and paralyzing you. Sadness is a healthy passing phase. Depression can become highly destructive.

The woman who was a makeup person for my television show called me recently to tell me that her brother, who had just graduated from high school and was planning to go to college, had fallen into depression. A year before, he'd had an accident while driving his mother's car. Then, recently, he had another accident with his own new car. He was so depressed about the second accident, which he felt made it impossible for him to look for work, that he got down on himself. He focused only on his problems and he became overwhelmed. Then, he took his father's sawed-off shotgun and killed himself. What a tragedy. This young man could have gotten another car, and he could have found a job, but he let his emotions become his tragic reality. There is no reason to choose death over life in such a situation.

Career Crises

For generations we have become conditioned to identify with what we do for a living. When you first meet someone, one of the first things that is asked is "What do you do?" Or, "Where do you work?" And, of course, our work provides our livelihood. It is our source of financial support for our homes, our families, the education of our children. It is not uncommon then to feel sadness and remorse at the loss of your job. But it is wrong to take job loss, or career failure, as an incapacitating emotional blow.

Often, when these situations arise, the person who has lost a job reacts in just the opposite manner that he or she might advise someone else to respond. I would like to present as evidence Mrs. Mamie Brown's baby boy, Leslie Calvin Brown. I had a double standard. One for me, one for everybody else. I have long advised other people that failure and defeat are only temporary conditions, but I took them on as permanent. I talked the talk, but at that time I couldn't walk the walk. I asked myself how this could happen to me.

After my show was canceled, there was a period when I felt I did not have the strength to get out of bed. I closed the shades and did not want to see the sun. I stayed in bed, I ate a lot. Television watched me a lot. I didn't want to talk to anybody. I retreated into the pain and into the anger and it paralyzed me. This went on for two or three weeks. I was in minor depression. I brought myself out of it, finally, by pulling out my own tapes. I listened to tapes entitled *It's Hard, Getting Unstuck,* and *You Gotta Be Hungry.* I also talked to friends and family members who told me it was okay. Without their help, I might still be in bed, watching old episodes of *I Love Lucy.*

Practicing Self-Defense

Earlier in this chapter, I wrote of my hurt when the L.A. radio announcer made fun of "The Motivator" losing out in the talk show game. And I noted that I responded to that hurt at first with anger, but then I realized that I had made more money in taking a risk and losing than that radio jock would ever see in his lifetime of blathering on the airwaves. That is what is called a "self-defensive thought." And, like sadness, it is a healthier way to deal with loss than negative thinking or being depressed.

Self-defensive thought is a way of rationally dealing with negative thoughts that creep in and try to drag you down during hard times. Self-defensive thoughts protect your self-esteem from negativity and paralyzing depression. Here are some examples of self-defensive thinking.

NEGATIVE THOUGHT	SELF-DEFENSIVE THOUGHT
1. *The deejay is right. I failed.*	1. *It takes courage to risk failure.*
2. *I can't get my life going.*	2. *I'm going to take time to recover.*
3. *I'm a failure.*	3. *I have come a long way.*
4. *I could have done better.*	4. *I'll do better next time.*

Taking Stock in Hard Times

In times of turmoil on the job, it is important to realize that your financial worth has nothing to do with your value as a human being. Who would you rather trade places with on Judgment Day, Mother Teresa or Donald Trump? It is fairly silly to judge yourself in terms of how much wealth you have, but it is also fairly human. It is perfectly normal and healthy then to feel sadness at job loss, but it is not healthy at all to feel depression and a sense of worthlessness. You are still worth something in the marketplace. Your challenge now is to go out and find the place where the greatest value is placed upon your skills, experience, and abilities.

Here are a few things to think about if you feel a sense of worthlessness come over you in times of turmoil in the workplace.

You are not worthless if you can:

- Make a list of three things you can do to help others.

Example: I can help others see that failure in your career is only a temporary condition and that by learning from failure you can actually benefit from it.

1. _____
2. _____
3. _____

- Make a list of three talents, abilities, and forms of knowledge that you can pass on to benefit others.

Example: I can teach others how to communicate through public speaking.

1. _____
2. _____
3. _____

- Make a list of three accomplishments you've had in life.

Example: I've provided for my mother and seven children so that they have all they need.

1. _____

2. _____

3. _____

- List three people who hold you in high regard.

Example: The wonderful Gladys Knight Brown.

1. _____

2. _____

3. _____

The point here is that depression brings a sense of worthlessness and it brings a sense of suffering, while healthy sadness generally does not. Sadness cleanses. Depression drags you down. By recognizing those feelings and refusing to accept them as fact, you can fight off depression that is not chemically caused.

Turning Away from Self-Destruction

Matthew had worked for many years for a corporation and he felt secure within it. Then one day he was named to serve on a committee that had to select employees to be terminated in a downsizing. Matthew felt badly because he knew so many of the people. But he would soon feel worse. After they finished helping select those to be fired, everyone on his committee was fired too.

He had worked at this place for twenty years and the loss of his job devastated him. He began drinking. His drinking caused his wife and children to move out. Matthew eventually lost his family and his home. He had to move back in with his mother. He was in a downward spiral. He hit bottom when he checked into a motel with a gun and a bottle of Scotch. He had only one bullet. He put it in the chamber, and spun it so he had no idea where the bullet was.

He was going to kill himself by playing Russian roulette. Several times, he put the gun to his head and pulled the trigger. But it did not fire. At one point, in his drunken state, he took a break from this deadly game and turned on the television set. He was flipping channels when he came to a program featuring a man who was going on about how people deserve to go after their dreams in life. Matthew quickly changed the channel, but something brought him back. Some last reserve of self-preservation.

The fellow on the show was encouraging viewers to *be hungry* for what they wanted in life. *Never, ever, ever give up on your dream!* he urged. The speaker was all over the stage, sweating, shouting, and laughing.

Distracted from his deadly game, Matthew laughed and cried with him. He cried for his losses, and he cried over what he had become. And when the man on the show finished his talk, Matthew threw the unfired gun and the unfinished bottle of Scotch in a wastebasket and went home.

I was speaking in Memphis a few months ago when this tall, handsome fellow with deep blue eyes came up and reached for my hand. I gave it to him, but instead of shaking it, he grabbed my wrist, turned my palm up, and dropped something into it.

It was a bullet.

Matthew then told me his story. Again, we laughed and cried together.

Life is a gift.

Hold on to it.

No matter what.

- *Maintaining perspective in hard times*
- *Learning to live with a long-term vision focused on your values*
- *Valuing those closest to you*

CHAPTER 7

A Call Home

When I was a child, my mother said I was a devilish boy. I wasn't evil or malicious, but I found all sorts of ways to cause her grief. I remember in particular one day when she went fishing with a friend, I decided to entertain my brother and sister by putting on one of her dresses, a set of high heels, and her best wig.

Wesley and Margaret Ann thought it was hilarious, until I picked up the leather strap Mama used to whup me and then began chasing them all over the house. I threatened to whup them unless they did the housework that she had told me to do. My little game ended quickly when I heard Mama coming up the steps outside. I hid in the bedroom, struggling to take off her dress, but one of the neighbors did me in. She yelled over that "Leslie has been cursin' and yellin' at the other kids, actin' like you Mamie!"

Mama came after me, and I had a hard time getting away because I was still wearing her high heels. I'm not sure I could have outrun Mama if I'd had a pair of Air Jordans, not that they were available back then. Well, my mother ran me down, and when she did, she put the leather strap to use on me. I didn't enjoy it, but Wesley, Margaret Ann, and the rest of the neighborhood seemed to have been amused.

It was around this time that my Mama decided that I was possessed of demons just as some of the neighbors had been insisting. On the advice of those same neighbors, Mama packed me off one day to a local "spiritual woman." She was a full-bodied, exotic-smelling woman, and she rubbed special oils on me and prayed over me while Mama and an even bigger-bodied assistant pinned me down.

As the spiritual woman did her incantations, she kept asking me if I felt anything trying to get out of me. I was confused. I thought she was referring to some bodily function I hadn't mastered yet. When I gave no answer, she sprinkled me with more weird-smelling oils. Still they held me down while the spiritual woman cried, "C'mon out of him demons!"

Finally, I got the picture.

"He's gone!" I screamed. "He's gone! The demon has gone!"

I then did my best approximation of a child cleansed of evil and fully infused with the Holy Spirit. My impression must have been convincing because suddenly I was no longer clamped down. As soon as they relaxed their grips on me, *I* was gone. As fast as my weird-smelling, freshly oiled little body could fly.

Later, when I misbehaved again, Mama would note that she'd paid $15 to have the demons removed, and since they had obviously returned, she was going to go get her money back!

Possessed by Real Demons

In the weeks following the cancellation of my television show, I was overtaken by many more adult demons. Depressed and totally self-absorbed, I was fixated on what had happened to me, and what I was going to have to do to recover. I did take some action to snap out of it. I scheduled speaking engagements all over the country in order to force myself to get back into the swing of public speaking. But I was still in denial and still grieving over the loss of my television show and all that went with it.

And then, life showed me what was truly important.

A call came from my son Calvin in Miami. He said my eighty-eight-year-old mother was very sick and that I had better come home because she refused to be taken to the doctor.

I knew from the tone of his voice that my son was gravely concerned.

"What's wrong with her?" I asked.

"Dad, just come home," he said solemnly.

It happens all too frequently. In the tumult of day-to-day living, you get caught up in what you are doing and where you are going. The press of so many small things consumes all your thoughts. And you forget about life around you. It's the same sort of feeling that comes after you arrive at a destination and then can't remember the process of getting there.

My son's telephone call brought me home both literally and figuratively. It brought me home to be with Mama in what would prove to be her greatest time of need. And it brought me back to remembering what is really important in life.

I had fallen into a pattern of self-pity and self-involvement and I did not really begin to find my way out of it until Calvin called me home. Getting his telephone call was as if an emergency room doctor had put the shock pads on my chest, jolting my failing heart back to life and shocking me into awareness.

There is nothing like the prospect of losing a loved one to force you into regaining perspective. Have you ever read about or encountered someone with a seriously ill child and then found yourself reflecting on your relationship with your own healthy children? Life runs in cycles of good times and bad, and the only thing predictable about those cycles is that they will occur.

There are times when life bears down hard on you like an unrelenting storm. I have just emerged from such a time, battered in both my professional and personal life. I have come through it with a much greater respect for the depth of my emotional wells. I've seen depths I never dreamed existed, but now I know I can come back up from those depths, wiser in life and more focused on the things that are the most important to me.

The Most Important Things

Too often we are focused on the wrong things; living a life out of perspective with what is really important to us.

Have you ever missed an important event in your child's life in order to go to a business meeting or a social event? What did you accomplish at the business meeting or social event? Write it down, if you can remember:

_____

What did you miss in your child's life?

_____

Now which event seems more important to you?
When your child or your spouse looks back after you are gone, what will they say about you?

_____

What would you like them to say about you?

_____

Take a moment now to write down the things that you have made the focus of your life, and then write down the things that you wish you had focused on more.

Past Focus

_____

_____

_____

I Wish I Had Focused On

_____

_____

_____

Before Calvin called, I had been wallowing in my disappointment with the talk show. Suddenly, the lost notoriety and the embarrassment were no longer even on the chart. They became as trivial as they had always deserved to be. I was no longer the fallen host of *The Les Brown Show*. Suddenly, I was my Mama's son again. And nothing else really mattered.

It is a bit sad to me now that it took my mother's illness to snap me out of my depression. But it did the trick. My perspective was restored. My long-term view came into focus and my short-term loss disappeared from my range of vision. We all need to develop a long-term vision that guides us, rather than always focusing on the short term and the day-to-day occurrences in our life. By focusing on our values and the long-term maintenance of them, we give ourselves guidelines. Should I take the family on vacation or should I catch up on housework? Should you go to your child's school play, or should you work late at the office? Which trip holds value over the long term? Which duty cannot wait or be done some other time?

Here are a few questions to ask yourself when pondering whether you are living according to long-term vision:

• Will the decisions I am making now look like the right decisions over the long term or will they seem selfish and short-sighted?

• When my children are adults, will they remember me as a parent fully involved in their lives?

• Can I name my children's best friends? Their schoolteachers? Their school principals?

• When is the last time I spoke with my parents and siblings? When is the last time I visited with them in person?

• What do my parents think of me as an adult? Do they feel they raised someone who appreciates their efforts?

Take a look at your honest answers to these questions, and evaluate whether you are investing your time in the most rewarding areas of your life, or are you frivolously throwing your most valuable commodity into pastimes and activities that will pay you no emotional return in the long term?

Hard Decisions Made Easy

When you live according to a long-term vision based on your values, some of the toughest decisions become the easiest. When I was in my third term as a state representative in Ohio, my mother fell seriously ill from severe food poisoning. The doctors said it was going to take her a couple of months to recover. I immediately resigned my elected position to go home to her.

I was living out of a long-term vision then, based on my great love for this woman who had rescued and raised me. But people were shocked. There were all kinds of rumors that I'd decided to seek higher office or that I'd been run out of town for being outspoken. It was sad that people of narrow vision could not accept that I simply had a greater view of life. I was needed by someone who had always been there for me.

When you live according to what is most important to you, you are secure in your decisions no matter what the pressures or opinions of others are. You carry confidence into life, knowing that you have strong guidelines. And you act without the baggage of guilt or negative thoughts weighing you down.

Other benefits of living with a long-term vision:

- Emotional factors, job pressures, peer pressure, none of these impede you when you have a long-term view that gives you a clear and conscious perspective.
- Once you have made your decision you are comfortable with it because it is based on a wise and well-considered frame of reference.
- Your decisions move your life forward in a positive direction because they are made with a view toward their lasting impact on your life.
- The confidence you have enhances your personal relationships as well as your ability to work with other people. Because you see the value in your life so clearly, you can also see the value in others.

Developing Long-Term Vision

How do you develop and maintain your long-term vision? It takes effort. As I demonstrated, it is easy to be blinded by the flurry of daily events, career upheaval, minor events that take up major amounts of your time. Here are a few tips for keeping your life in the proper focus.

Imagine your loved ones gathered together after you are gone. Maybe your children with their own families. What do you hear them saying about you? Write down what you think they might say about you and their lives with you.

1. How will they describe your *character?*

_____

_____

_____

2. How will they describe your *attitude* toward life?

_____

_____

_____

3. What will they say your *priorities* were in life?

_____

_____

_____

4. How will they describe your *values?*

_____

_____

_____

5. When your children talk about you to their own children, which of your characteristics, attitudes, priorities, and values will they hope their children also develop?

_____

_____

_____

6. Which of your characteristics, attitudes, priorities, and values will they hope their children do *not* develop?

_____

_____

_____

7. Assume that you discover you have only five more years to live. How would you spend that five years? What would the focus of your life be?

_____

_____

_____

8. Now, assume that you have only one more year. How would you live it differently than the five-year period given you above?

_____

_____

_____

9. Look at all of your answers above. Is there anything that surprises you? Is there anything that concerns you? Anything that you wish was different?

_____

_____

_____

10. Considering what you have learned in this exercise, how might you approach life differently? How might your focus change? Write out your long-term vision plan, a road map for how you will live your life.

   Example: I will never lose focus of the people and things that I value most in life. I will always place the welfare and love of my family above all else.

_____

_____

_____

Investing in Loved Ones

When you invest your love and time and attention with your loved ones it pays back the greatest dividends. When you don't, you risk losing something valuable. A doctor I know from Phoenix, Ron, had gotten so busy with his life that he kept putting off visiting his father, who lived just on the other side of town. Ron had his medical practice, charities, golf, so much to occupy him.

He had promised to take his father golfing and just hadn't found the time to do it. He talked to his father on the telephone every day, but hadn't gotten over to see him like he intended. Recently, Ron had let several months slip by without seeing his father. Then one day, he got a call notifying him that his father had died.

Ron was devastated. Suddenly, he realized that he had been neglecting what was most important in his life. And all those hours spent in the office, or working for charities, or playing golf with friends seemed like wasted time.

I'd heard stories similar to Ron's from other friends and associates, and long ago I had made up my mind that my mother would always remain a priority. I owed her so much. And I consider her to be a remarkable woman. I'm going to tell you a little more about her now, so that you will understand what is to follow.

My Mother's Way

Mama had a tremendous appreciation for life and she lived it with passion. She had an unstoppable spirit and her gift was to convey that spirit to the children she took into her home. She grew up in the wetlands of central Florida. Her own mother died "and left me a crawling baby," she said. And so Mama lived mostly with relatives while her father traveled doing migrant farmwork. She learned to take care of herself early on, and she learned to take care of us any way she could.

When it became too physically demanding for her to work in the tomato fields, or to cook at the M&M cafeteria, Mama started a little business in her home, or at least, in our backyard. Mama hooked up with some moonshiners from Georgia, who would deliver their homemade liquor to our house in big one-gallon tin containers.

Our house was up on blocks with a crawl space underneath. Mama had a piece of linoleum cut out of the kitchen floor so that she could open up a hatch and hide the moonshine under the house. The customers would come to our back window with quarters for a shot, which Mama would pour into whatever they held in their hands.

The customers would then hang around the backyard, talking trash, playing cards, or listening to Mama's stories and holding their sides from laughter. It was like Mrs. Mamie Brown's Juke Joint, without the jukebox, or the joint, for that matter. Mama also worked with the local numbers runners in the gambling game that preceded official lotteries. You don't hear much about neighborhood numbers games anymore. Because of all the legalized gambling, there has been a lot of downsizing in the numbers business, apparently.

But back then, Mama kept track of who had what numbers when the runners came to pay up. To keep the customers happy, Mama made homebrew too. She made it out of raisins, rice, and yeast, and any fruit she had around the house. She was a microbrewer long before it became fashionable. My brother and sister and I were the bottling division. We'd pour her homebrew into bottles we found and cleaned, and then we'd cap them. Neither my brother nor I drink alcohol, and I think it is probably because we watched so many people get drunk and make fools of themselves in the backyard. We'd wait until they went to sleep and then we'd play pranks on them, hiding their shoes or tying the laces together.

Our fun, and Mama's entrepreneurial backyard juke joint, came to a fast end when two big fat policemen raided our house one day. It was a scary time. They hauled Mama off, leaving the three of us with Miss Catherine next door.

To our horror, Mama was convicted and sentenced to jail. It was a sad time for us. We visited her every week, talking to her through the bars at the Dade County jail. There was always a lot of crying on both sides of the bars. Mama looked so miserable in there. When she got out, she brought her jailhouse drinking cup with her, and she kept it on a shelf to remind her of what had happened, so that she wouldn't be tempted to go back into the moonshine and homebrew business. She took in ironing instead, and sometimes worked at cooking and making pies for other folks. My Mama had a great deal invested in us. She invested love without wanting anything but love back.

The Storms of Life

As I packed to leave for my mother's home in Miami, it dawned on me that what I had been going through with the loss of the talk show was nothing compared to the storm that was about to hit.

Emotional storms are as much a part of life as nature's storms. They often catch you unprepared. They strike so swiftly, and before you know it nothing else matters but surviving this storm. The news from my son was stunning to me, but then Mama and I had a relationship that went beyond even the love of the typical mother and son. Mama was far more than my adoptive mother. She was my rescuer, my provider, the source of my perspective on the world, and the deep well from which I draw spiritual strength.

When my brother and I were born unwanted, Mama took us and vowed never to separate us, and to take good care of us. She rarely talked to us about the circumstances, but over the years she gave up bits and pieces. Like most adopted people, I've sometimes wondered what happened to the woman who delivered us into the world, and to the man who was our father. I have made some attempts to locate them since my mother's death with the clues I've picked up.

Mama did tell us that the woman who had delivered us would come to watch us from afar when we were young. She said that she had three other children after us. And the woman told Mama that one day when we were adults, she would come up to us and tell us something that would let us know that she is our mother. Mama told us what she would say, and no one has ever said it to me yet. One time in Dallas, though, someone came up behind me and said something very similar. I jerked around and said, "Why did you say that?"

I realized when I turned around that she was too young to have been my mother. She must have wondered why I reacted the way I did. If you are wondering what that secret phrase is, keep on wondering.

I still wonder about my birth parents, but I never consider them my real parents. Mrs. Mamie Brown earned that distinction. She is all the parent I'll ever want or need. My trademark sign-off "This is Mrs. Mamie Brown's baby boy" has never been a gimmick. It goes to the core of who I am.

Mamie's Boy

Growing up, I was always known as "Mamie's boy." I took that as a considerable compliment, but I think it referred to the fact that

I was bull-headed like her and every bit as talkative. Mama was a storyteller and when I became a radio deejay telling stories and entertaining people just as she had, I began using the sign-off that is now my signature. I didn't use it to win over the mothers in the audience, but it had that effect. They'd say, "I wish my children were as devoted to me as you are to your Mama."

The devotion came easy. We were so much alike, I sometimes find it hard to believe she did not give birth to me. She certainly gave me much of my character. In particular, I learned to tell stories from her. I'd sit on the kitchen floor while she cooked or as she cleaned collard greens or picked stringbeans. She would tell us stories about the alligator in the swamp that she fed like a pet, or the day she saw a mermaid in a water barrel at a fish shop. My mother always had wonderful stories, and she told them in great detail. I hear her voice whenever I take a stage to tell my stories, which, to a large degree, are hers too.

For her part, Mama was proud of my speaking career, although she showed her pride in what you might call an "understated manner." She'd say, "Boy, you always run your big mouth. You are sure my baby!" When other people would comment about my referring to her in the sign-off, she would say, "Yes, he's my baby, but I used to beat his butt so much because he caused me so many problems." I was her pride, and her problem. We probably became so close because she had to spend so much time working on me and whaling on me. She'd say, "Why are you so bad?" I'd say I didn't know, and she'd reply, "Well, I'll just beat your behind until you figure it out! A hard head makes a soft behind."

There was no "quiet time" in those days, believe me. Quiet did not figure into my Mama's notion of childrearing. In fact, my child rear was her primary target, although she was more than willing to slap her disciplinary tools upon whatever portion of me was within reach. I'd run from Mama when she came after me. She'd come to beat me and I'd run to the windows and yell "She's killing me! Help! She's killing me! I can't breathe!"

Our neighbor Miss Catherine would come to the door and say, "Don't beat him no more, I'll take the boy in." I'd try to appeal to neighborhood sympathy, and I'd try to wear Mama out so that by the time she caught me it wouldn't hurt so bad. By the age of eight or nine, I could outrun her most of the time, but she was crafty. She'd play the angles and cut me off. She had once dated a military martial arts instructor, so she knew a little judo, and if she caught me by the arm, she could flip me on my back with just a twist of her wrist. I'd hit the floor *Boom!* and then it was all over but the crying.

And I didn't weep alone. My brother and sister would join in the crying. They were worse than me—and they were just watching! Mama didn't have to beat them because witnessing what happened to me gave them all the discipline they needed. They'd even start crying at the thought of me being beaten. I'd come home after being out too late because I'd be playing checkers and yakking like I had something to say with Mister Will Hines and Mister Henry and Sonny Boy, the old men who sat every day outside Richard's Grocery at the corner of Tenth Street and Fourth Avenue. I was supposed to be home before the street lights came on, but I seldom made it. I was always having too much fun entertaining the old men, making them laugh with my impressions of neighborhood folks and telling them stories of my adventures.

When I walked in the door late, I'd quickly open all the windows to alert the neighbors that I was about to become a child in deep trouble. Wesley and Margaret would begin whimpering on my behalf. "Mama's going to beat you," they'd say, and when they saw her coming after me, they'd start crying. As a result, they never got beaten. One day after complaining about my mother whupping me because I spent too much time in their company, the old men I played checkers with decided to give up the game and play with my young and foolish mind instead. They told me that if I put a special little "wontbeatcha" flower that they got by the railroad tracks behind my ear, Mama wouldn't beat me. So I got three or four of those wontbeatcha flowers and put them behind my ear, and when I got home late I told my brother and sister that I wouldn't be getting a beating because "I've got the wontbeatcha flowers."

This time, I didn't run when Mama came after me. I stood my ground with my special flower power in place. And when Mama proceeded to whup me, I yelled, "The flowers, Mama! Stop beatin' me, I got wontbeatcha flowers!" She did not break her rhythm on my behind, "What are you talking about, you fool? Those flowers don't mean anything!"

I was in pain, and also a state of shock. They'd set me up! The old men outside the grocery store had lied to me! They laughed for months over that one. Those whuppings hurt. But it was worth it, I guess, because I truly enjoyed hanging out with the old men at the grocery store. It was like eating ice cream. I was allergic to it, and it made me sick. But it felt so good going down, I was willing to take the bad with the good. I was Mama's boy, after all.

Mama's Window of Opportunity

Her love was obvious in all she did for us. My mother adopted us although she had no visible help and resources. She was a single woman who had a desire to have a family even though her marriage had failed. She simply knew she wanted to do it. There is a saying, "Leap and the net will appear." My Mama lived like that, and the nets did appear. The help, resources, everything she needed to make it happen . . . it came, although I don't know how, but I think it had something to do with the fact that my Mama had a deep reserve of love and faith that guided her.

My brothers and sisters tell me constantly that I'm just like Mama. She was creative. She was relentless. I remember that after I had moved away and done well in the world, she decided that I should help her build an addition to her house so she would have more room for visitors. I didn't pay a lot of attention. But Mama kept after it, and one day when I came to see her, I walked into her house and there was a big old window sitting in her living room. I said, "Mama, what is this here for?"

"When you build me my addition, you won't have to buy a window because here it is."

My dynamic Mama had seen someone tearing down a house in the neighborhood and she paid two men five dollars to bring that window to her. That was my Mama. She knew she was going to get that addition. Of course, before I could build the addition, her vision grew into me buying her a whole house, one next door, where her visitors could stay.

As I flew from New York to Miami to be with Mama, I reminisced about her and our life together. I thought again of how I never had been able to keep her in a house I'd bought for her. As a boy, it had always been my dream to buy my mother a house. I had purchased one for her early in my career as a radio deejay, but shortly after she moved in we discovered that there had been a lien placed on it because of the previous owner. Mama had to move out, and she told me she was glad. She had always had one-story houses and the stairs bothered her, she said. I bought her a house in Columbus when I lived there, but she refused to stay in the cold weather. There were others over the years that she scorned. The fanciest came when I got a big advance for my first book. I bought her a five-bedroom house with a Spanish tile roof on a golf course in a fancy subdivision outside Miami. She told her friends at first "I'm living like Mrs. Rockefeller."

It had a big yard with fruit trees and a screened-in swimming pool. Mama had her own wing of the house so she could have quiet when she wanted it. We had a minor problem in that she wanted to keep all of her old furniture, but I smoothed that over by letting her keep her old house in Liberty City so she could go there to visit neighbors. I moved her into that new house, along with my oldest son, Calvin, so he could watch out for her. I was so proud especially when Calvin called and told me that Mama enjoyed going into the yard and picking mangos. But about three months later, Mama announced that she was going back to her old house in Liberty City because "I don't like living in that big old barn in the country. It's too quiet." She missed her friends in the neighborhood where she could just talk out the window.

Mama didn't care much for the trappings of success. And I never became a celebrity in my Mama's eyes. She was proud of me and she would talk me up to her friends, but in her house, I was no big stuff. I was still her baby boy in that house. It was still "Yes Ma'am" and "No Ma'am." I might have had a syndicated talk show on television, but she still ordered me to go to the store to get her things. In fact, I didn't really feel I'd made it to the big time until one day my Mama said she would be willing to watch my show, even though it came on at the same time as the show of her boyfriend, Bob Barker of *The Price Is Right*. She had me get her another television so she could watch us at the same time. My Mama had always kept me grounded.

And now, I was going home to her for what would be the last time.

- *Tips on dealing with the trauma and pressures of a serious illness in the family*
- *Dealing with the grieving process*

CHAPTER 8

By Mama's Side

I was not surprised Mama would not go to the doctor. She had always preferred to treat her own ailments rather than face the probing indignities of modern medicine. My son had called me to come to Miami this time because she was obviously seriously ill. She had been sleeping a great deal, and was not eating. Always plump, she began to lose too much weight. But she refused to go to the doctor out of pride and modesty. "You all better get out of here because I'm not going to have no doctors looking under my dress and sticking me with needles," she insisted when I arrived at her house in Liberty City.

I tried to enlist my twin brother and sisters and their families, and some neighbors too. There were ten of us coaxing, but she wasn't buying. I'd like to tell you that through tact and gentle persuasion, I convinced my mother to go to the doctor. But I can't lie. I had to *bribe* her to go. I told her I'd give her $2,000. Mama didn't need money, but she liked having it around for a rainy day. I knew this, so when tact and persuasion failed, I offered her the money. There was one biblical verse that Mama used. It is the one with the phrase that goes "Money answereth all things."

And so Mama said she'd take payment, but I had to pay up front. Mama dealt with me on a cash-only basis. "Don't you write me one of those bouncing checks," she told me. She wouldn't go to the doctor until I went to the bank and brought her the cash. I loved her more than I can communicate. And, although I was relieved that she had finally agreed to go to the doctor, my relief was short-lived.

After examining her, the doctor said that Mama had breast cancer, that the cancer had spread to her liver and perhaps her brain, and that it was going to kill her within a matter of months. My sister held my arm to hold herself up, but my knees were buckling. The doctor said they could operate, but Mama had told him she didn't want it, and he said it was her call. Either way, her time was limited. When Mama listened to the doctor's diagnosis, she became defiant. "You talk too damn much," she told the doctor. "Let's go home."

The Deepest Pain

In my family, I am supposed to be the positive one—the motivator. But during this stormy period, I started doubting myself and my faith. I remember one night, Mama was in so much pain, she was crying out "Oh Lord, help me." I was by her bed, and I began to pray out loud that God would take the cancer from her and give it to me. I told God that I could handle it. Mama stopped me and said, "No son, I'll be all right. I don't want you to have this." Then she went back to sleep, breathing in those deep, deep sounds that you could hear all over the house.

There are very few times in a life as difficult and painful as those in which a loved one lies gravely ill. Even though death is part of life, it is a trigger to emotions ranging from hurt and guilt to rage. As in any period of difficulty in your life, the most important thing is not to allow your emotions to rule your thoughts and actions. These are hard times for everyone involved, and too often families are torn apart by the emotional pressures rather than being drawn together to share their feelings and to console each other as well as the stricken family member.

The stages family members go through upon learning of the terminal illness of a loved one mirror those experienced by the person who is dying—shock, disbelief and denial, fear and anger, resentment and guilt are all relatively common, though they may not follow any particular order. There are many ways of responding because each of us brings a unique set of experiences to the situation.

Here are some of the most common emotions that arise in such situations.

• Shock. After hearing from the doctor, my sister Margaret Ann walked my Mama to the car after the examination. Then she came back and got me. I was in such bad shape. I was crying but I couldn't move from my chair. My Mama saw me and she reverted to the parental toughness that had gotten her through so much in life. "Come on boy, get in the car," she commanded.

I am always being asked to help folks who are going through hard times. I get twenty to thirty calls a day from people who have listened to my tapes, or people I know who are going through a tragedy. I can't tell you how many suicidal people I have been asked to help. Sorrow is constantly being laid in my lap, and generally I am able to walk people through a process for handling the storms in their lives. But I was not able to walk myself through this. I was in a state of shock and confusion. I could not understand why this was happening to a woman who had devoted her life to making a home and family for children who had none.

I'd been in a similar situation a few years earlier when my second son, Patrick, had been stabbed while trying to break up a fight. I'd flown back to Columbus where he lived and I'd rushed to the hospital nearly out of my mind with panic. Ironically, when I got to the hospital, there were several people in the emergency room who recognized me from the days when I'd been a radio deejay and then a state representative from Columbus. They said, "Look, here comes The Motivator, Les Brown." They had yet to see the grief-stricken panic in my eyes, but when they did, they stopped their requests for my autograph, and simply stepped back to let a very worried father pass. That's what I became when my son was hurt, simply his father, boiled down to that very essential role. And that's what happened when I went home to be with my sick Mama, simply her son. Her heartsick, lost, and useless-in-a-storm son.

In this preliminary period of grief, it is wise to avoid making important decisions without the guidance of calmer minds. You can hardly expect yourself to be as rational and thoughtful as you need to be. I know I wasn't. At one point I fell to the ground in front of my nine-year-old son and said, "I can't deal with this pain." My brother, Wesley, told me to get up, but I told him I couldn't deal with this. He said, "Don't you know God? Get up." He said it was easy to have faith when all was well, but she needs us now as we once needed her. Be still, he said, and turn to God, and know he will give us the strength to pull through.

• Denial. As kids we used to say we wanted to die before Mama because we didn't think we could handle it if she died. I think a lot of kids are like that, they can't envision a life without their mother. At first, I did not believe Mama was going to die this time because she had always beat the odds before. She had ptomaine poisoning years before and survived. Well versed in old ways of healing handed down for generations, Mama was skilled at medicating herself. I remember watching her working up concoctions with camphor, and wrapping herself in Palmer Christian leaves. For fifty years, I'd had her with me and, in spite of what the doctor said, I thought Mama could pull this one out too.

Denial is a natural reaction and we look everywhere for hope. Some may look to clergy, "healers," or spiritualists to disprove the medical diagnosis. It is important in this stage for family members to communicate with each other and the loved one who is ill so that important issues are not overlooked in the emotional upheaval. Counselors advise the family members to keep the loved one informed of medical information, and to share it with *all* in the family rather than trying to protect anyone. The grieving process includes what counselors call *preparatory grief*, a key step in easing the transition toward acceptance. "The more this grief can be expressed before death, the less unbearable it becomes afterward," writes Dr. Elisabeth Kübler-Ross, author of the classic book *On Death and Dying*. As part of their denial, some family members tend to put a mask on their grief when they visit with the loved one, but the patient generally sees through this "happy face." It is generally better for both individuals if feelings are discussed and aired. Sharing of the sad times as well as the good times assures the patient that he or she is still very much a part of the lives of loved ones.

• Anger. Mama refused to stay in a hospital, so we honored her request to come home. We arranged for a hospice nurse to tend to her medical needs at home. The nurse, Miss Betty, told us that Mama's condition was critical. She said the cancer was causing Mama's stomach and liver to swell. The sight of Mama slowly dying was crushing to me. I agonized and I became angry because I did not understand. Mama didn't understand either. She would cry out, asking "Why is this happening to me, Lord? All I've ever done was to take care of other people's children." I comforted her, "Mama, you haven't done anything to deserve this." I felt so helpless and powerless. I could not stop the pain and I could not take her place. All I could do was be there and hold her hands.

Modern society, with all of its medical technology, has learned to put off death so successfully in many cases that often there is a strong sense of resentment and anger when it appears that death cannot be denied. In other times, when death was not so often denied, people were generally more accepting of it as a natural process, a part of life. There is likely to be anger now when a loved one is diagnosed as terminally ill. Anger at doctors, anger among family members, anger at the patient for not seeking treatment earlier.

• Guilt. Shortly after my Mama's terminal condition was determined, a friend who'd been through a death in her family suggested that I should make funeral arrangements before Mama died. The friend said that there is so much pressure and stress after the death of a loved one that you don't think clearly. My sister, Margaret Ann, was open to that but Wesley was outraged. "Where is your faith? Why are you throwing dirt on Mama's face when she is still breathing? Don't you believe in asking God for miracles?" he said.

I didn't argue with him. I was stunned. I had not meant to "bury" Mama prematurely. Wesley said I was sending her to an early grave because I had lost faith. Wesley did not want any negative energy around Mama. He didn't want any sad, long, doomsday faces in the room. He laid a heavy guilt trip on me, one that lingered for many days and nights. The sense of guilt over missed opportunities, past disagreements, and lost time together can be overwhelming in these times. Often, family members feel guilty for not detecting medical problems earlier themselves, or for not insisting on regular medical examinations. One day I tore into Margaret Ann out of the blue. "Margaret Ann, you knew two years ago that Mama had a lump in her breast but you didn't do anything about it." She started crying. It wasn't her fault and I knew it. Mama wouldn't cooperate. I know it hurt Margaret Ann when I said it but I was dealing with my own guilt and anger.

Counselors say it is healthy for family members to discuss this feeling and all others in order to clear the air and allow the grieving process to move along. "If members of a family can share these emotions together, they will gradually face the reality of impending separation and come to an acceptance of it together," writes Kübler-Ross.

• Holding on and letting go. The family members and loved ones, like the patient, typically go through cycles of hope and clinging to life and then through the final stages of resignation and "letting go" of life. Some never give up hope. Some become resigned immediately to death. There are intense emotions involved in both cycles, but it is important to recognize that they are valid and neither is more courageous or worthy than the other.

The Dying and Death of a Loved One

Not everyone responds in exactly the same way to hard times in their personal life, particularly when it involves the imminent death of a loved one. Often, roles change and some family members who previously did not play leadership roles may step forward while recognized family leaders are consumed by grief and unable to take charge. That is what happened in our family.

Although he had never been a source of strength for the family before, Wesley stepped up during this period. A former military man, he came into town like a soldier taking his post. He became the primary caretaker while I spent most of my time grieving. When he saw me breaking down he would ask me to leave the room. While I was not of much use even though I wanted to be with him by her bedside day and night, Wesley was the pillar of strength.

By contrast, one of our younger adopted brothers, Leonard, simply could not deal with Mama's dying at all. He would come to the house but he could not bear to go into her room for fear of seeing her suffering. He said he could not take seeing her suffer, hearing her moans. His behavior made me angry at first because I didn't understand it. But the problem was mine, not his. Leonard took a lot of heat for the way he acted, but since then I have come to understand. We all handle the death of a loved one in our own way. It is not at all unusual for loved ones to be repelled by the indignities of dying and the pain it can bring to someone close to you. There are many people who grow weak-kneed at the sight of intravenous tubes, bed pans, oxygen tanks, hypodermic needles, and at the sounds of the labored breathing and groans of the loved one. It is difficult to see someone you care for in this situation and some people handle it better than others. Leonard was not being cold, not at all. He was simply dealing with it as best he could. He loved Mama too, and in his love he had no tolerance for seeing her suffer.

There is no right or wrong or standard method of grieving. It is as personal as the way you laugh or cry. How you react to grievous news such as a terminal illness or a death depends to a great deal on your relationship with the person. It is not unusual then for each family member to exhibit grief in a different manner. It is unfair to say that one family member isn't showing enough emotion, or that someone else is overreacting. You simply cannot judge what others should do, you can only be patient and accept that they are responding in their own, appropriate way. There are many reactions that arise in times of personal crises and grieving; frustration, fear, quick temper, powerlessness, loneliness, panic, sleeplessness, and isolation are all common.

If you are going through a time of personal hardship, it is critical to be conscious of your thought processes so that you remain in control of your actions and your life, particularly if those around you need your help and support. It can be of value to take time each day to either keep a journal or to write down the emotions you are feeling in order to maintain a sense of control.

Dealing with the Coming of Death

Here are some key things you need to keep in mind during the first few weeks of adjusting to the terminal illness of a loved one.

1. Make sure essential business is taken care of. There are medical, legal, and financial matters to be taken care of when death appears to be imminent. You may not be capable of dealing with these matters, but someone should be put in charge of them.
2. Don't give up your own life. Stay in touch with people and matters in your own life. Don't unconsciously punish yourself for a loved one's illness by neglecting your own affairs or by unnecessarily giving up sleep, meals, and your own physical needs.
3. Do not focus solely on the issue of death. Try to stay balanced by also thinking and talking about the life and relationships of the loved one. Do not be afraid to be playful or to bring humor to the bedside.
4. Find an outlet for stress. Express your emotions. Find someone to confide in, or a punching bag to hit. Get away now and then to air out your brain and your emotions. Set aside a quiet time of isolation for yourself every day.
5. Understand that situations can change rapidly in the case of a terminally ill patient. A change in the condition of the patient can alter plans or call for drastic action, so be aware that there may be no pattern for living in the time to come.
6. Bring the family together for prayer. We found it to be calming to come together each day and pray at Mama's bedside.

Tending to the Dying and the Grieving

In the case of a terminally ill loved one, sometimes grieving family members are so overwhelmed by their own emotions that they forget that the loved one too is still in need. My Mama, of course, was iron-willed down to the near-end, but she also had emotional needs. Mama did not want to be a burden on us; she had always done for herself, and in many ways, she continued. She was not going to relinquish that independence easily. Only when she no longer resisted us carrying her and putting her into bed did I know the fight was going out of her. At one point, we had to start taking her into the bathroom. She cried in humiliation that these kids she had cleaned as babies would see her in this condition. She had so much pride. Mama was proud that she had handled all that life had thrown at her. She had not bent to it, she had stayed on top of it and not let it get to her. Her body was giving out, but her spirit was still indomitable, and still she was working on a goal.

Mama had decided that she wanted me to buy the house just around the corner. She wanted it so other family members could stay there when they came to visit. I had told her that we didn't need to buy the house, but she had enlisted Gladys in her plot, and unbeknownst to me, she had Gladys talking to a real estate agent. My Mama never gave up. I think she is up there in heaven still trying to work out a deal with some angelic real estate agency.

We were getting all kinds of advice from people on how to help Mama in her final days. Some were telling us she needed to be on a diet with broccoli and carrot juices, but when we'd set a glass of that next to her, Mama would say "Get this trash out of here, I want some pork chops and collard greens." One night, my brother and I, some other family members and friends gathered as the Reverend Johnnie Colemon from Chicago led us in prayer over the telephone. We were reading books on spiritual healing and about the power of prayer. When she awakened and saw us all gathered there in prayer, Mama told us how much she loved us. And she told us she would be all right. It was a touching moment.

I'll be truthful, during this period with her, we had many somber and melancholy moments, and we had a lot of laughs too.

When the pain subsided mercifully, Mama would return to her old spunky self and I could tease her just like I always had. When she was feeling good, I'd pretend like I was going to snatch the wad of cash that I knew she always kept tucked inside her blouse. "Get out of there you little thief!" she'd say, slapping at my hand. She'd tease me back by threatening to call the police.

One day as we sat with her, we talked and joked about her old friend "Arthur." When I was a boy, sometimes early in the morning, especially when it was rainy, as she got ready for work, Mama would walk with a limp and I would ask her what was wrong. "Arthur is bothering me," she'd say. As a loyal son, of course, I'd want to find this Arthur and pound him into sawdust. But Mama would never tell me where Arthur was. "If you live long enough," she'd say, "you'll know Arthur." It took me years to realize that when Mama complained of Arthur, she was referring to her *arthritis*.

Making Peace

In the final phases of dying, many people go through a slow period of separating themselves from the living world. This is really a period of making peace and accepting death. Sometimes this is exemplified by the person calling in loved ones one at a time or in small groups to say goodbye. Often, this is misinterpreted by family members as some sort of last-minute rejection or shunning, but it is not. They should take comfort in this action because it means that the loved one has accepted death.

Dying people need to be understood. In my readings during my Mama's illness, I came upon a story about a dying elderly woman who stubbornly clung to life in her hospital bed. Her daughter could not bring herself to speak to her mother because of old anger and hurts. Finally, a counselor spoke with the dying woman and learned that she had a great fear of dying, but only because she had this phobia of "being eaten alive by worms" after she'd been buried. Now, it was not reasonable for her to think that she would even be aware of what was going on after she'd died and been buried, but the counselor did not tell the woman that. Instead, she listened patiently. Just being able to express this fear put the dying woman at ease. With the counselor's help, she and her family worked it out so that her body would be cremated rather than buried, and shortly after those arrangements were completed the woman died in peace.

My family was fortunate, in many ways, because we had a lengthy period of time in which to bid my Mama goodbye and to express our love for her. We spent a lot of time talking with Mama about her life and about her grandchildren. And about our relationships. She liked Gladys and she urged us to elope. She saw a lot of herself in Gladys. Fondly, she called her "that big-mouth singing woman." Mama would say, "Boy, that girl can sing with her big-mouth self." She was proud to have Gladys in the family, and she was looking forward to Gladys being her daughter-in-law. They were like two peas in a pod. During her final illness, Mama came to rely on Gladys to do things for her that she did not want any man to do. She could talk to her like she couldn't talk to us. My mother was only vaguely familiar with Gladys's singing career, and she was amazed at people's reactions to Gladys as someone famous. Mama would say, "That child can sing, but she is country just like me. She says 'Yes, ma'am, no ma'am,' and she has good manners."

The Final Hours

The day Mama died, I never left her room. I stayed there and held her hand until the end. The people from the hospice said there was no way she could keep breathing without her heart giving out, she was so weak. I didn't want her to die alone so we called everyone into the room. "Those who have the strength and the love to sit with a dying patient in the *silence that goes beyond words* will know that this moment is neither frightening nor painful, but a peaceful cessation of the functioning body," writes Kübler-Ross. "Watching the peaceful death of a human being reminds us of a falling star; one of a million lights in a vast sky that flares up for a brief moment only to disappear into the endless night forever."

Around 8 P.M., the hospice nurse said that we should call a minister because it appeared that Mama didn't have long. The minister came in with his Bible opened, and he started reading the Psalms. Wesley was there with me and my sister, Margaret Ann, and her husband, Alex, and my sons Calvin and John Leslie. Mama was in pain again and she was thrashing and her eyes were opened wide. She went on for a long time. We were having trouble keeping hold of her hands because she kept hitting the rails of the bed. I said, "Mama, let go." I felt so bad for her. I wanted her to have that peace, finally, forever.

Wesley began saying Psalms as Mama thrashed in pain. I couldn't say anything but "Mama we love you!" Wesley was strong until the end. He recited those Psalms with a powerful spirit. Later, I thought that Old Man Death probably came down early on, but then sent back for help because my brother Wesley was praying so hard. I think Death had to send a whole gang of angels to get Mrs. Mamie Brown. After a while, though, Mama began to breathe in rasping tones, and all of a sudden she got a look on her face, a look that no longer contained pain but peace, a peace that surpassed all human understanding.

I had never seen anyone die before, and I wasn't prepared for the beauty of it. When Mama took her last breath, there was such peace in her facial expression. It was as if she could see what lay ahead. Her countenance changed from the expression of pain she had worn for the last few weeks, to looking again like Mama. It was a look so serene, it halted my grief. Then, I felt her hand go limp, and she was gone. I said, "Bye, Mama. She's gone. Bye Mama." All of us in the room began to cry and to hold each other and pray, saying, "We love you, baby. We love you."

I closed her eyes and sat there and talked to her for a long time about what she meant to me, how appreciative I was. Even though I loved her and felt very close to her, in many ways she was a mystery. Who was she really? Why did she take in strangers that she did not know and love them and take care of them? She took in people, children, and animals and never wanted anything in return. She never said "you owe me." And so, her passing was a celebration in a sense. We all prayed after she crossed over. It was like it was a victory, it was like she stepped to a better place, a place of rest for her spirit. Mama used life up, there was no doubt about that. That was her legacy to us. Her spirit will always be a part of me.

The Grieving Process

Just as we all dealt with Mama's terminal illness in our own ways, we all responded differently to her death. It was interesting, because Wesley and I again switched roles. I had wept and grieved and been pretty much out of my head during much of her last few weeks, while Wesley had been strong. Upon Mama's death, however, I felt a surge of energy and strength, while poor Wesley fell apart. He had not done enough preparatory grief. In fact, a few days after Mama's burial, Wesley went to the cemetery and said he wanted to dig her up. He was nearly berserk with grief. In trying to be so strong, he felt he had not taken adequate time to say goodbye. His reaction was not all that uncommon. Frequently, some close relatives and loved ones isolate themselves from all the other grievers. They talk about the deceased as if he or she is still alive. They dwell on memories and even make up stories of intimate times with the deceased. We gave Wesley room to act out his grief in his own way. It does no good to do otherwise.

Grieving is not accomplished quickly. It is a transitory emotional wave that can be excruciatingly slow to unfold, but it is a healing process. Here are a few suggestions to consider when a loved one dies:

• All individual family members and loved ones should be allowed to express grief in the manner that is most comfortable for them, short of condoning alcohol binges or other self-destructive behavior. Let the person cry, scream, weep, or go into isolation if that is what he or she needs to do.

• Be ready to serve as a friend and counselor. Sooner or later, nearly everyone needs to talk through grief. You too may need to do this, so it can be a mutual process.

• Do not think you can *handle* it alone. I tried this, to some degree, without being aware of it, and as a result, my grieving period was extended much longer than it might have been. Grieving is a process that can take years, but your initial and most intense grieving period generally will last only a few weeks unless you "handle it" as I did; then you are prone to spontaneous outbursts of grief over extended periods.

• Be ready to bear the brunt of the anger of family members or loved ones of the deceased. Often, those who fail to release their anger prior to the death need to vent eventually. By tolerating it, you do the person a great favor. By criticizing or rebuking that person, you only prolong their grief.

To prepare myself, I read many books about death, dying, and grieving during the period when my Mama was dying. The experts generally agree that there are four elements that are important in grieving and healing.

1. Monitor your feelings during the grieving process. The loss of a loved one has much the same emotional impact as any other loss or defeat in life. A very important part of your life has been taken away and this can trigger a vast range of feelings running the gamut from anger to hurt to guilt and overwhelming sorrow. It is not at all uncommon for people to be angry at the deceased for "abandoning" the grieving party.

   It is important to monitor your thoughts carefully during times of grieving in order to negate distorted thinking that can lead to self-destructive actions such as binge drinking or suicidal thoughts. How often have you heard someone remark after the loss of a loved one, "I don't think I can go on"? That sort of thinking needs to be carefully monitored.

2. Take time to acknowledge the significance of the death in your life. One of the mistakes I made after my Mama's death was to not take a few days to thoughtfully sort through all that had happened. The weeks leading up to her death were a fog of preparatory grieving. Upon her death, I went through a period of elation because she was out of pain finally, and in a sense that was good because it allowed me to get my life back up and running again. But, several months after Mama's death, I underwent a period of delayed mourning in which I began breaking down and weeping at the mere thought of her being gone from my life. This even happened while I was at the podium delivering a speech.

My problem was that I had not taken the time to acknowledge what the loss of her in my daily life had meant to me. I was still reaching for the phone to call her every day. I had not said goodbye properly, even though physically I had eulogized her and attended her burial. Emotionally, I had not made peace with her death and what that meant for my life.

3. Sit down and remember your times with the deceased. It can be helpful to clear your mind of memories by sitting down and telling the story of your relationship with the loved one who has died. You can do this either by writing it out or by telling it to a close friend or counselor. Or you can write a letter to the lost loved one expressing your feelings directly to them. By doing this in detail and relating the emotions as you go, this process helps wash out all of the pent-up feelings.

   The loss of a loved one can also set off emotional memories of past losses that may not have been dealt with at the time they occurred. If this happens, you may need to tell the story of these relationships too in order to release guilt, anger, or whatever has kept them locked within you.

4. Vent your emotions over the loss whenever you need to. Grieving takes time and it has cycles. Feelings that subside in the weeks and months after a death may return in intense waves on anniversaries, birthdays, and holidays. Don't try to ignore these emotions or to override them. Acknowledge them by visiting the burial site and talking things over with the spirit of the deceased, or by conducting some sort of personal ritual on special occasions to acknowledge the loss and grief you feel for the person.

5. Do not isolate yourself. We all need encouragement and companionship. You need not feel embarrassed for your grief, but seek out those who understand your feelings and share with them rather than with someone whom you don't know as well.

6. Take steps outside the emotional realm to move on with real life. These might include:

• Clearing out the belongings of the deceased, keeping mementos but otherwise acknowledging that this person is gone for good.

- Selecting favorite photographs of the deceased and putting them in honored places.
- Visiting the cemetery when the urge arises.

Mama's Spirit

I had never doubted the strength of Mama's spirit in life. It was equally formidable in death. The second that my mother's grip on my hand relaxed and she passed on to the next life, one of her dogs, Rags, began howling in the yard outside her window. I've been told dogs can sense the passing of a master and that it is not unusual for them to howl, so I was not that surprised. We even laughed a bit about her power over the dogs. But I was not at all prepared for the display of her spirit's power over me.

Later that night, we were all gathered around the kitchen table, talking about Mama and the funeral arrangements, and relaxing. I had my shoes off and my feet up in a chair. I wasn't fully conscious of it because so much else was going on, but my foot was throbbing. I became aware of it, though, when little John Leslie said, "Come look, Daddy has Grandma's foot!" My foot was indeed swollen just as Mama's had been from arthritis. This had never happened to me before. Soon, word spread. Even the neighbors came by to look, "Yeah, that's Mama's foot all right."

Wesley took one look and said, "Man, she's got you now."

On the morning after the funeral, I went to the hospital for tests on the foot and the doctors had no explanation for it. Later I went to the Mayo Clinic, and they couldn't figure it out either. The swelling stayed around for two or three months. I couldn't wear socks on that foot during that time because it was so tender. I couldn't understand what was going on with it, until I happened to pick up a book on metaphysical symptoms. The book said that swollen extremities were a common expression of grief. Wesley was right. Mama and her spirit still had a grip on me, but to tell you the truth, it was comforting to still be sharing something with her, even if it made me limp.

- *Answering your calling in life*
- *Adopting an undefeatable attitude*
- *Making the leap in your life after hard times*

CHAPTER 9

It's Not Over Until You Win!

I'll never forget the look in my Mama's eyes in the moments before she died. There was such peace. A tear came from the left eye; one last tear for the hard life she led on this earth. That look of peace was such a comfort to me. I had grieved so much at the thought of her dying, but when her time came it seemed she was telling me to let her go where there was no more pain, where there would be peace for her. In the hours after her death, and most of the days that followed, I grieved some, but mostly I felt a sense of relief and inner strength. I wanted to celebrate Mama's life rather than focusing on her long and painful dying.

I had a sense of being filled with Mama's dynamic spirit, and not just in my aching and swollen foot. I felt her perseverance and her relentless drive and passion for life surging back into me. I had been down so long with the loss of my television show and with her illness, I think Mama was sending me a message. It was time to move on with my life.

Throughout this book, I have been coaching you on how to handle hard times in your job and in your personal life. I have given you suggestions, tips, and guidance on how to deal with hard times, and now I want to suggest to you that when hard times have had their lock on you for a while, the best thing you

can do is to charge ahead with your life. Rather than slowly ease
back into your old life, I recommend taking a leap and going after
life with as much relentless energy as you can. Don't settle for
getting back into the old routine. Change your life for the better.
Make the leap!

After Mama's death, a new clarity came into my mind. All of
the remorse and depression that had come with her illness and
the loss of my show lifted. I was inspired to look forward to challenges and the adventure of life. When my Mama became ill and
Calvin called me home, I was forced to snap out of a depression. I
was reminded that my perspective and priorities on life had become skewed. With her death after so much suffering, I was en-
ergized. If this powerful woman could live such a dynamic life, I
could hardly allow mine to remain mired in self-pity. Mama had
taught me the lessons earlier in life. I had learned that indomitable philosophy from her, but in going through hard times,
I had temporarily lost my way. Her passing put me back on
course.

As I reflected on my Mama's life and death, it occurred to me
that she had passed her fighting spirit on to me, but also to my
youngest son, John Leslie, who is now eleven years old. He was
once a very easygoing child but he has grown into a highly com-
petitive young man. Recently, I went to one of his peewee football games and I was amazed. He was mauling the kids who got in
his way. He was like Mean Joe Green in short pants. My little
John Leslie was knocking kids down left and right out there. After the game I asked him what made him so aggressive. "They
used to knock me down all the time, Dad, and I just decided I
wasn't going to be knocked down anymore. Now *I* do the knocking down!"

Kids grow up on you, don't they? Of course, I have to admit, I
have tried not to baby him. He and I go after each other when we
play. I think it is a natural thing for the son to always be testing
his strength against his father, and for the father to push and test
his son's strength. When he and I go at each other, I'm always reminded of a buck deer and its male offspring locking horns in the
woods. I really began to see my Mama's spirit in John Leslie one
night when he and I were locking horns over his favorite board
game, Connect 4. I was laying it on John Leslie. I'd beaten him

ten straight games and if it had been a National Football League game, I would have gotten a flag from the referee for taunting.

"Just play, Dad."

I was talking trash to him. "Don't you know I am the greatest? Not only in this state but across the entire planet, Jupiter, Mars, and—wait! This just in, a telegram saying Mr. Les Brown is Master of the Universe in Connect 4!"

"Just play, Dad."

"No, let's go to bed, son, I am *tired* of beating you mere mortals."

John Leslie was having none of it. Of course, I wouldn't have teased him if I didn't think he could take it. He looked up at me with defiance in his eyes.

"You can't go, Dad," he said.

"Why not?" I asked.

"Because it's not over until I win!" he demanded.

The gauntlet was down. "Young man, I am not going to go lightly on you," I teased. "I am invincible. As long as you stay here I am going to whip up on you."

"Be quiet, Dad, sit down and play," my son replied.

I beat John Leslie five more games, stood up and said, "The Master will now retire to his chambers while you treat the wounded."

"Keep playing, Dad," he said.

Ten more games I beat him.

"No, Dad, one more."

I wasn't going to let him win, really. I wanted to go to bed with my crown still on my head. But sooner or later, the son surpasses the father. I relaxed and lost my concentration and the boy wore me down.

John Calvin beat me the next game. He gave himself a high five, stood up, stretched and said, "Dad, I'm ready to go to sleep now."

I was shocked. I checked the board.

"Get up and go to bed, old man," he said.

Reflecting later on that night, I was inspired by my son's determination and grit, and I was a little ashamed of the way I had been handling the hard times in my life. We all suffer losses and defeats in life. We all experience rejection. Doors slam in our faces. Banks reject our loan applications. Employers cut back and lock us out. Divorce, downsizing, disasters, and disappointments are part of life. But if we hang on to that spirit, that determination that says "It's not over until I win!" the hard times will never get the best of us.

It's Not Over Until You Win!

That kind of courage and resiliency, that kind of unstoppable spirit, is there within all of us but very few of us reach past the pain and disappointment to tap into it. You can't spend your life tiptoeing around hard times and hurts. You can't simply build a wall of pillows around you and settle for what is comfortable, average, and ordinary. How will you ever know that you have really lived to your fullest potential? You have to go after life and live it as if it owes you every minute. You have to spend every last bit of talent and energy before your body is spent and your spirit summoned. You have to answer your calling.

I'd been blessed with a calling in life. My purpose had been made clear through my success as a public speaker. I needed to get back to that calling. There are few things as important as answering your calling, whether it is to lead governments or to care for children. We all have a purpose, a reason for being here, our role in the greater plan. And we all have the responsibility to pursue that calling with all the energy we can summon. When people are answering their calling in life, they are living dynamically. They are driven. They accept no defeat or setback as a finality. They push on. These people are not just making a living, they are living their making. They are doing what they were made to do and they are doing it with everything they have. There is no doubt that I was born to be a public speaker. The tools were all there, all I had to do was hone them and learn how to put them to their best use. I must have known this all my life, consciously or unconsciously. If I hadn't, where do you think I would have been? A slow learner, held back twice in grade school and kept in special education classes all through high school? A product of poverty? An adopted child? Where would I be if I had not identified my calling and gone after it?

Take a minute now and consider whether or not you are answering your calling? What is your calling? Write it down.
My calling is:

_____

Now, what is the ultimate you can achieve with that calling, how far would it take you if you pushed it to its greatest level?

_____

_____

_____

The truth is, you probably have no idea how far it can take you because, as I have discovered, when you keep pushing all of your life to develop your calling, it takes you places you never dreamed you would go. But for now, write down five levels that you think you could achieve if you answered your calling. For example, my calling as a communicator has taken me to:

1. radio deejay
2. state representative
3. motivational speaker
4. public television personality
5. talk show host

Try to come up with five levels that you might reach:

1. _____

2. _____

3. _____

4. _____

5. _____

The interesting thing about going after your calling and pushing and pushing it, is the way unexpected opportunities open up

to you. As a young man, I may well have dreamed of being a radio deejay but I never would have thought I'd end up as a state
representative, television talk show host, or the author of a best-
selling book. Take one of your projected levels listed above and
list three things that might grow from it. I'll provide an example
based on a few opportunities that have presented themselves to
me just recently.

1. syndicated national radio host
2. network television co-host
3. multilevel marketing entrepreneur

Now, make your projections of unexpected levels that might
open up to you. Go ahead, dream!

1._____

2._____

3._____

Of course, none of this can come about if you allow hard times
or defeats and disappointments to knock you on your back completely. Look what I would be missing if I hadn't come out of my
depression, hurt, and distorted thinking. When I regained my
focus and returned to my calling, it amazed me the opportunities that opened up. I discovered that the loss of a television talk
show was actually taken as a victory by many who knew me and
cared about me. They could see the format wasn't right for me.
They could see that it didn't fit my calling. I actually received letters saying *Congratulations!* after the show was canceled. "Now
you can go back to speaking and inspiring people," one of them
said.

To my surprise, many of those who had followed my speaking
career could hardly contain their joy at the cancellation of the
show. One lady came up to me and said that it *hurt* her to watch
the show because she could see how painful it was for me to work
in the constraints of the talk show format. She said she actually
had to get up and open windows because it looked like I was having trouble breathing! She and her family would gather around

when the show started and cheer for me to come on, she said, but *"the real Les never showed up."*

Now I look back and wonder whether I was awake. It's like the time I was on a raft in the ocean in Florida and fell asleep. I woke up and I was way out from shore. I realized I had some serious swimming to do to get back where I belonged. That happens in life, we've all been there. You drift aimlessly along, thinking you're safe, and then you end up in serious danger of becoming shark bait. When you find yourself adrift in life, you can't wait around for the tide to bring you back. You have to start kicking and swimming because it is your life and if you throw yourself to the sharks, it'll be all over. One day you'll wake up inside the belly of a beast, digested and wasted. Don't doubt it.

Once I made the leap and started taking life on, I caught a huge wave going my way. One of the best talent agents in the country contacted me. She has shown me doors that I never dreamed of pushing on, opportunities that I never dreamed existed. I am now involved in entrepreneurial businesses that have added a great deal to my income. In addition, my public speaking career has not only resumed, it has gone through the roof. And I have discovered that no one took the cancellation of my television show as a sign that my career was over. In fact, I'm still getting offers from the radio and television industry. And to think, I could still be flat on my back, wondering what went wrong. Moaning and groaning and sending out announcements for my next pity party!

After eulogizing my mother at her funeral and contemplating her life and her spirit, I began to see again. My vision was restored, and I began to find the doors flying open in front of me. I got up and back into life with a renewed passion and energy and commitment. I began to stretch and challenge myself and even though there were occasional setbacks and flashbacks to the painful things that had happened, they did not knock me backward, they only propelled me forward. The harder the battle, folks, the sweeter the victory.

Because of my recent hard times, it has become more clear to me than ever that the only limits we have are those that we accept. I heard recently a story about two boys who had gone ice skating. One skated into a danger zone and fell through. His smaller friend saw him thrashing in the icy water and then saw him go under the ice. The smaller boy tried to break the ice with his skates and his fists but he could not do it. Then he spied a big tree limb at the side of the pond. He went to it, pulled it to the spot where his friend was trapped under the ice, and, amazingly, lifted it over his head and threw it, shattering a hole in the ice so that his friend could get to the air. Then he pulled his friend out. Later, people in town marveled at how the smaller boy had been able to lift the huge limb. How did he do it? they asked. "I know," said one of the older fellows. "He did it because there was no one there to tell him he couldn't do it."

Tuning Out Negative Voices

Many people allow themselves to be defeated by much less than what life threw at that young man. Often, they allow themselves to be defeated simply by the negative voices and thoughts that come from within. These are the voices that say *You've been fired, you'll never get another job! You can't start your own company! You don't have the skills to do that! You'll never find someone to love you!*

Those who block out negative thoughts, those who look ahead with optimism and conviction achieve the impossible. You can't listen to those negative voices. You can't give up on life. Giving up is not an option, it is a waste of God-given talent. You have to be able to say, I lost. So what? GET UP! My television show was canceled. So what? GET UP! You lost your job, so what? GET UP! Your spouse left you, so what? GET UP!

In the blanks below list any recent setbacks or defeats you have had. Then read aloud the message I've provided. Clear out the cobwebs. Pull yourself out of the mire and the self-pity. Answer your calling.

I _____ So what? GET UP!

I _____ So what? GET UP!

I _____ So what? GET UP!

I _____ So what? GET UP!

I _____ So what? GET UP!

An Embarrassment of Riches

Looking back now, I am embarrassed at how I responded to hard times in my life. How many people have even had the opportunities to lose what I lost? What would you give to have your own television talk show for even just three months? I failed at a format that was not right for me, so what? Do you know that as soon as I got back up, I began getting offers for television shows with formats that are much more suited to my style? It could happen anyday now, and this time I'm again prepared to give it all I've got. What have I got to lose in trying again? I've already lost but I did not accept defeat as permanent, I only accepted that there were better things to come. Television is an option, but I will never consider giving up my calling as a public speaker.

It's been said that in life you are either experiencing problems, just leaving problems, or heading toward a problem. Considering that this is the cycle of life, that problems are always going to be a part of life, you only have one choice. You have to learn to deal with them by saying: So what? Give me all you've got. Unload on me. Because I am going to take it, deal with it, and then I am going to get back up! When bad things happen to you, you can roll over and die, you can go on Ricki Lake's show and cry on the world's shoulder, or you can get busy getting over it. You can wallow in life like one of those whining, complaining, little helpless rubber-boned people who allow circumstances to dictate life to them. Or you can decide to get up and get on with life, going after your calling, pushing your talents, defying those who think they have defeated you. You can lie down and give up, or you can say, "I'm tired of being knocked down, I'm going to do the knocking down from now on."

A Child Lost, and Then Found

I'm proud of the spirit that my Mama passed on to us. I see signs of it even in some of the saddest situations in our family. At Mama's funeral, all of her children gathered, even Linda, who had been the question mark at family gatherings in years past. Often, in recent years, her chair at the family table was empty. Linda was the lost one. She had temporarily let the worst of Liberty City get the best of her. She became an alcoholic and crack addict. But she has come back. One of the happiest moments in my life occurred a few years ago in a drug rehabilitation clinic in Miami. I was speaking to a group of former addicts in the program at the clinic, when a pair of familiar eyes caught mine.

"Excuse me," I told my audience with my voice cracking. "I just found my sister among you." I had no idea that Linda had gone straight. I'd lost touch with her, as had most of the family. But there she was putting her life together after years of abuse. No one had taken her there. She had done it on her own. I was shocked to see her there. We had tried over the years to get through to her, but she had not listened.

Later, we talked and I asked what had finally motivated her to take control of her life. "I have had it," she said simply. "I was tired of it." I knew that she was not giving herself enough credit. Sure, she had grown tired of it, but in her heart she knew that she did not deserve to live like that, that she was better than that kind of life. And finally, she admitted it by reclaiming her life. She'd had it with the worst of life. And she knew she could have far more of the best.

Whether in your personal or work life, you have to have the strength to face hardship and say, "I've had it." You have to walk away from it. *"Where are you going?"* I don't know, just away from this life that I don't deserve.

Study this list of questions and answer those that apply to you.

- What area of your life is no longer satisfactory?
- Is your job paying you what you are worth?
- Are you growing personally and professionally?
- If you keep on your present track personally and professionally, where will you be in five years?
- Do you have toxic people in your life?
- Are there enough nurturing and stimulating people around you to keep you growing?
- Are you the kind of person you want to be?

- Will your children admire you?
- Have you prepared yourself to compete over the next decade?
- Is it time to make a leap?
- Is the thrill gone in your relationship or is it just buried in neglect?

Write down what you've had it with in your life and then what you are going to do about it.

I've had it with: _____

I'm going to: _____

Now, write five steps you can take to get away and get back up on life:

1. Today I'm going to: _____
2. Tomorrow I'm going to: _____
3. Next week, I'm going to: _____
4. By next month I'll: _____
5. By this time next year, I'll: _____

Make the Leap

Once you decide that you have had it with conditions being dictated to you, you can set out to change your life. When you have the "I've had it" mind-set you prepare yourself to take risks and to make the leap back into life. No money? No problem. Most of us start out with no money. Some of the richest people in this world didn't have a dime when they made the leap. I've had it. I've been without it. Having no money won't hold you back. Only your own self-doubts can do that. You can't be afraid of making mistakes. You have to take extraordinary measures in order to make extraordinary changes in your life. You have to give up the old familiar ways and try new tools to get new results. You cannot simply keep doing what you've done before, unless you want to keep getting the results you have been getting. You can't even go to your strengths, because they obviously haven't been strong enough to get you where you really want to go. You have to try something entirely new. You have to make the leap. You have to be bold.

You can risk failure or you can risk wasting your potential and talents and watching your dreams slip away. Would you rather end life sliding down an old mountain or climbing a new one? We all have great potential but there is no guarantee we will fulfill it. You have to nurture, develop, and keep pushing your abilities to get beyond the ordinary. You want to be extra ordinary and un-conventional in your life. You want to make the leap that makes life thrilling. Most people never achieve greatness in life because they never take the leap to get beyond what is handed them, or what comes easy, or what is comfortable. What about going be-yond the limits of your vision of what you can do?

People who achieve greatness act as though there are no boundaries to what they can achieve. So few people are willing to go for it if they can't look at what lies ahead or below them. They need the security. But if you make the leap by pushing yourself beyond your vision, you experience the full excitement of life. You bring passion to what you do, and that passion can push you even further into whatever it is you do or dream of doing. You can do this in whatever you pursue. By making yourself the best and then better than the best, you set the momentum of your life whether you're a janitor or a junior executive. We all know wait-ers who brought more to the table than the menu. We've all had co-workers who brought more to the job than the basic require-ments. We've seen athletes such as Michael Jordan and Larry Bird who have become *masters* of their sport because of the joy, dedi-cation, and drive they bring to it.

We have all had moments when we say "I can't believe that I am doing this," moments when we transcend our own vision of ourselves and what we believe is possible for ourselves. Just think, I used to watch Phil Donahue on television and even though I had the highest-rated, fastest-canceled talk show in the history of television, I was there. I was on the big tube all across the nation. I have accomplished things I didn't even know I could do. You have the same potential, perhaps even greater potential. You have talents and abilities and skills that you have not yet tapped into. You have a song within you that has yet to be sung.

You have to make the leap in order to live out that potential and to even drive beyond it.

What can you do to bring passion and mastery to your life? List five things you can do to bring greatness into:
Your relationships:

1. _____
2. _____
3. _____
4. _____
5. _____

Your work:

1. _____
2. _____
3. _____
4. _____
5. _____

If You're Not Making Mistakes You're Not Going Anywhere

Warning from the Surgeon General, Leslie Calvin Brown: When you make the leap and go into action in life you are going to make mistakes. Guaranteed! When I went into business I didn't know anything about running a multimillion-dollar operation. I made a lot of mistakes, and I became a millionaire because of those mistakes. *In order to get where you don't know you can go, you have to make mistakes to find out what you don't know.* You have to risk mistakes. Maybe you have forgotten that. Surely when you were a child you knew it. And when you first entered the job market you had to know that you weren't fully prepared, but you were willing to take risks and make mistakes in order to learn and grow. Why is it that we forget that as we get older? Is it because we think we are supposed to know everything by a certain age? How ridiculous does that seem?

Mistakes are teachers. You cannot learn without discovering what it is you need to know, and the older you get the more difficult it is to find out what more there is out there for you to learn. That's why taking leaps is so important, especially if you are a middle manager who has been downsized out of a job, or a late bloomer looking to get beyond the glass ceiling. Make the leap! Don't look! Leap! If you fail, so what? Life is an experiment, find out what doesn't work and you'll have narrowed the search for what does work. Your greatest gift is your ability to choose and to create your own destiny so why accept limitations placed on you by a label or a job classification or an employee assessment form?

Would it be better to go through life frustrated and angry and bitter because you never took the leap? Better to blame other people, circumstances? Better to be a wimp, lazy, or small-minded? H. B. Fuller, the motivational writer, said that unless you attempt something beyond that which you have already mastered, you will never grow. And I say if you are not growing, you are withering on the vine.

Mistakes on Take After Take After Take

When we started doing *The Les Brown Show*, I had a terrible time reading the TelePrompTer. When you are standing in front of a studio audience aware that the show is being taped for millions of viewers, the job does not get any easier. As I struggled to read the TelePrompTer, I could actually hear people in the audience reading the words aloud to themselves! And they were a lot further away. I would stop and stumble and the audience would laugh at me and the producers would get red in the face, and I had to act like it was all just part of the fun. In my mind, I could hear the audience members thinking to themselves, "They are paying this guy millions of dollars and he can't even read his lines any better than that?"

I was making MISTAKES! Imagine, me, the guy from the Dodo Ward, making mistakes. So what! Mistakes are as much a part of my life as my fingers and my toes. Sometimes they get me into trouble, but sometimes they make things happen for me. I wasn't really making mistakes, you know. *I was going through a learning curve.* When you step outside of your normal realm of experience, you are certain to feel discomfort and nervousness. Don't be afraid. It's the same sensation you get when you are about to take the plunge on a roller coaster or water slide. It's an experience that can make you uneasy, but it can also be thrilling and energizing. If you always stay with what is comfortable and easy, you may never know how far your talents will take you. Far too many people sit back and coast just when they should be moving to the edge of their seats and hitting the accelerator. I've had more opportunities in my life open up in the last twenty years than I'd dreamed of as a younger man, but I've discovered that small dreams lead to grander dreams if you keep pushing and stand poised to leap when opportunities appear.

Sure it can be scary. Sure there will be times when you feel you are in over your head. Sure it will take time to feel you have mastered that new job or business or new relationship. But you can do it. Life is not for the faint of heart. You have to be prepared to do whatever it takes as long as it fits within your value system. If your current habits are producing results that you don't want, change those habits. Push yourself until it hurts, and then keep pushing until it feels good. Recently I had to speak at the National Speakers Association convention. Now, I've been a public speaker for a long time but I still can be intimidated by *that* audience. Unlike most professional speakers, I don't have a memorized speech or speeches. I do a lot of research to custom-design my presentations and I adjust them based on the needs of the audience. That can make for some exciting moments—and for some serious stage fright. Before I went out to give the speech I had a moment of panic. I began to think I should have prepared something else for this speech. When you are speaking before a group of professional speakers from around the world you want to look your best in order to justify why you are up there, and in the middle of my speech I made a glaring mistake. I called the founder of the National Speakers Association, Cavitt Roberts, the wrong name. I called him "Dick Cavett," whom I'd seen on television the night before. I did it not once, but twice. But I just kept on going. *You wouldn't be here if you weren't among the best of the best. You have done this hundreds of times before. These people are among your biggest fans because they know what it takes to be asked to do this.* And I did it.

Later, I felt some embarrassment. A few members mentioned it, but most of them said it didn't matter. And they agreed it would have been a bigger mistake to stop. Back in my radio days, I had a friend who was a deejay and if he came to a word he couldn't pronounce in the newscast, he'd just say "hard word" and keep on ripping.

As I prepared myself to go in front of the audience at the National Speakers Association convention, I reminded myself that there are always going to be more geniuses sitting down than standing up at my speeches. There will always be people in my audiences who have a better education and more business credentials than I do, but few started where I began, and few have made it so far through so much adversity. You have to put yourself in a frame of mind where the only thing that matters to you is what lies ahead. You have to be prepared to jump and hope that land will appear beneath your feet. You don't want to come to the end in life saying, *Boy, if I had it to do all over again . . .* You want to be able to say *I took life on and squeezed every second out of it!* You can't be afraid to make mistakes, to get some knots on your head, or to get your hands dirty.

Angels Appear When You Go After Life

One thing I have discovered is that when you take leaps in life, angels appear to help you. When other people see that you are challenging life, they want to help you make it. That has happened to me repeatedly in my career. There are always people showing up to help me at key times because winners want to see other people win. When you become conscious and alert to the possibilities in your life, these angels appear. I've had enough of them to fill a heavenly choir, from Mama, to Mr. Washington, to my friend Mike Williams, to my agent, Jan Miller, to Dr. Talmadge McKinney, to Robert Henry of the National Speakers Association—all of these people, and many more, have served as my angels. And most have also been willing to let me know when they thought I was wrong. In most cases, these angels appeared in my life only after I had taken some risk. Of course, when you make a leap in life, you tend to be looking for help, so it is easier to find these angels. You will never find them if you are wallowing in depression or locked in a room feeling sorry for yourself. Bitterness blocks out blessings. Author Jim Roane has noted that success is a condition *that must be attracted, not pursued.* He means that we achieve rewards not by our intense pursuit of them, but by preparing ourselves for them. When you are prepared, opportunities come your way, they find you. It is what you become that determines what comes to you in life. At some point in time, then, the pursuit of your goals becomes secondary and what you have become in the process of preparing yourself is what is most important.

The growth you achieve, the faith, courage, and confidence you build, the skill and knowledge you acquire—these are the things that can never be taken away from you. These are the things that make the journey exciting and worthwhile. When I lost my television talk show, I failed at doing something that I wanted to do. I lost that show, but I did not lose the experience, the knowledge, the relationships that came with it. I walked away a better person and I walked away with better goals. I walked away also with my values intact. I did not sell out to that show. I walked away with my integrity and peace of mind. I did not cave in. I did not do trash television. I did not let anyone corrupt my values and beliefs. I held strong to what I believe in. When you take life on in that manner, you never lose.

How do you open the door to opportunities in your own life? Here are a few suggestions.

1. Become clear on what it is you want out of life. If you don't know, who does? Write down what it is you want and think about it. Make sure. And then begin thinking about how to attract what you want to yourself.

Example: I want to one day have a youth empowerment program designed to help people solve problems in their lives and to help them reach their goals.

_____

_____

_____

Now, what can you do to prepare yourself for that opportunity?

Example: I read everything I can on this topic and I talk with experts in the field.

_____

_____

_____

2. What is it that you have to change about yourself in order to attract what you want? What sacrifices are you willing to make?

Example: I have to control my tendency to speechify as a talk show host and I have to learn to help guests get their stories out quickly.

_____

_____

_____

3. Evaluate what you bring to the table. What skills do you have now and how do they invite opportunity?

Example: I now have experience in television talk shows and I know what needs to be done to make a show successful.

_____

---

4. Where will you draw the line? What is it you will not do to become a success in your chosen endeavor?

Example: I will not do trash television. I will not pander to the lowest common denominator simply in order to get ratings.

---

5. Make certain, finally, that this is something you really want—or is it something someone wants for you?

Remember, there are times in life to listen to your heart as well as your head. You have to have a passion for what you do and you have to be able to push past common thinking and reasonable objections. You have to think uncommonly and unreasonably in order to pursue what you are passionate about. And when you act in that manner, driven by your heart, you will find life opens up to you. Angels appear and your leaps into life land you on goals that had seemed impossible to achieve. Your heart fires the imagination and lifts the spirit. Too often, in your mind you can think of only what has happened in the past instead of being triggered by the possibilities ahead. Follow your heart. Make the leap at life.

CHAPTER 10

Dancing Up Life!

I have not often admitted this, but I was inspired to become a public speaker by perhaps the *worst* motivational speaker I've ever heard in my life.

This fellow is still working, surprisingly, so I won't give his name. He was the opening speaker in a seminar I attended early in my speaking career and he nearly closed the show early with his monotone, unenthusiastic presentation. As he spoke, the room grew as quiet as a graveyard between funerals.

I went to sleep to be awakened by what could only be called courtesy applause for his presentation. You could make more noise clapping with one hand. After the less-than-stirring speech, I leaned over to the guy sitting next to me and said, "That was really boring." And he said, "You should be so boring for the kind of money he makes." The fellow told me this terrible speaker was making $5,000 for each terrible speech.

After hearing how much money a really *bad* speaker could make, I decided it was time for me to go after this dream. A few days later, I caught a Greyhound bus from Miami to Orlando where I'd signed up for a seminar for beginners held by the National Speakers Association. It seemed like the bus ride took weeks. I know it took every last dollar I could scrape together. And so I was road-weary but eager to hear some inspiring, motivational, and dynamic speaking when I finally took a seat at the event. But who should walk out to lead the first session but that same terrible $5,000-per-speech speaker? I could not believe it.

All that time on a stinking bus, stopping in every one-horse town between Miami and Orlando, to hear this guy again? I nearly got up and walked out. By the time he'd gotten halfway through his speech, nearly half the audience had fled. But I stayed on until the bitter end and the speaker's parting shot, as it turned out, was worth the price of admission. He obviously had noted the exodus of the audience and the drooping eyelids of those who remained because, as he built up to his anticlimax, he stopped suddenly, looked out at the remaining numbers of aspiring public speakers and said, "You know, the only reason that I am standing up here and you are sitting down there is that I represent the thoughts that you have rejected for yourself."

I don't know about the other dozen or so people in the audience, but Mr. Monotone hit me right between the eyes with that shot. It was true. He had acted upon something that I had only dreamt of doing. I'd spent years dreaming of becoming a public speaker. But dreaming was all I had done. This guy may not have had any talent for it. He may have been the most undynamic public speaker in history. But he was up there while I was still dreaming. And so that is how I became motivated to start a new career by perhaps the worst motivational speaker I have ever heard.

Throughout this book, I have stressed the fact that the only thing that can possibly keep you from going after your dream is the person standing in your shoes, wearing your clothes, and thinking your negative thoughts. That is what that really bad motivational speaker was talking about. There was no denying that he was right. His words reminded me of something that had occurred a few days earlier. I was with someone in a car when we drove past a really fat man who was "jogging" down the street. It was more of a slow waddle really, a pitiful pace. The other person in the car made fun of the fat guy. But it occurred to me that at least the fat guy was out there trying. He was doing something about his problem, and if he kept at it, eventually that waddle would become a jog, and that fat guy wouldn't be so fat anymore. I thought then that I'd rather be a fat guy working on a dream than a skinny guy going nowhere in life.

If you don't work on life, it will certainly work on you. The preceding chapters have offered ample evidence of that. I've offered you a great deal of advice on how to deal with hard times in your personal life and in your work. In Chapter 9, I urged you to get back up and make a leap at life once you'd been knocked down. And now, I want to conclude by offering you tips on how to keep at life no matter how hard it slaps you around.

A Plan for Dynamic Living

LESSON ONE: PERSONAL REALITY CHECK

Johnny is a highly successful jazz drummer and a really miserable person. He got where he wanted to be in life, but after scratching and gouging and kicking to get there, he didn't much like himself. So many people become so wrapped up in trying to get where they think they want to go, they don't pay any attention to who they are becoming along the way. So check yourself and check your goals regularly. Are you living the life you want to live right now? Are you the kind of person you want to be, or need to be, in order to get what you really want in life? What you get in life is a direct result of the person you become. Therefore, if you lose all of your possessions tomorrow you can easily replace them because you acquired them not because of what you have but because of who you are.

Life gets better only when we get better. To attract success, you have to be ready for it. If you are a positive, dynamic-living person, you will attract people who will bring opportunities to you. Or you will make the opportunities yourself. Make it a regular practice to take inventory and to look at what you have become. What sort of people do you attract? Are you respected by co-workers, family, and friends? Do people ask your advice or do they give you advice? Do you listen to people? Do your conversations always deal with events in your life or do they focus on the events in other people's lives as well? Success must be attracted, not pursued. And you will never attract success if you repel other people with a self-centered attitude.

I had a friend who has made vast sums of money, and lost them too. He has been a millionaire several times over, and when it was over, he'd pick himself up and try again. He never let his roller-coaster life keep his spirits down. He used to quote one of Elizabeth Taylor's ex-husbands, Michael Todd, another guy who'd experienced many ups and downs: "I've been broke," Todd said, "but I've never been poor." He viewed what was happening to him as a challenge to his creativeness but he didn't see himself as a poor person. Whenever I've been broke in my life—and there have been a few times along the way—I've never said I was broke. I've always said that I was simply "overcoming a cash flow problem." Check yourself. Is that your attitude in life? Are you an optimistic, self-motivated, dynamic person?

It also helps to every now and then take an inventory of what is required to make you happy. Too often, we decide we need a new car or a new and bigger house, or some other material thing to make us happy when all we really need is the love and respect of others. But with the following Happiness Inventory checklist, you can at least get a handle on where your happiness factors are at any given point in time. Rate each item from 1 to 5 with 5 being the most important to you. After you have done that, go over each one again and put a check mark next to those items which are not now being satisfied. Commit yourself to going after those things that make you the happiest.

The Happiness Inventory

To be happy, I need to be:
1. Physically fit.
2. Creatively challenged.
3. Active in athletics.
4. Quiet for regular periods each day.
5. Involved in intellectual discussions.
6. Living in a nice, safe place.
7. Working at a challenging job.
8. Traveling extensively.
9. Feeling loved by my partner in life.
10. Assertive.
11. Needed by others.
12. Getting along with others.

13. Well organized.
14. Active spiritually.
15. Satisfied with my level of education.
16. Skilled in communication.
17. Around children.
18. Aware of the world around me.
19. In solid shape financially.
20. In the outdoors, enjoying nature.

LESSON TWO: CONTROLLING YOUR INNER DIALOGUE

Back when I was just starting my radio career in Miami and only beginning to dream of becoming a major broadcast personality, I went for the first time to see a motivational speaker in person. And as I sat in the audience listening to the booming voice of Dr. Norman Vincent Peale talking about his classic work *The Power of Positive Thinking* I was mesmerized by this man who was small in stature but a giant in inspiring people worldwide. Excited by his presentation, I began to feel as though I could do that sort of speaking for a living. But in the days that followed, the further I got from that auditorium, the more remote my chances seemed.

My negative inner dialogue took over. *Les Brown, you can't do that, you don't have a college education. Les Brown, you can't do that, you don't have the experience. You don't have the money. You've never done anything like that. What makes you think you can speak to thousands of people about living their dreams or about being wealthy and successful and fulfilled when you are still struggling just trying to make ends meet?*

Those negative inner voices can be relentless. How many times have you thought about doing something only to convince *yourself* that you couldn't do it? Only that inner dialogue has the power to keep us from living our fears rather than our dreams. So after you check yourself and your happiness, check for traces of those negative inner voices. My own negative voices began haranguing me after I first heard Dr. Peale, and it took me fifteen years to shut them out. Those negative voices had me tied up with procrastination and fears and all sorts of incredibly logical reasons for not doing what I really wanted to be doing—what I am doing now.

Those negative voices made so much sense. What made me think that AT&T, McDonald's, General Electric, Xerox, IBM, and other Fortune 500 companies would hire me to speak to their employees? Me, a product of the ghetto, a former special education student? Years passed before I even dared to set out on that dream of becoming a public speaker. But one night I found myself at a public speaking seminar in Columbus featuring Denis Waitley and Zig Ziglar. I had listened to their tapes and I'd read their books. They were the most inspiring speakers I'd found, and yet when I met them afterward, I couldn't bring myself to ask all the questions that I had for them on how they'd gotten their own careers going.

Oddly enough, considering my history as a motormouth, I became tongue-tied when I had the opportunity to talk to these two great speakers. The only thing that I could get out was "Wow, you guys were great!" Then I rushed out of there and sat in my car in the parking lot and listened to the questions I should have asked. *How did you get started? How do you market yourselves? What should I do first to get my name out there? Do you have any suggestions for developing clients?*

The questions poured out of me and onto the parking lot pavement. My inner voice had said, *Don't open your mouth in front of them, they will think you are stupid.* The negative voices held me back just as they can hold anyone back. You have to recognize those voices and you have to tell them to be still. Or they will stifle your growth. Once, early in my speaking career, I went to speak to a group of children in the Watts neighborhood of Los Angeles. Upon arriving at the school, their principal warned me that I could be facing a hostile audience. He told me these kids were gang members. He said murder and violence were part of their daily lives. They had thrown things at previous speakers who had failed to realize that these were not your typical innocent schoolchildren. Believe me, the negative inner conversations took that and ran with it. And they advised me to do the same thing: *Run! These kids won't want to hear anything you've got to say. They'd just as soon put a bullet in you as hear what some aging Dodo might tell them.*

You know, even today, I have to deal with those voices before I step out in front of an audience. And although they never are silenced completely, I have learned to tune them out just as I finally tuned them out that day. I went backstage at that high school in Watts and looked in the dressing room mirror and drowned out the negative inner voices with a positive pep talk. *Don't allow this to intimidate you. You are the Intimidator! Mesmerize them. Hold them in the palm of your hand. You can get to these young people because you have walked these streets. They need someone to show them the way that you found. They won't boo you. They won't shoot at you. They need you.*

My positive outer conversation went on a little long. And it must have gotten a little loud because the principal came knocking on the door wondering if something was wrong. But I went out there and I hit those kids right where they needed it. Right between the ears. I told them my background. I told them that gangs and violence had lived in my neighborhood too. But I told them also that I had not allowed those things to live in me. I told them that when they pick up a gun, they are only picking up a gun that I threw away, and that if they were smart and if they cared anything at all about their lives, they would throw those guns away too. *You don't have to end up in a premature grave, but that's where you are heading when you pick up a gun,* I told them.

I advised them that life is full of negative distractions such as drugs, alcohol, gangs, and violence, but those things only keep them from finding their greatness. When they fall into the gang life they become servants to the needs of other people. Their own lives mean nothing in that environment. I told them that they have to keep their minds focused on their own growth and development. *You have to believe in yourself and the power of your potential. And you have to go after what you want. You can't do that in the streets. You have to do it in school, in the library, in the home, in your hearts.*

They never knew what hit them. Later, some of the teachers said they had never seen anyone silence those young people for so long. In fact, I got to the teachers too. Four of them quit to chase their dreams after hearing me speak! And to think, I nearly ran away because my own negative voices had been working on me.

LESSON THREE: LIVE DYNAMICALLY

Have you ever been stuck in the snow or mud? If you can't get out by spinning the tires what do you do? You get out and push.

And if pushing doesn't work, you get someone to pull you out. You change your approach until something works to free you from whatever rut you are in. Why then, when you get stuck in life, would you just keep doing the same old thing?

We all know people who have a good education and a proper background but for some reason don't get anywhere in life. That's because they do not live dynamically. They don't take life on like Mama did. They don't decide what they want and go after it constantly, relentlessly, with everything they have. Too many people do less than they should and as a result they are less than they should be. Mama always seemed to be doing more than it was possible to do. She never seemed to sleep. Unlike most people, she considered rest something that eventually became necessary, but it was not at all an objective. She was always waking us up early in the morning saying, "Get up, get outta here."

Mama was always involved in life. When she was done raising us, she took in more children. For a long time, she took in handicapped children, watching them while their parents worked. She had more ways to make money than a Chicago politician. She baked sweet potato pies and sold them. She took in ironing. She was always looking ahead and thinking about things she could do. At one point when I was experiencing one of my cash flow problems, she said she wanted to help me out by getting a job as a cross-country truck driver. She was nearly eighty years old at the time. You see, Mama had once dated a truck driver who would sometimes let her drive his semi. She liked being way up there on the highway and she often talked over the years of getting her license to be a long-haul trucker. When she offered to drive a truck to help me out, I didn't help her get a license, but I did get in gear myself. If my Mama was willing to hit the road for me, I had to do more for myself. Mama motivated me with her dynamic attitude. And she reminded me that when you are stuck in life, the way to get unstuck is to change your approach.

LESSON FOUR: LIVE WITH A SENSE OF URGENCY

I ran into an old acquaintance from Columbus at a funeral recently. Terry had spent most of the last two decades drinking wine and hanging out under a tree on a street corner. He didn't look good. He is an articulate, intelligent man but there was no light in his eyes. Life had passed him by. We were at the funeral of a mutual friend who had been a dynamic businessman and philanthropist in Columbus. Terry told me that he and the businessman had gone to school together and had even been in business together. We both wept at the funeral but I think Terry wept for the life that he had wasted—his own. I asked Terry at what point their paths had diverged—at what point Terry had decided to spend his most productive years in idle, drinking booze and chasing women.

Rather bluntly, I said, "How did you waste thirty-five years of your life?" He said, "I didn't waste thirty-five years. I wasted a second, then a minute, then an hour, then a day, and the days grew into weeks, and here I am. It happened gradually and one day I looked around and all those years had passed me by."

That is how it happens to most people, time is sneaky. Once you pass thirty-five, you no longer get twelve months out of the year. It cuts to nine. I swear! And if you don't pursue your dream with a sense of urgency, time just disappears. It does not slow down and wait for you to catch up.

There will come a time in your life when you will have more yesterdays than tomorrows. Make a list NOW of three things you are going to do TODAY to get you started after your dream.

Today I am going to:

1. _____

2. _____

3. _____

NOW, make a list of three things you are going to do TOMORROW to follow up:

1. _____

2. _____

3. _____

NOW, make a list of three things you are going to do NEXT WEEK:

1. _____
2. _____
3. _____

NOW, make a list of three things you are going to do NEXT MONTH:

1. _____
2. _____
3. _____

NOW, make a list of three things you are going to do NEXT YEAR:

1. _____
2. _____
3. _____

NOW, make a list of three things you are going to do over the NEXT FIVE YEARS:

1. _____
2. _____
3. _____

NOW, make a list of three things you are going to do over the NEXT TEN YEARS:

1. _____
2. _____
3. _____

That may seem like a lot of advanced planning now, but I guarantee you it will go fast whether you pay attention or not. My friend Phyllis has a nurturing spirit, and she has always had a passion for medicine. She started out taking premed classes in college but she became pregnant and dropped out. Several years later, I saw her and she appeared to be defeated by life. Having the responsibility of a child had weighed her down. In talking to her, I remembered how excited she had been when she had talked in the past about going to medical school. She had always shown such fire and determination when she had spoken of a career in medicine. And so I asked her if she planned on one day returning to her dream. "One day I'm going to go back," she said, without much conviction.

How many times have you said that? How many times have you heard someone else say it? I've got news for you. That *One Day I'm Gonna Day* never comes. You have to go after your dream now! You have to take the first step now! You have to live your life as if the clock is ticking because, guess what? It *is* ticking! And the older you get, the faster it ticks.

In only a few years, I'll be facing the prospect of my thirty-five-year high school class reunion. *Thirty-five years!* But I still feel like I'm sixteen years old. I may not look it, I may not be able to do the same things physically, I may even be a grandfather, but it doesn't seem like that much time has gone by. Where does the time go? I don't know, but I know that if you're waiting around for that One Day I'm Gonna Day, you're liable to miss out on a whole lot. Most people never achieve their goals because they waste most of their most productive years thinking that they'll get down to serious business later. BIG MISTAKE!

You have to go after your dream with an urgency. That doesn't mean you can't take time out for fun every now and then, but you have to think of fun as a part of the process, rather than thinking I'll have fun now and work later. Fun is finding what you most enjoy doing in life and making it your life's work. Fun is chasing your dream. It's been said that we spend the first half of our lives learning and the second part living what we learn. But if you spend your twenties and thirties chasing the good times, you'll probably spend your forties, fifties, and sixties working for those who took life more seriously.

People invest in wardrobes, boats, cars, CD collections but they neglect investing in their personal growth and development in the form of education, books, self-development tapes, classes, seminars, or workshops. And they wonder why they aren't getting anywhere? Many people go through life in a hypnotic spell, mesmerized by the totally incorrect thought that they are going to be young forever. Do these people think life is going to wait until the party is over? By the time they lose their edge and their energy, they are imprisoned by self-destructive habits that are hard to shake. Then they want to get serious about life and if something good doesn't appear, they become cynical and claim that somebody did them wrong, but they did it to themselves.

Marcus Aurelius said, "Stop living your life like you have a thousand years to live." One of the most vital things to remember: What we know and what we feel does not matter if we do not act upon it with a focused sense of urgency. Every day move forward! Every hour of that day move forward! Every minute of every hour of that day move forward! Look at your life. Ask yourself: Are you where you want to be given your abilities and what you know? Look at where you want to be and where you want to go and ask, "How much time do I have left?" You don't know, do you? None of us do. You must seize the moment. You must make time count by getting all you can out of each day rather than simply "getting through" the day.

Are you on schedule? What must you do to pick up the slack and close the gap? Once you determine where you are and where you want to go, you have to create an agenda for your life. If you don't create an agenda for your life you will find yourself buying into the agendas of others. You have to map out the things you need to do each day, each week, every month, two months, six months, one year, and five years. You have to know where you want to go and what you need to do to get there, and, most importantly, when you need to do it. Making a declaration doesn't do it. You have to go after it with a sense that the clock is ticking on you. If you don't start chasing that dream today, it will be all the further away tomorrow.

One of the things I've always done to give a sense of urgency to my life was to be a relentless overachiever. If I had to come up with $10,000 for a business venture, I would create a plan of action to make $70,000. That way, if some aspect of my plan fell through, I'd still likely be ahead of the game. I've always done the same thing when budgeting my time. I set my watch fifteen minutes ahead because I would rather get there fifteen minutes early than show up when everyone else does. That attitude puts me ahead, both in my mind and in the minds of my competitors.

Make a list NOW of five things you can do to live your life more urgently, and after each item note what the results of that action might be:

1. I can _____
   It will result in _____
2. I can _____
   It will result in _____
3. I can _____
   It will result in _____
4. I can _____
   It will result in _____
5. I can _____
   It will result in _____

Lesson Five: Make It Okay to Fail

Although you should go after your dreams with a sense of urgency, let me warn you that you are likely to encounter defeats and failure along the way. There is no reason to be afraid of failure, not if you view failure as part of the process of reaching success. I think one reason people are afraid of failure is that we live in an impatient culture, one in which failure is looked upon only as a negative. Everybody wants to be a winner right now, but in truth, winning is a process in which failure plays a large role. In the scientific community, failure is an accepted part of the process of experimentation, evaluation, and solution-seeking. Whether you are trying to find a new vaccine or a new method for processing steel, you are expected to encounter failures that open the way to eventual success. It has been said that a high percentage of people allow their fear of failure to outweigh their desire to succeed.

They don't want to be perceived as failures so they don't even try. People who make it okay for themselves to fail are not people who don't give their all, they don't set out to lose, but they understand to get to success you have to pass failure. All of us experience more failures than successes, but those failures give meaning and texture to our successes.

When I was a state legislator the older legislators would discourage me from debating the more experienced people on the floor of the state house. But I knew that when I lost it was because of what I did not know. On the other hand, I knew too that when I won it was *because I had learned something.* When I shoot pool or play chess, I like to play people who I know will beat me because they make me reach, they make me become more creative and imaginative. I don't mind losing to them if I can take some of their skills away from the table with me. If you are willing to view losses as something to learn from, then you have no fear of either failure or success. Those who strive make a lot of mistakes and have a lot of failures but all failures are guideposts that leave clues to a better path to follow next time. Failures, it has been said, are low stumps that you can stand on to reach new heights.

I find it amusing when people talk about my public speaking as if it was just something I started doing naturally one day, without going through any training or difficult times. They don't stop to consider that I spent many years being a miserable failure so that one day I could be a big success as a motivational speaker. I did not take the stage on my first day as a public speaker and wow the audience with my poise, projection, and wondrous talent. As my schoolmates back at Booker T. Washington will attest, I was not born with a boom box in my throat. This voice took years to develop and so did my confidence in my abilities. When I say that anything that is worth doing is worth doing badly, I am not advising you to *purposely* do something poorly. If you know how to do it, do it right, but if you have yet to climb the learning curve, know that it is worth it to struggle and falter as you learn to get it right.

The book of success is filled with the names of former failures. Walter P. Chrysler failed in the automobile industry forty-two times. Winston Churchill failed his grade in school three times. Where would this world be if everyone allowed failure to mean defeat? Hank Aaron struck out more times than he hit home runs. Les Brown failed twice in school. He failed as a photographer. He failed as a concert promoter. He failed as a political consultant. He failed as a talk show host.

I experimented with failure as a formula for success. Just as doctors inject people with a virus in order to make them healthy, I took massive doses of failure as an elixir for success. Failure made me the success I am today.

Because of failure, I am a lot stronger today. I need to be. And so do you. If you have never been knocked flat on your back through some major disappointment in life, you have no way of knowing what you are made of. Your talents and abilities are gifts handed to you but your *character* is formed under fire and tested in turmoil. There are many people who crawl away or play dead after life knocks them down. Others get up to fight again. Are you a crawler or a fighter? How do you know? Have you ever risked failure?

LESSON SIX: MAKE YOUR MOVE BEFORE YOU ARE READY

Carl had a good job selling medical equipment in the Midwest, but his dream was to open his own fitness center. A longtime weightlifter, Carl had worked for seven years as a personal trainer at a posh health club on Chicago's North Shore. He had enjoyed working with people and helping them become fit, and so, at the age of thirty-one, with a wife and one-year-old child, he decided to move on his dream.

Some of his family and friends argued that he wasn't ready. He didn't have a large reserve of cash. He didn't have a big clientele built up. There were a lot of risks involved. But Carl knew that if he waited for the perfect time, he might have a very long wait. He believed, as I do, that if you go after your dream with a commitment and dedication that others can see, you will create momentum and the universe will open up to you. Things come to you when you make your move and you are ready for it to happen. When Carl began moving on his dream by talking to friends and business contacts, he soon found financial backers lining up to support him and to bring in their own contacts. People believed in Carl and in his abilities. When they heard him talk of his dream, they bought into it. In very little time, he found an accountant to help him with his business plan, an architect to lay out the building, a banker to help him with financing, and other assistance. Many of those people traded their resources for Carl's talents. He helped the accountant's son get in shape for soccer season. He trained the banker and some of his financial supporters and got them into better physical shape. And he found that the more people he exposed to his dream, the more momentum his dream picked up.

Many talented people have spent their lives standing on the sidelines of life saying "I am not ready yet, I need more money, I have to put together my business plan." And far too many of them are still standing on the sidelines when the clock runs out and their playing time is over. They stand there still waiting for the perfect time to get started on their dreams. They failed to recognize that the perfect time is now. If you have an idea, a dream, something you want to do, listen to your heart and go for it. Start before you are ready, keep your mind open and focused, and the way will come to you.

Too many people think about what they want to do and then ask *But how?* The answer is that the *how* is none of your business. The *how* will come. The resources will appear once your dream picks up momentum. Do what Carl did. He wasn't reckless. He wasn't irresponsible. But he went after his dream, and when he did he attracted others who believed in him.

The only other requirement is that you must have passion for your dream because if you have passion for it, then no matter what happens it will be worth it. I remember one of the first out-of-town speaking engagements I had was for a law enforcement convention in Houston. I was sharing the speaker's podium with a psychologist. I'd been recommended by a Miami police officer who had heard me speak, but I was intimidated by the size of the audience, several thousand top police officers from around the country. I had actually tried to avoid going, but the Miami police officer tracked me down in my hiding place and left a ticket and hotel reservation at my door. He got me. I couldn't give the ticket back, so I went. I was nervous because it was my first large group on the road, and also because this noted psychologist was supposed to be speaking to them too. As it turned out, he was a no-show. And I was the hit of the convention. I talked to the cops about dealing with stress, a subject they are extremely interested in. I used stories and examples they could identify with, the stress of raising children and making relationships work and they applauded and laughed. It built my confidence and I felt myself get stronger. That speech was a breakthrough for me. I thought, "I can do this!" I never looked back after that. What if I had waited until *I* was ready? To this day, that Miami police officer who tracked me down and gave me a ticket—an airplane ticket to my breakthrough speech—does not know how much his pushing me helped me in my career.

Lesson Seven: Eliminate Toxic People

You know, when I was a child, I couldn't understand why my mother was so upset and why she beat me so severely when she caught me running with the Fourteenth Street Gang. I was only hanging out with them. I wasn't stealing or jumping people. But she said if I stayed with those guys, eventually I would be doing those things too. She beat me to make sure I wasn't tempted. "If you keep running with them, you'll end up like that," she said between applications of her switch. "If you run with losers, you'll end up a loser." Whether you realize it or not, people rub off on you.

As usual, Mama was right. I have seen studies that show that an individual's best friends generally have nearly the same income. And I have also heard it said that you can't soar like an eagle if you flutter around with the pigeons. There are many things that can stifle your growth and keep you from chasing your dreams: if you feel unworthy, if you are blocked by fear, if you allow negative circumstances to overwhelm you—but nothing can be as devastating as *toxic people*. They are the anchor around your neck, the cement on your shoes. They will weigh you down.

I have a great respect for toxic people. The same sort of respect

I have for poisonous spiders, rattlesnakes, and hungry grizzly bears. Toxic people will get inside your bloodstream and convince you that nobody wants you but them, that you can't live without the pain they bring to you. They are dream-busters and heart-breakers. They suck the joy out of any situation. Even one toxic person can ruin your life. I know an attractive young lady with a promising career and an academic scholarship to a good college. But then she hooked up with a toxic guy. She became pregnant with his child and stayed with him even after he got another girl pregnant. Brokenhearted and broken in spirit, she fell into drug abuse. The toxic man in her life left her, cleaned himself up, and never looked back. Meanwhile, her life was in ruins.

Often the toxic people in our lives are not actively seeking to destroy us, it's just that in allowing their own lives to be a mess, they weigh us down too. This is often the case with relatives or children. My sister Linda caused a great deal of ill feelings in our family until she finally cleaned up her life. And she didn't come around until she was ready. All of my mother's crying and yelling and fussing at her did no good. Linda did it when she finally grew tired of living that toxic lifestyle. You can't change people. It is a waste of time and energy to try. You can try to motivate and in-spire them, but you have to be wary. If you can't bring the people in your life up, don't let them drag you down.

Jake was in a toxic relationship with Janet, a woman who was sleeping with all of his friends. He was so distraught over her in-fidelities that he decided to kill himself. I called him and went to see him. "What is she providing you that you can't get anyplace else on this planet?" I asked him.

"I love her," he said.

"Oh, you are so much in love that you want to kill yourself? Gee," I said, "ain't love grand? Don't you think you could find a much healthier love elsewhere? What good is a love that makes you suicidal? You are talking about going after a permanent solu-tion to a temporary problem. There are others to love out there, people who will love you in return."

It took some talking, but I brought Jake around. He came to see that this was not really love and that his suicidal urges were irra-tional. This woman in his life was simply evil. There are evil people in this world and my advice is not to get locked into battles with them. Walk away from them if you can. If you are stuck working with them, take it as a signal that it is time to look somewhere else. It makes no sense to allow one person to drag you into misery. Toxic people contribute to stress and heart attacks and strokes. They will age you overnight and turn your hair white.

Sadly, sometimes these toxic people can be your own children who may put you on guilt trips and find reasons to justify their toxicity. Kenny has supported his children all their lives. He has supported them as adults. He is their meal ticket, and they have no appreciation of him. They treat him like dirt. They do not respect his feelings or his privacy. They prey upon his guilt because he was not around a lot when they were younger even though he would do anything in the world for them. They blame him for everything that goes wrong in their lives and he blames himself too. I say his children are toxic. Toxic people are great blamers. They will justify their behavior by saying they were abused or neglected or somehow made the way they are because of the actions of someone else. These toxic people are great for unprincipled talk show hosts, but they destroy the lives of everyone around them. My advice is simple, but effective: Get as far away from these people as you possibly can.

I was jogging in Central Park in New York City and another jogger recognized me and ran alongside. He was a doctor, and had heard me speak on the evils of toxic people. He thanked me profusely. "I had one in my life and after I heard you talk about them, I realized what it was doing to me, and I left that person. I have never been happier in my life," he said. On another occasion I was at O'Hare Airport in Chicago when a woman came up to me and said that after hearing me talk about toxic people she left her husband and her grown children, severing all ties to them, because they were destroying her life. She said she has never looked back.

When you clear your life of toxic people you add years to your life. I was once involved in a toxic relationship and I know what it is like. When I finally walked away from it, I felt a sense of relief that blew me away. I had to ask myself later, "What level of darkness was I walking in when I allowed that person to dominate my life?" But don't take my word for it, prove it to yourself.

Look at the relationships you have now and examine them for toxic people.

List the five people closest to you and note whether they are beneficial or toxic to your life. (If you have more than five toxic people in your life, I have only one word of advice: *Run!*)

NAME	BENEFICIAL/TOXIC
1. _____	1. _____
2. _____	2. _____
3. _____	3. _____
4. _____	4. _____
5. _____	5. _____

The detoxification process includes several steps:

1. Ask yourself: "What kind of person am I becoming because of this relationship?" Evaluate your relationships and rate them as either beneficial or toxic for your life.
2. Try to figure out how to stay away from toxic people. Respect their toxicity. Try to remain emotionally detached. State clearly what your problems are with this person.
3. Admit your own responsibility for allowing yourself to become influenced by the toxic person.
4. Talk about what you expect from the person in the future, and what you expect from yourself in the relationship.
5. If you find that you can't make the break on your own, seek some help and guidance either from family members or friends, or professional counselors associated with your church or social service agencies.
6. Work on your courage and confidence. Remember, no one deserves to be mistreated by others.

Now, for each of the toxic people in your life, write what you can do to *detoxify* that relationship. Remember that you can't change people, but you can change your relationship by distancing yourself from them, or by not allowing your actions and feelings to be controlled by them or their words.

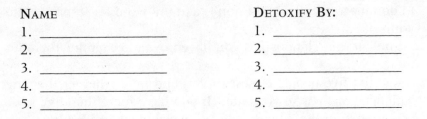

NAME

1. _____

2. _____

3. _____

4. _____

5. _____

DETOXIFY BY:

1. _____

2. _____

3. _____

4. _____

5. _____

Recently I was speaking in California and after my presentation a woman approached me and told me that in hearing my speech she realized that she was involved in a highly toxic relationship in which her husband was physically abusive. He dominated her to the point that she was not permitted to leave their home in order to pursue her own career interests. She had dreamed of suicide as a way of freeing herself. I spent hours talking to this woman, taking her through a method for escaping, asking questions to make her think more clearly. "What about your children? What impact would suicide have on their lives? Do you want to leave them alone with this man who has abused you?"

I can't understand the logic of people who would rather leave life than leave a toxic relationship. I would hike to Australia rather than contemplate suicide. Who does that really hurt? That warped, suicidal thinking indicates how toxic relationships befuddle people. You don't have to be there! Go somewhere else. It is a big world with a great many nontoxic people. I know a woman who had no money and six children but she walked away from a toxic relationship and guess what? She thrived! Even if you have no resources, you will find them. Take one step, and help will appear. Get away from toxic people. Get away.

LESSON EIGHT: TRUST IN A GREATER POWER

As a child, I often watched my mother ironing the clothes of the families she worked for, and I remember her praying to herself as she did this work. She would also quietly hum and sing gospel songs. And I remember also that in dire times when the power company had turned off the lights or when there was no food in the refrigerator, Mama would have us pray with her. It seemed to give her strength. It fueled her belief that, in spite of our present condition, everything would be all right. With all of the uncertainty and hopelessness and fear in the world today, I think we might all look to my Mama's example. We all need to be grounded mentally, emotionally, and spiritually. Whatever your beliefs, whatever faith you practice, tap into it and draw strength as my Mama did.

Some may deny that there is a power greater than all of us, but I am not one. I know that power has been influential in my own life, though I have no physical proof. As you work toward your goals and answer the calling of your life, you can see that power at play too if you are looking for it. People come into your life at the right time. Friends show up exactly when you are in need of them. Coincidence, it has been said, is God's way of staying anonymous. Often God is present in our lives but we are so distracted by other things that we fail to notice.

All of us have been in situations that appeared hopeless, and yet we survived. We found a way. Or perhaps the way was shown to us. Prayer works. "Pray as if everything depends upon God and work as if everything depends upon you," said Mary McLeod Bethune, the great educator. Prayer to me is talking to God just like you would talk to someone you respect. You can do it on your knees, walking around, or lying in bed. Make prayer and quiet reflective time part of your day. I suggest that people pray first thing in the morning, and then later in the day take twenty minutes for prayer or quiet reflection.

When you take time to meditate and focus on words such as *peace, love, God, faith,* you feel strength come into you. Sometimes I meditate on a passage from the Bible, *The Lord is my shepherd, I shall not want.* Or *The Lord is the strength in my life of whom shall I be afraid.* God has given us a spirit of power and love and of sound mind. I am blessed and highly favored. Create something that will dispel your fear and anxiety, anxiousness and nervousness, and that will bring a sense of peace and calmness into your life so that you can block out anything that troubles you.

And when you pray, let your prayer be one of thanksgiving, not one of begging God. *Father, thank you for giving me the gift of oratory, for being able to reach people for the power of the spoken word. I thank you for the discipline necessary to reach my goal. I give you thanks for all the right people, all the right relationships in service of you and in service of humankind.*

When you pray, visualize the goal you are working on as being completed, and then go about your business and work and do what you can. Trust a power greater than yourself to deliver all the things that you need and you will be surprised at all that takes place. Take a card around with your goal written on it and then on the other side of it give thanks for your accomplishments so far and a favorite affirmation or line from Scripture. Mine says: *Ask and it shall be given, seek and ye shall find, knock and the door shall be open, for everyone that asketh receiveth and he that seeketh findeth and for him that knocketh the door shall be open.*

Read the goal out loud and speak the words with power, feeling, and conviction. See it in your mind's eye as complete. Through prayer, through meditation, through focusing your thoughts and speaking the word, you are positioning yourself for the universe to work through you. And to attract to you all the things you need. You are becoming a magnetic force for good in your own life experience. When you expect things to get better they do. So expect miracles and blessings to happen in your life. Every day say *Good things are supposed to happen to me!* We live in a world where cynicism is the norm and blessings are abnormal. When someone gives you a gift don't say "You shouldn't have" but instead "Thank you for being so thoughtful." When someone pays you a compliment, don't downgrade it or dismiss it, accept it. Welcome good things. Keep in mind that life is on your side, that good things are supposed to happen to you and that you are blessed and great things are coming your way because you deserve them.

Whatever goals you have in mind, write them down and meditate on them. I have little writing tablets all over my house and in my hotel rooms when I am on the road and I am always writing my goals down on them and then I write down ways I am going to accomplish those goals. When you are focused like that and in alignment mentally, emotionally, and spiritually things come to you. But ships don't come in on rough waters, they come in the calm. That is why I get most of my ideas early in the morning or late at night, at times when you are contemplative and quiet and your mind is ripe. When I first began thinking about a public speaking career, I picked up a newspaper while on a contemplative walk and I saw an article about a youth program that was looking for creative ideas to motivate and inspire young people. My mind was open to innovation and challenge, and so that article led to a $125,000 contract with the city. It got me going again in life. Be open and receptive for new ideas and listen to your first mind.

And start working on yourself. We work harder on our jobs than on our dreams. Faith, prayer, and positive expectation without works will not produce any results in life. You have got to go into action and go all out, don't hold back on yourself. The motivational writer A. L. Williams once said, *All you can do is all you can do and all you can do is enough but make sure you do all you can do.* When you go all out, you will pass an invisible boundary and you will begin to see blessings coming your way from all directions, but that only happens when you do all you can do.

Find several people, family members or friends, who are in tune with you, and meet once a week for a session of praise, progress, and prayer. At this session, you can discuss what you have accomplished in the previous week, what you feel good and proud about. The group can offer positive reinforcement by acknowledging your progress toward your goal. Then, you can pray together, each taking turns thanking God for the power, the strength, for the people, for the ideas, for the resources for making your blessings take place. There is power in prayer, particularly when people pray together. All over America, people are forming groups to pool their investment capital for financial gain. I am suggesting that you do the same with your spiritual capital, to gain the sort of leverage that brings even greater rewards. These praise, progress, and prayer groups will bring heavenly returns.

LESSON NINE: DEVELOP A LARGER VISION

All of the things I am doing today in my career were within the reach of my talents ten or fifteen years ago, but I did not see myself as capable then. I had a limited vision of my own abilities and that restricted my growth. I was stuck in a mud hole of my own creation, trapped in a cage I'd constructed myself. I wasn't doing all that I could because I couldn't see beyond the wall of my limitations to the horizons of my possibilities. For a time back then, it seemed like everything I tried, I failed. I didn't know what to do and whatever I was doing, I felt I couldn't do it any better. Fortunately, I had somebody, a friend, Mike Williams, who looked at me not as I was, but as what I could become. And through that person's help, I learned to see myself beyond my circumstances. I engaged in a self-development process to overcome my negative inner conversations. When I wanted to be a motivational speaker, I had this voice inside saying that I didn't have the education or the resources or the time to develop my career. I had never run a business before. That negative voice controls our lives if you listen to it. But as I worked on my career, I came to believe I deserve to have it, and that sense of deserving gave me a sense of mission. What you get in life is a direct result of what you subconsciously believe that you deserve. As we increase our sense of deservingness we will see a difference in our lives.

Ask yourself: What do I deserve from life? From my relationships? From my job or career? If you are in a business just to make money, you are in the wrong place. You have to *love* what you are doing. The things that we enjoy most in life are the things that we feel we deserve. You have to know what you stand for. Most people don't know what they want in life. If you don't know where you are going you are going to end up somewhere else. When you know what you want in life and go after it, things that you cannot anticipate will happen to you. You will run into obstacles and people will stand in your way. You have to look at what you feel you deserve, and then fight for what you want. I encourage you to write down five reasons why you should reach your goals:

1. _____

2. _____

3. _____

4. _____

5. _____

When you become discouraged, and you will be discouraged, when people make commitments to you and don't keep them, your heartfelt reasons for doing what you are doing will be your salvation. They will keep you going if you make up your mind that nobody—no person, place, or thing—will steal your dream.

Write down five reasons why you are not going to give up:

1. _____

2. _____

3. _____

4. _____

5. _____

Once you have established a larger vision for your life, go for it. Don't give yourself an escape hatch. Make a *commitment* to go after your dream relentlessly. Remember, the uncommitted life is not worth living. Uncommitted people don't leave a trace on this planet. You have to stand up for your dreams, your business, your family. Stand up for what you believe in because you can fall for anything. If you have no values, your life will be valueless.

Ask yourself this crucial question: What will cause you to give up? Where will you draw the line? You need to set the boundaries so that you know how far you need to go before stopping. There is risk involved in giving up what you have for something you believe to be better. You have to be willing to give up life as it is now for what you want it to be.

When you stand for something, for integrity, for hard work, you will leave a legacy of success. You can't *try* at life, you have to go at it with all of your spirit. You have to have juice in your life. You have to live with passion, drive, and energy. You want to make a difference because you can make a difference. You want to be unreasonable. If you want to be successful, if you want to manifest your greatness, you have to be unreasonable. There will be people telling you that you cannot achieve your dream because it is not reasonable, and you can say, that's fine, because I am an unreasonable person. The Wright brothers were unreasonable enough to think they could fly. Nelson Mandela was unreasonable enough to think he could change an entire nation by standing by his beliefs. My Mama was unreasonable because she thought she could raise seven children even though she had few resources by most standards.

Far too many people are held back because of their entirely reasonable inner conversations. You have to watch your inner and outer conversations. They affect you. The Wright brothers encountered conversations that said they would never fly. Mandela was mocked by his jailers. My Mama's friends encouraged her to take me to the state authorities because I would never be anything but a problem child. Understand the power of words. We have to monitor our inner conversations of defeat and negativism. If you can't say something good, something productive that builds you up, don't say anything at all! The people who make it in life are the people who decide to be unstoppable.

LESSON TEN: GET OUT OF YOUR COMFORT ZONE

When I was a little boy, my twin brother and my sister and I would sit on the porch of our house and pick out our cars as we watched traffic. *That Cadillac's mine! I've got that Mercedes! I want that convertible!* We did the same with the fancy hotels on Miami Beach. Ours was sort of like Monopoly without the board, the pieces, or, particularly, the cash. Even the play money.

That's my hotel there with the fountain. Mine is taller. I've got the one with the doorman. We were dreaming and fantasizing, of course, but that is what most children do. The problem is that when we become adults, we stop dreaming. We become logical and rational and limited.

If it is childlike to dream and to think that you can take on the world, then I advise you to become a child again. You have to be willing to do things you have never done, because when you push yourself, you expand your talents and the opportunities for your life. Most people follow the path of least resistance; they say it's too hard and it would take too long. My friend Scott told me that he had always dreamed about going to medical school but he was already forty, and he said he didn't want to be forty-eight and looking for his first job in medicine. I found that to be irrational thinking. "How old will you be in eight years?" I asked him. "Forty-eight," he said. "Well, if you plan on living to be forty-eight wouldn't it be better to be that age and doing what you dream of doing rather than being that age and wishing you were doing something else?"

It is amazing to me sometimes how people will hang on to what is comfortable or at least familiar rather than letting go and going after what really excites them. Why do we do that? All of us dream. Why do so many of us hide from our dreams? Who is going to do it for you if you don't do it for yourself? How do you know you can't do it if you don't try? What are your limits? Have you tested them lately?

Until you risk giving up what you have now, you will never know what you might have if only you had pushed yourself out of the comfort zone. We are all born unique but the majority of people die as copies. They go through life doing what everybody else is doing because of laziness, fear, or a lack of vision. Unlike gold and diamonds, you cannot bury your talents in order to preserve them. Those gifts do you no good if you don't act upon them and develop them to their greatest potential. If you don't use them, you will lose them. During the year that I was involved in *The Les Brown Show*, I didn't do much public speaking, and I got rusty. If you think Michael Jordan looked a little out of synch in the first few games of his comeback in basketball, you should have seen me when I returned to the podium. It seemed like I'd forgotten everything I'd known. My timing and rhythm were off. I could not pull my thoughts together as readily. Slowly, though, I began remembering things I didn't know I'd forgotten.

We all have abilities and talents and we all have to work to not only develop them but to push them and to push ourselves as far as we can go together. These are times that require constant growth personally and professionally. I saw a television program recently in which an eighty-year-old woman was on an Outward Bound wilderness expedition. She was climbing mountains and rafting. She was part of a team and in this program if one person on the team failed to make it through, the entire team had to go back and start all over. The others in the group were in their twenties and several of them fell back. They lost their gumption, as my mother would say. But the woman in her eighties kept plugging on because she had deeper reserves to call on. She had obviously tested life constantly. Her spirit was powerful because of it.

You have to push at the outer edges of life constantly, because you never know when life might give a little and open new passages for you. I know. I've been pushing all my life, and believe me I'm not through with life yet. As a child, I was always talking, always jabbering, always making people laugh, always saying something to make other people feel good. I was especially good at making my brother and sister laugh when I mimicked the local preacher: *I talked to the Lord today, huh! and he told me to come by and tell you this morning, huh! that you have to believe in Him, huh! if you don't want to go straight to hell, huh!* My brother and sister would be rolling on the floor and acting like the choir, *Preach Brother Les, preach on!* And my Mama would walk in and warn us about being irreverent toward the reverend. *You are all going straight to hell!* she would say.

But I wasn't going yet.

My ability to talk to people got me a job as a paperboy, selling the *Miami Herald* door-to-door and on the street corners of my neighborhood. *Hey get your paper today right now! Find out right now the latest scandal at city hall in Miami!* It was a good job for me then, but I thought I could do more.

From that job, I convinced a friend to give me a job making BIG MONEY working for the City of Miami Sanitation Department. I told the guy I could do it, but I found out real soon it wasn't my kind of work. Next, I got a job selling used television sets door-to-door in Liberty City. *Hi, would you like to buy a nice working television set? No money down. Emerson, Westinghouse, Motorola . . . These are the best television sets you'll ever get. The pictures are so sharp your neighbors will be watching through the windows.* I made some good money, $30 a week, doing that job.

But I knew I wasn't done yet.

I applied for a job at Sears selling appliances. And I quickly became the *top* salesman in the appliance department. My specialty was knives. Electronic carving knives. I'd stand on the floor of the store holding a giant juicy red tomato and demonstrate how to carve that tomato up with precision, speed, and no mess. *Come right over, ladies and gentlemen. Here is a carving knife extraordinaire. You can actually skin a live chicken without causing a cluck! You can take the feathers right off a pigeon without a flutter. See here, I'll hold this tomato in one hand and the knife in the other and slice it without spilling a seed. Hurry, come right over here and see this! I've got something for you, what a gift for somebody you care about.* At one point, I did cause a mess when, while carving the tomato, I carved my finger too. I tried not to scream. Really, I did. A customer was watching and he wanted me to carve him another tomato, but I had to excuse my-self to go to the bathroom and bleed!

Still, I did so well selling those carving knives that the store manager decided to put me in charge of unloading a thousand or so alarm clocks that hadn't been selling. *Excuse me sir, you look like a man for whom time is very important. Not only will this clock wake you up but when you wake up and push the snooze button to get a few more winks that might cost you your job it will wake you up automatically and say "C'mon Get up! Get off the sheets and on the streets!" How many alarm clocks would you like today sir? And in what color?*

Oh, I moved some clocks. But time, and Les Brown, march on. I started hanging out at the local radio station, working for noth-ing, running errands, biding my time, waiting for a chance to get on the air. And then one day my opportunity came. And when it came, I was ready to roll. *Look out, this is me, L.B. triple P. Les Brown, your platter-playin' papa. There were none before me and there will be none after me, therefore that makes me the one and only. Young and sin-gle and love to mingle, certified, bona fide, indubitably qualified to bring you satisfaction, a whole lot of action. Look out, baby. I'm your LOVE man!*

Within a very short time, I was given my own show on that Mi-ami station where I became a radio celebrity. After a few years, I was offered a higher-paying job as a deejay at a station in Colum-bus. But I wasn't done yet. It was the early 1970s and a time of unrest in the country. I began urging my listeners to get involved politically, to stand up for their rights. I wrote political commen-tary about voter registration, police brutality, providing food for the needy, talking about issues on a regular basis to make people aware of how we can act as a force for change: *Hi, this is Les Brown, without the vote we are without hope. If you are not involved in the process you have no right to complain about what is going on in our com-munity. Either you are part of the solution or you are part of the problem. Get involved!*

My talents were so well suited for political activism that I got fired from my radio job in Columbus for stirring up too much controversy. But I wasn't done yet. No sir. At the urging of my listeners and supporters, I ran for a seat in the Ohio legislature. I had no political experience, no financial backing, and no party support, but I had the ability to motivate people to take action and to support me: *Hi, this is Les Brown. When I was on the air as a radio personality in Columbus, I had no fear of speaking out against the wrongs in this community. I am still speaking out, now as a candidate for the House of Representatives where I will be your voice. I encourage you to stand up for what you can believe in because you can fall for anything. Let me stand up for you in the State House.*

I won the election by a landslide. I slaughtered the incumbent. Not only did I win that first election, I won two more. In my first term, I passed more legislation than anyone. But I wasn't done yet. There were more human resources out there that I wanted to reach as a national and international public speaker. I dreamed of becoming a catalyst for action and a messenger of hope.

And so, after leaving the Ohio legislature in order to take care of my mother during an illness, I began developing my skills as a motivational speaker. I preached the gospel of greatness: *We all have talents and abilities and genius in us that we need to unleash on the world. We have to push back our fears and doubts and develop unstoppable attitudes and resilient spirits. We have got to be HUNGRY!*

After several challenging years of training, I won the highest awards bestowed by Toastmasters International as well as the National Speakers Association. I was selected among the top five public speakers in the world. My popularity as a motivational speaker led to a public television special called *You Deserve!* which not only won an Emmy but also became the most effective fundraising program of its kind.

But I wasn't done yet.

The success of my public television specials led to a book contract with a New York publisher and to the publication of my first book, *Live Your Dreams!*, which, in turn, led to even more public speaking engagements across this country and around the world. Soon, all of the major television production companies were in hot pursuit of me as a television talk show host. And as you know, I signed on with King World Productions to do a solution-oriented program: *Hi, welcome to* The Les Brown Show. *Today we are going to talk to people about how they can be successful by pushing their talents to the limit. We'll be right back after these words from our sponsors.*

As our ratings indicated, viewers bought into our concept, but the producers didn't. Yes, I had the highest-rated, fastest-canceled talk show in the history of television. Yes, the loss of my television talk show and the death of my beloved mother knocked me for a loop. But I am here to tell you folks: I survived! And Les Brown is *not done yet!*

It's not over until YOU and I win!

About the Author

Les Brown is a highly acclaimed and dynamic public speaker, who conducts personal and professional seminars for leading corporate and business clients and public audiences around the world. He is well known to television audiences through his PBS specials and was the host of the nationally syndicated *Les Brown Show*. He lives outside Las Vegas, Nevada, with his wife, entertainer Gladys Knight.